Death in the
Blood

Death
in the
Blood

The inside story of the
NHS infected blood scandal

CAROLINE WHEELER

HEADLINE

First published in 2023 by
HEADLINE PUBLISHING GROUP

2

Cataloguing in Publication Data is available from the British Library

Hardback ISBN: 978 1 0354 0524 4

Designed and typeset by EM&EN
Printed and bound in Great Britain by Clays Ltd, Elcograf S.p.A.

Headline's policy is to use papers that are natural, renewable and recyclable
products and made from wood grown in well-managed forests and other
controlled sources. The logging and manufacturing processes are expected
to conform to the environmental regulations of the country of origin.

HEADLINE PUBLISHING GROUP
An Hachette UK Company
Carmelite House
50 Victoria Embankment
London EC4Y 0DZ

www.headline.co.uk
www.hachette.co.uk

For Luke, Sam and Grace

'They tried to bury us,
they didn't know we were seeds.'

Dinos Christianopoulos

Contents

INTRODUCTION

The first time I spoke to Mick Mason, I wrote him off as a conspiracy theorist. It was 2001 and I was a naive twenty-one-year-old trainee reporter who by chance picked up a call from him to the newsroom. I had quite recently joined the *Sunday Mercury* newspaper in Birmingham as a rookie reporter, and part of my initiation was to answer random calls from the public.[1]

It was a conversation that was to change my life and the course of my career. The thirty-four-year-old told me he was a haemophiliac who had been infected with hepatitis B and C, and HIV, after receiving blood products via the NHS that had been riddled with the deadly diseases. A near-certain death sentence had been passed on him as a teenager. As if that wasn't bad enough, he had recently received the devastating news that he may also have caught vCJD after receiving blood from a donor who later died of the human form of mad cow disease.

It was the stuff of nightmares, and such an impossibly heartbreaking story that I found it hard to believe. But every word of it turned out to be true – just like the dozens of other harrowing accounts I have heard from the victims of this easily preventable scandal, which has claimed thousands of lives in the UK and destroyed tens of thousands more.

Over the past twenty years, I've helped to campaign for justice for these innocent men and women, and their families. Many of them, already facing terminal illness, have suffered the indignity of being forced into financial hardship, while all the time being ignored and stonewalled by the authorities whose negligence caused their suffering in the first place.

At the heart of this tragedy is contaminated blood. In the 1970s and 1980s, nearly 5,000 UK haemophiliacs contracted HIV or hepatitis C after being infected by tainted blood-clotting products. Factor VIII was seen as a miracle cure for haemophilia, a genetic disorder in which the blood fails to clot. But demand far outstripped supply, and much of the product ended up being sourced cheaply from the US.

Across the Atlantic, America operated a dangerously deregulated donation system. People were paid for their blood, which meant much of it came from donors who badly needed cash. As a result, blood sourced from high-risk groups – including prisoners, sex workers, drug addicts and alcoholics – was packaged up and sold around the world. As early as 1975, the TV programme *World in Action* revealed that the NHS was buying blood harvested on 'skid row' – the poorest part of a town, where drug addicts, alcoholics and homeless people typically live – leading to a hepatitis epidemic among haemophiliacs.[2] Much of the blood sold to British hospitals came from high-security prisons in Arkansas, where a large number of inmates were infected with hepatitis and HIV. To make matters worse, the donations were pooled, which meant a single batch of factor VIII could include blood from up to 20,000 donors. If just one of those donors was infected, the entire batch could be contaminated.

In the same year as the *World in Action* broadcast, David Owen, the then-Labour health minister, promised Britain would become self-sufficient in blood products to ensure vulnerable patients were put at minimal risk. It never happened. By 1980, Britain was importing twice the quantity of blood products it produced domestically. This failure to act was bizarre, particularly as Owen's pledge came amid widespread warnings about the risks of contaminated blood.

One example can be found in a letter from Dr Joseph Garrott Allen, an expert on blood and professor of surgery at Stanford University in California, to Dr William Maycock, head of the transfusion service in Britain, dated January 1975. The American expert warned Maycock of the dangers of using US-pooled plasma from 'skid row' donors, and said the products were 'extraordinarily hazardous'.[3]

By 1983, British government experts knew that those receiving clotting factor concentrates were also at risk of infection with the deadly new AIDS virus, and recommended that the blood products undergo heat treatment to kill infection-causing viruses. However, implementation was delayed because of cost. Even after a British haemophiliac who had contracted HIV from blood products died of AIDS in August 1983, the government still refused to accept that the disease was blood-borne.

It wasn't just haemophiliacs who were at risk: contaminated blood was also used in transfusions for the general population. About 35,000 people in Britain are believed to have contracted hepatitis C from contaminated blood, including Anita Roddick, the founder of The Body Shop.

The businesswoman was infected by a transfusion of blood after the birth of her daughter Sam in 1971. For decades, Roddick was unaware she had the disease; she only found out three years before her death in 2007.

Medics believe many thousands of others could have suffered a similar fate without ever being diagnosed, meaning the death toll of this tragedy is likely to be far greater than official estimates. So far, more than 2,800 people in the UK alone are known to have died after receiving contaminated blood products in what Lord Robert Winston, the eminent scientist, described as the 'worst treatment disaster in the history of the NHS'.

The number of people who have lost their lives makes it the deadliest man-made disaster in post-war British history, far outstripping the combined death tolls of other more well-known tragedies, such as Hillsborough, Grenfell and Lockerbie. Yet no organisation or individual has ever been held to account. Instead, the victims who were lucky enough to survive have spent the last forty years desperately searching for answers.

The same is not true in other parts of the world. Michel Garretta, the former head of France's blood transfusion service, and his deputy, Jean-Pierre Allain, went to prison in 1992 for knowingly distributing AIDS-infected blood products to haemophiliac patients. Seven years later, the former French socialist prime minister Laurent Fabius, the former social affairs minister Georgina Dufoix and the former health minister Edmond Hervé were also charged with manslaughter. Hervé was the only one found guilty, but he received no sentence.[4] In Japan, three former drug company executives – including one who was a former government official – went to prison in 2000.[5] In the United

4

States, private drug companies have paid out millions in out-of-court settlements.

When British victims launched litigation against the government in 1989, they encountered a very different response. Ministers decided to ignore advice from Britain's chief medical officer, who warned the government that it should compensate thousands of victims of the contaminated blood scandal. Government memos from the time reveal that Sir Donald Acheson told Ken Clarke, the former health secretary, that the disaster was a 'unique catastrophe', and advised ministers to provide financial support to the victims on 'humanitarian' grounds. 'I hope the Secretary of State will take account of my view that the problem of HIV infection in haemophiliacs can in fact be regarded as a unique catastrophe,' he wrote. 'The key feature . . . is that HIV infection, in addition to almost inevitably causing a very unpleasant progressive illness and death, results in a substantial proportion of cases in infection of the female sexual partner and also on average one-quarter of the subsequently conceived children. In both the wife and children, the infection will also prove fatal.'

He added: 'The tragedy goes beyond anything which has ever been described as a result of a therapeutic accident and is very likely indeed never to occur again. I hope, therefore, that for humanitarian reasons the government will find some way to make an ex-gratia settlement to the infected haemophiliacs in relation to this unique tragedy.'[6]

Once again, ministers decided to prioritise the public finances over other moral or legal considerations. Clarke rejected Acheson's advice on cost grounds. 'I agreed broadly with the points he was making about the strength of the humanitarian needs and I shared the desire to help victims if we could,' he later reflected. 'But I did also have to remember all the other worthwhile claims for health expenditure, and my overall responsibility for public funds.'[7]

The victims and their families eventually received limited ex-gratia payments in 1991. But even when the state finally offered support, it left a stain. Among those awarded payments were 1,200 patients who had been infected with HIV. They were forced by government officials to sign a contract preventing them from making any future legal claims in return for a cash payment of around £24,000.[8] It was only after they had signed the contract that they were told they had also been infected with hepatitis C – a fact the Department of Health had known about two years earlier but failed to pass on.[9]

This apparent stitch-up would have fatal consequences. Patients with both HIV and hepatitis C died more quickly than those with just one of the viruses. Advances in treatment also meant HIV was now less deadly than hepatitis C, which causes severe liver damage. Campaigners say the government was desperate to keep the scandal away from the courts for fear of the publicity, criminal charges and compensation claims that might follow. Jason Evans, the founder of campaign group Factor 8, whose father died in 1993 after being infected with both hepatitis C and HIV, said: 'It was the greatest trick the Department of Health would ever pull on them.'[10] Had patients found out earlier, they could have been given treatments to encourage their immune systems to attack the hepatitis C virus. Although the drugs available were not as advanced as those we have today, they would have significantly improved the patients' survival chances.

And so the victims' battle for justice continued into the twenty-first century. Even back in 2001, when I interviewed Mick Mason, justice was his main preoccupation. 'I want the government to launch a public inquiry so we can discover the whole truth,' he told me. 'It is an absolute scandal that this was ever allowed to happen when there are so many checks that could have been done.'[11]

•

Although Mick Mason's story first opened my eyes to the scandal, it wasn't until nearly nine years later that the enormity of the tragedy hit home.

By 2010, I had left the *Sunday Mercury* in Birmingham and moved to London to work in Parliament as a lobby correspondent for Northcliffe Newspapers Group, which included the *Hull Daily Mail*. Not long after joining Northcliffe, I got to know Diana Johnson, the Labour MP for Hull North, who was interested in the campaign for justice for the victims of the contaminated blood scandal. She introduced me to her constituent Glenn Wilkinson. The former engineer had been given factor VIII in 1983 to prevent excessive bleeding when he had three teeth removed at Hull Royal Infirmary. Like many of those victims who contracted deadly diseases through contaminated blood, he was delivered a death sentence after undergoing a routine operation, in this case during his lunch hour. At a meeting in Westminster, Glenn told me that he only discovered that he had hepatitis C twelve years later, when it showed up on blood tests. The married father of two, who runs the Contaminated Blood Campaign, was devastated when he was first told the news. His horror turned to anger when doctors told him he should never have been given the blood product in the first place, as his haemophilia was so mild.

By the time I met Glenn, he was already an active campaigner and frequently came to Westminster to meet with ministers and civil servants to discuss the government's inadequate response to the scandal. During one visit, security staff forced him to remove a protest T-shirt before allowing him on to the parliamentary estate. Glenn was determined; he knew that lobbying the government or seeking legal redress were the only options if those affected were ever to get to the truth of what had happened. With the support of his MP, he used every available opportunity to push the issue up the political agenda. Looking back, Glenn admits he was often concerned that the campaign was futile and would never get anywhere. 'The harder we went at them, the more the government seemed to push back and obfuscate. It felt like we were bashing our heads against a brick wall, and to be honest, many of us felt that the government was just waiting for us to die so that they could avoid giving us answers and avoid paying out any more money,' he told me.

When I made my next move to become the political editor of the *Sunday Express* in May 2014, I was determined to try to help raise the profile of the campaign further. The injustice of Glenn's story as he battled through ill health to draw attention to the scandal had touched me deeply. It seemed incomprehensible that such ongoing suffering by a group of people who had contracted deadly diseases through no fault of their own could continue to be ignored indefinitely. With a new job at a newspaper with an illustrious campaigning history, I wanted to see if it was possible to use the clout of a national title to finally effect change. Within my first month at the paper, I persuaded the news desk to run the first of what would become a long series of articles on the contaminated blood scandal.

Meanwhile, as I started to look more deeply into the controversy, Glenn introduced me to another veteran campaigner, Mike Dorricott, who was to leave a lasting impression on me. Like Glenn, Mike had mild haemophilia and had been given contaminated blood in 1983 during a routine dental operation. He had been infected with hepatitis C and had struggled to cope with a string of serious health complications, including cancer. The former high-flying executive with United Biscuits eventually found himself physically unable to work after having a second liver transplant. At the age of just forty, he had to forego his comfortable salary for a modest pension that meant he was unable to service his mortgage. The inheritance he had dreamed of leaving to his children was gone.

Despite his travails, Mike retained a *joie de vivre* that seemed incongruous with the hand life had dealt him. Even as his health deteriorated, he took part in the World Transplant Games in 2013 and won double gold at golf. By the time we were introduced, the father of two had terminal liver cancer. Doctors had told him he had just months to live. But if he was going to die, he was going to go down fighting.

With his family facing an uncertain future, Mike pulled no punches in an interview with me, published in the paper in June 2014. He urged David Cameron to introduce a fairer compensation scheme for those infected by contaminated blood products. 'My life has been ripped apart by a wholly avoidable situation. Mr Cameron, you can – and should – put this right.' Mike implored the then-prime minister: 'My time is now up as the prognosis of terminal cancer will mean I won't get to see my children grow up into adulthood.'[12]

Mike, who lived with his family in Sedbergh in Cumbria, had been determined to live long enough to hear the outcome of the Penrose Inquiry, a major inquiry into the infection of Scottish patients with contaminated blood. Although the inquiry would have had no direct benefit for him and his family living in England, he and other campaigners had hoped the findings would put pressure on the Westminster government to act.

But on 25 March 2015 – the very morning the Scottish judge Lord Penrose was due to deliver his findings – Mike collapsed and was rushed to hospital in Newcastle upon Tyne. He spent the last days of his life at the Freeman Hospital surrounded by the people he loved most: his sister, wife and two daughters. His skin had long since turned yellow from liver failure and he could no longer breathe unaided. He was reduced to speaking in a whisper. Even as his major organs began to fail, and he drifted in and out of consciousness, Mike appealed to his sister, Jane, and wife, Ann, to get in touch with me to remind me that his dying wish was for justice for him and his family. 'Tell her to keep going,' he implored them, in an effort to ensure that his voice, even after death, would continue to be heard. Mike was just forty-seven years old when the end finally came.

His daughter Sarah, who moved to Leeds to be closer to her dad in the final stages of his illness, has now taken up the fight on his behalf. Speaking to me on the phone several years after his death, her feelings were still raw. She told me: 'He was a very kind and very humble man, and he strove to do the right thing, so I am trying to take a leaf out of his book. I need to know, for myself and my family, that I have done right by him. I need to get justice and closure for myself.' Sarah, who found out she was expecting a baby shortly after her dad's death, added: 'It's a joke that it is taking this long . . . There are suspicions that it is being drawn out so that victims will have passed away by the time some kind of resolution is found. There doesn't seem to be any speed or urgency. I don't give a monkey's chuff about the cash – it's about the liability, the apology, [having] someone to say: "I made a mistake and this is the reason why."'

Sadly, the Penrose Inquiry raised more questions than it answered. Having cost at least £11.3 million and taken six years to complete, it made only one recommendation: to test patients who had a blood transfusion before September 1991 for hepatitis C if they had not already been examined. The report was also reluctant to apportion blame, angering victims and their loved ones, who branded it a 'whitewash'. However, far from derailing the campaign, it made those fighting for justice more determined than ever.

It was at this point that Angela Farrugia, who had seen her three brothers die after they were all infected with contaminated blood, came forward to tell me her own agonising story. Angela, an exuberant redhead, was retired and living with her second husband, Michael, when she joined the campaign in July 2015. She revealed her desperately sad story during a long and emotional telephone conversation.

Barry Farrugia, a gas engineer from Dagenham, east London, was the first of her siblings to die in 1986, aged thirty-seven, leaving behind five sons. Like his brothers, he was a haemophiliac. He became infected with HIV, hepatitis B and C, cytomegalovirus and the human herpes virus after receiving factor VIII. Soon after Barry's death, Angela's other brother Victor, a former merchant seaman who lived in East Ham, was diagnosed with HIV. He was infected with contaminated blood after undergoing hospital dental treatment and died in 2002 in the same hospital where he is thought to have been infected. It was not until after his death, at the age of sixty-three, that his family, including his son and daughter, discovered he had also been infected with hepatitis C. A third brother, David, who worked for London Underground for more than forty years and lived near his sister in Aveley, Essex, died in 2012, suffering a brain haemorrhage linked to the hepatitis C he had contracted after receiving blood products. He was sixty-nine and left behind a daughter and grandson.

'We never got over Barry's death, and when my brother Victor was diagnosed with HIV . . . it was almost too much to bear; it was unreal,' Angela told me in an interview with the *Sunday Express*. 'My mother, Violet, died shortly after Victor was diagnosed, after the rapid onset of cancer. I am convinced she died of a broken heart.'[13]

Angela's nephew Tony Farrugia said he 'lost everything' when his father Barry found out he had been infected. Tony, now a father of two, who does not suffer from haemophilia, ended up in the Brambles Children's Home in Luton after his father suffered a mental breakdown following his diagnosis and was detained under the Mental Health Act. Tony, a larger-than-life character who became famous for painting himself blood red during protests to draw attention to the scandal, is desperate for justice. 'None of this was an accident, it was all completely avoidable,' he told me. 'It's a constant reminder every time one of the victims dies of what we have been through. It's difficult. You are dealing with it every day. You are around people who are dying. It needs to be dealt with. These people need justice; they need closure; they need to be able to live their lives not having to fight every day. They need the truth. We deserve the truth.'

•

For years, many patients who contracted HIV from contaminated blood lived in secrecy and fear because of the stigma surrounding the disease. But as families like the Farrugias decided to tell their stories, so others were inspired to do the same. Having been contacted on social media by numerous individuals who were willing to go public, I decided, in late July 2015, that it was time to launch a crusade calling for a full and final settlement for the victims.

Nick Sainsbury, Ade Goodyear, Joe Peaty and Richard Warwick helped to launch the campaign in the *Sunday Express* with the harrowing story of their school days. The boys were all pupils at Treloar School in Alton, Hampshire – a school with a devastating past. For half a century, Treloar's has been one of England's leading centres in caring for disabled youngsters. The four men all suffered with haemophilia and had been sent there as children because it offered them the best chance of leading a normal life.

But many of their school friends died before they reached their thirtieth birthdays, killed by diseases including HIV and hepatitis C transmitted by the very blood products that were supposed to save them. In total, eighty-nine boys with haemophilia attended this pioneering school in the decade after 1975. Only sixteen are still alive.

Ade, who attended the school from 1980 until 1989, lost not only most of his school friends; his two brothers, Jason, who had AIDS, and Gary, who had hepatitis C, also died. But the contaminated blood scandal does not just inflict physical harms. Ade now suffers from what he describes as 'lifeboat syndrome' and feelings of 'guilt' about still being alive. 'I've watched so many people die,' he told me quietly. 'I stopped counting at forty – and that was just at Treloar's.'

The parents of Colin Smith, who was just seven when he died of AIDS in January 1990, weighing less than a four-month-old baby, were the next brave family to back the crusade. Colin, a haemophiliac, was only ten months old when he received factor VIII during an operation to fit grommets at the Royal Gwent Hospital in Newport, south Wales. In one of the most harrowing interviews of my career, Colin's mum, Jan, revealed that towards the end of his short life he could barely hold up his own body, and had to be picked up in a sheepskin to avoid being hurt.

When Colin fell ill in the mid-1980s, public concern around AIDS had reached fever pitch. The stigma of being associated with the tabloid-styled 'gay plague' was devastating. The Smiths were soon dubbed the 'AIDS family'. The terrible four-letter acronym that had come from nowhere to become such a harbinger of doom was scratched on their door and daubed on the side of their house. The parents of the children at the school Colin attended threatened to boycott it. As he approached his final days, even Colin's medics objected to the family bringing him home to die. The reason? They said no undertaker would take his funeral.

Colin is buried in the cemetery close to the family home. The epitaph on his gravestone, which the family still visit every week, reads: 'Keep smiling, freckle face. Miss you always, sweetheart.'[14]

Colin was not the only little boy whose life was devastated by the scandal. Chris Cornes was an orphan by the age of ten after losing both parents to infections that were contracted from contaminated blood donors. Chris was once part of the biggest haemophiliac family in the UK. His father, Garry, who contracted HIV and hepatitis C from infected blood transfusions, was one of seven brothers. Six suffered from the disorder; five are now dead. Chris's mother, Lee, discovered she had contracted HIV from Garry when she was seven months pregnant with Chris. She died in 2000. The orphaned boy eventually saw out his childhood in hostels for the homeless, with barely enough money for food and clothes.

Chris, who first spoke to me when he was thirty-one, eventually found work as an account manager in Northfield, Birmingham. But he told me that the contaminated blood scandal had 'shattered his life' and led him to contemplate suicide. Although he escaped any physical consequences of the scandal, he has been mentally scarred by the experience and still suffers from post-traumatic stress disorder. He remembers his mother clearly: 'She used to dote on me. It was as if she was trying to make up for the fact that she and Dad weren't going to be around very long.' Sadly, he has fewer recollections of his father. 'I have almost no memories of him except for one vivid image of us together when he lay dying in bed.'[15]

Over the next few months, I pored over the details of the broken lives of the victims and their families. Among them were widows who had lost husbands, parents who had lost children and children who had been orphaned. Almost a year after the launch of the campaign, it still looked like Kleenex was going to be the only winner. But with every story, I felt we must be getting closer to a breakthrough.

Eventually, David Cameron used his last act as prime minister to unveil a £125 million package to increase the ex-gratia payments to those affected. While the additional funding was welcome, it did not provide closure for the victims and their families. And as Theresa May took over as prime minister in July 2016, the chances of achieving justice for the victims looked further away than ever.

Everything changed when May lost her majority following the snap 2017 general election. Less than a month after May re-entered Downing Street, I bumped into Diana Johnson in Parliament – a chance meeting that would alter the course of the campaign. I had worked out that the Democratic Unionist Party (DUP), which was propping up May's government in a 'confidence and supply' arrangement, was supportive of a public inquiry. When I mentioned this to the Hull North MP, by now the co-chair of the All-Party Parliamentary Group on Haemophilia and Contaminated Blood, she offered to ask the leaders of all the main political parties to sign a letter calling for a Hillsborough-style inquiry.

By now, my home was *The Sunday Times*. In my second week as deputy political editor, the newspaper published the letter.[16] Among those who had signed it was the DUP's Nigel Dodds. Little did I suspect that just days later – and more than seventeen years after I had written my first story about the scandal – the government would finally agree to the inquiry. It seemed almost too good to be true when the prime minister's special advisor rang me to deliver the news an hour before May announced it on the floor of the House of Commons. 'Well done,' he said. 'Just two weeks into your new job and you have got your inquiry.'

At the time of writing, that inquiry is now preparing to deliver its verdict, due in the autumn, 2023. Hopes are high among campaigners that justice will finally be achieved for the families, many of whom want closure after decades of howling into the wind. Some simply want the answer to the crucial question: why? How on earth was this allowed to happen? Was UK blood policy one of the most monumental cock-ups in modern British history? Or is there a more sinister explanation, one that may make more sense when viewed alongside the countless warnings issued by eminent experts about the deadly effect of contaminated blood products?

Ministers have already paid interim compensation of £100,000 to each of the surviving victims, or, in the case of those deceased, their partners. This was the first sign that the government, which for decades had been ducking responsibility for the tragedy, is prepared to accept liability. The current prime minister, Rishi Sunak, is now under pressure to extend the same interim payment to orphans who have lost parents and parents who have lost children. This would be in addition to any final financial settlement recommended at the conclusion of the public inquiry. However, the question remains: can any sum of money ever be big enough to compensate for the trauma and the broken lives the scandal has left behind?

•

This is the story of four decades of tragedy, lies and cover-ups – but also of the brave victims and their families who refused to be silenced by the authorities, no matter how much they despaired.

In order to tell their harrowing story, I have interviewed dozens of those whose lives have been torn apart by this scandal, as well as reviewing thousands of documents, interview transcripts and statements provided to the Infected Blood Inquiry.

It is the story of a determined group of campaigners who never lost faith, and how they enlisted the support of politicians such as Diana Johnson and Andy Burnham, the former health secretary and current Mayor of Greater Manchester, who threatened to go to the police with a dossier of evidence that exposed what he described as a 'criminal cover-up on an industrial scale'. In what was his final speech in the House of Commons in April 2017, Burnham provided examples of inappropriate treatment given to patients, tests being done on people without their knowledge or consent, and results from such tests being withheld for several years. He labelled these 'criminal acts' and compared the campaign by relatives of infected people to the efforts of the families of Liverpool football fans crushed to death in the Hillsborough stadium disaster of 1989.

I am proud to have played a small part in that campaign, and I will continue to hold the authorities to account on behalf of the families of the dead and those victims still alive: decent people like Sue Threakall, who lost her husband, Bob, after he contracted HIV; Su Gorman, whose husband, Steve Dymond, died decades after being infected with hepatitis C; Mark Ward, who was told aged fourteen that he had contracted HIV from infected blood products; and of course Mick Mason, whose story inspired a young journalist to join a two-decade-long fight for justice.

Anita Roddick.

1

BLOOD MONEY

1960–75

The birth of a healthy, bouncing baby is cause for celebration. The arrival of Anita Roddick's second child was no exception. It was July 1971, a year when the Soviet Union launched the first space station into orbit, the Disney World theme park opened in Florida, and the UK's little-known education secretary, Margaret Thatcher, took the controversial decision to end free school milk for children. Roddick, who years later became a household name as the founder of The Body Shop, had not had an easy time in labour after she was admitted to hospital on the south coast, close to her home in the seaside town of Littlehampton, West Sussex. She had suffered significant blood loss and required an emergency transfusion, but memories of her daughter's traumatic birth soon faded as she held her newborn child for the first time.

The euphoria of welcoming a new arrival into the world would come to be tinged with heart-rending grief, however. Roddick did not know this at the time, but while giving birth to a precious new life she had also become one of thousands of innocent patients to be handed a death sentence – an avoidable tragedy that would not be discovered for another thirty years.

Roddick's transfusion had not been screened. The apparently life-saving blood had, in fact, been infected with hepatitis C, a virus that can cause fatal liver damage but can also circulate undetected in humans for many years. The virus did not appear to inflict any immediate effects on Roddick. Five years after the birth of her daughter, Samantha, she opened her first shop in Brighton. A self-confessed hippy who used natural ingredients to make cosmetics she sold in reusable plastic bottles, Roddick's goal was to earn an income for herself, Samantha and her other daughter, Justine, while her husband, Gordon, spent two years riding horseback from Buenos Aires to New York.

It was not an easy start. Roddick's premises in Brighton were so derelict that she once joked that she chose green as The Body Shop colour to camouflage the mould on the walls. She then had to sell fifty per cent of the business to a local garage owner to raise money for a second shop after a bank rejected her application for a loan. When Gordon finally rode back from his Latin American sojourn, he suggested franchising branches. It was a fine strategic decision.

The Body Shop was ahead of the curve on environmental issues and expanded rapidly. The company was one of the first to prohibit the use of ingredients tested on animals in some of its products, and one of the first to promote fair trade with developing countries. The Body Shop franchise eventually grew to more than 2,000 shops in fifty countries. By the 1990s, Roddick was the fourth-richest woman in Britain. She became a dame in 2003, and in 2006, she sold the business to L'Oréal for £652 million.

It is not known whether the decision to divest herself of

the thriving business was linked to a terrible discovery two years earlier.

The blood transfusion Roddick had received during Samantha's birth had finally come back to haunt her. The entrepreneur was diagnosed with cirrhosis of the liver. The debilitating illness was detected following a routine blood test that was ordered as part of a medical examination to assess her suitability for a life insurance policy. The blood test indicated abnormal liver function – and subsequent tests uncovered the hepatitis C virus in her blood.

The diagnosis came as a complete bolt out of the blue for Roddick and her family. The only explanation she could find for the illness was the blood transfusion she had received thirty-three years earlier – long before blood donors were routinely screened for the disease.

Roddick was diagnosed in 2004 but did not reveal details of her illness until Valentine's Day 2007. 'I have hepatitis C. It's a bit of a bummer but you groan and move on,' she wrote in a post on her website. 'I had no idea I had this virus. I was having routine blood tests when it showed up.'

She added, with her characteristic optimism: 'I do have cirrhosis. I could still have a good few years – maybe even decades – of life left, but it's hard to say. I could be facing liver cancer tomorrow.'

Roddick also announced that she had become a patron of the Hepatitis C Trust, a charity she had discovered when she first found out she had the virus. She called for hepatitis C to be taken more seriously as a 'public health challenge', and questioned the success of a government awareness campaign.

'Having hepatitis C means that I live with a sharp sense of my own mortality, which in many ways makes life more vivid and immediate,' she said. 'It makes me even more determined to just get on with things.'

Less than seven months later, Roddick was dead. She suffered an acute brain haemorrhage at around 6.30p.m. on 10 September 2007, after being admitted to St Richard's Hospital, Chichester, the previous evening suffering from a severe headache. She was just sixty-four.

The entrepreneur's death left a huge hole in her family's life. Speaking after her untimely demise, her husband Gordon said: 'It's as if somebody has reached into my heart and turned out the lights.'[1]

Her youngest daughter, Samantha, was utterly devastated. In an interview for *The Sunday Times* almost a decade after her mother's death, she told me how she struggled with 'unconscious guilt' stemming from the knowledge that the blood transfusion during her own birth ultimately led to the early passing of her indomitable mother. Samantha, who has rarely ever spoken about her mother's death or the contaminated blood scandal, spoke slowly and articulately as we discussed her plight in an emotional telephone conversation. 'I was in my late thirties when she was diagnosed and she was in her sixties, and I knew it was to do with my birth,' she said. 'It was quite a tender subject for my mum, and I didn't really dissect how she found out, but I know it really rested very heavily on her heart.' Samantha, who bears a striking resemblance to her mother, with dark, curly hair framing her face, told me that the greatest tragedy of her mother's illness was that she had not been diagnosed until it was too late to effectively treat the virus. While Roddick had initially undergone groundbreaking treatment, she had to stop taking the medication after it was found to exacerbate her high blood pressure.

'The tragedy around my mum was she didn't get diag-nosed until she had cirrhosis,' Samantha told me. 'If she had known she had hepatitis C when she was a lot younger, she would have been able to have treatment.' Samantha, who founded the lingerie brand Coco de Mer, added: 'How can you think that something as innocent as a woman going into hospital to give birth can lead to someone coming out with hepatitis C? My mum was one of tens of thousands of people who were basically on a Russian roulette.'[2]

Although the origin of the blood Roddick received is unknown, much of the contaminated blood that entered the UK supply chain was imported from America. 'There is a cruel irony that my mum got poisoned by a supply chain, because The Body Shop was the first company in Britain to hold their supply chain properly to account,' Samantha told *The Sunday Times* in another interview.[3]

•

Blood, the elixir of life, is at the centre of this unimaginable tragedy. Since the dawn of humankind, curiosity about the mystical and biological functions of blood has led to both dangerous mistakes and revolutionary discoveries.

The ancient Book of Leviticus, the third book of the Torah and the Old Testament, observes that 'the life of the flesh is in the blood'. Many clinicians would agree with this statement. Red cells carry the oxygen that is required for our bodies and our brains to function. White cells defend us against invasion by lethal pathogens. Platelets and proteins in plasma form clots that can prevent fatal bleeds.

Blood is constantly being renewed by stem cells in our bone marrow; red cells renew every few months, platelets and most white cells every few days. Since marrow stem cells spawn every kind of blood cell, they can, when transplanted, breathe new life into a dying host.

In the verse from Leviticus, the word '*nefesh*', translated as 'life', can also mean 'soul', anointing blood with an intrigue that fascinates to this day. The British journalist Rose George has written extensively about the unique biology of blood and its connections to the origins of the Earth and of life itself. 'The iron in our blood comes from the death of supernovas, like all iron on our planet,' she writes. 'This bright red liquid . . . contains salt and water, like the sea we possibly came from.' George estimates our blood courses 12,000 miles through our veins every single day, while the body's network of blood vessels runs to about 60,000 miles long – more than twice the circumference of the Earth.[4]

Ancient humans were not aware of this science. Nonetheless, they were sure of blood's importance. For them, blood was something mysterious – visible only when dripping from a wound, or during childbirth, miscarriage and menstruation. It was a symbol of life and death.

In pre-modern times, blood was not only a target of treatment but also a source of medicine. In ancient Rome, the philosopher Pliny the Elder reported that gladiators who survived duels in the Colosseum would drink the blood of the fallen in the mistaken belief that it would ward off epilepsy.[5]

Throughout history, the blood of martyrs was also believed to cure disease. *The Golden Legend*, a thirteenth-century account of the lives of saints, attributed healing powers to water used to wash the bloodstained clothes of Thomas à Becket, the Archbishop of Canterbury, who was murdered in 1170. In 1483, King Louis XI of France, a paranoid religious fanatic, reportedly drank vast quantities of blood collected from healthy children in a desperate and ultimately unsuccessful attempt to stave off death from leprosy.[6]

The year 1628 marked a major scientific breakthrough in the history of blood. 'An Anatomical Essay on the Motion of the Heart and Blood in Animals' was published by the English physician William Harvey. His revolutionary insight – that blood circulated from the left side of the heart through arteries and returned to the right side through veins – is often cited as the greatest single discovery in medicine.[7]

Armed with that knowledge, physicians began to consider the possibility of blood transfusions. In 1666, at the Royal Society in London, Richard Lower revealed that he had transfused blood between two dogs, using a goose quill to connect an artery in the neck of one to the jugular vein in the neck of the other. One year later, French physicians introduced blood from a calf into the vein of a young man. The man's pulse rose, sweat formed on his brow, and he complained of severe back pain before dying shortly afterwards.

Such failures led the Royal Society, the French Parliament and the Catholic Church to suspend blood transfusions for human beings. The procedure was banned from orthodox medicine for 150 years and did not become viable again until 1900, when Karl Landsteiner, a physician at the University of Vienna, discovered blood types. Over the next few years, Landsteiner and his colleagues identified the main blood groups we know today: A, B, AB and O. They showed that the interactions between the different groups determined whether a transfusion would be safe. AB blood carriers were universal recipients, able to receive blood from any donor; O carriers, like Landsteiner himself, were universal donors. Now blood could be more safely administered to patients and become, for the first time, a true therapy.

More discoveries followed. In 1914, it was found that sodium citrate prevented blood from clotting, allowing it to be collected from a donor and stored until it was needed by a recipient. In the First World War, this discovery saved the lives of countless wounded soldiers.

By the 1930s, scientists had learned how to separate blood into its constituent parts, including red cells and plasma – the agent that prevents excessive bleeding when a blood vessel is injured. Platelets and proteins in your plasma work together to stop the blood flow by forming a clot over the injury. This vital breakthrough was greeted with much excitement by a particular group of people who, for centuries, had suffered from a terrible blood disorder that seemed to be passed between families.

•

Incidences of excessive or abnormal bleeding were first recorded hundreds of years ago. The Talmud, a collection of Jewish rabbinical writings on laws and traditions from the second century AD, stated that baby boys did not have to be circumcised if two of their brothers had previously died from the procedure.

In 1803, John Conrad Otto, a physician in Philadelphia, was the first to recognise that a bleeding disorder primarily affected men and ran in certain families. He traced the disease back to a female ancestor living in Plymouth, New Hampshire, in 1720. Otto called the males 'bleeders'. In

1813, John Hay published a paper in the *New England Journal of Medicine* proposing that affected men could pass the trait for a bleeding disorder to their unaffected daughters. Friedrich Hopff, a student at the University of Zurich, and his professor Dr Schonlein, are credited with coining the term 'haemorrhaphilia' for the condition, in 1828, later shorted to 'haemophilia'.

Haemophiliacs suffer from an inherited genetic disorder that impairs the body's ability to make blood clots – a process that is needed to stop bleeding. The female is the carrier of the defective gene. If she bears children, a son has a fifty per cent chance of inheriting haemophilia, while a daughter has a fifty per cent of being a carrier herself, which means she can pass the defective gene on to her children. Male children of a man with haemophilia do not inherit this condition.

Blood is made of different types of cells, including red blood cells, white blood cells and platelets, which are all suspended in a straw-coloured liquid called plasma. Platelets are the cells responsible for making blood clot. When a blood vessel is injured, platelets clump together to seal the injury site. They also initiate a complicated chemical reaction to form a mesh made of a substance called fibrin. This reaction always follows a precise pattern, with each clotting protein, known as coagulation factors, turned on in order. When all of the factors are turned on, the blood forms a clot that stops the injury site from bleeding any further. Ordinarily, there are a number of coagulation factors circulating in the blood, waiting to be turned on when an injury occurs. However, if one of the factors is missing, the chemical reaction cannot occur as it should. Each coagulation factor is given a number from I to XIII. The effects of any missing factor will vary, but can include blood loss, which can be severe and life-threatening.

There are two main types of haemophilia. Haemophilia A, which occurs due to low amounts of clotting factor VIII, and haemophilia B, which occurs due to low levels of clotting factor IX. Haemophilia B is also known as Christmas disease, after Stephen Christmas, the first patient to be described with the condition. Both types are typically inherited from parents through an X chromosome carrying a non-functional gene. However, sometimes a new mutation may occur during early development, or haemophilia may develop later in life due to antibodies forming against a clotting factor.

In more recent times, haemophilia became known as the 'royal disease' because the haemophilia gene was passed from Queen Victoria to several ruling families across Russia, Germany and Spain.

Haemophilia was a life-threatening disease at the time, and those who suffered from the condition were often at risk of bleeding to death. Prince Friedrich of Hesse and by Rhine, a haemophiliac, died before his third birthday in 1873 after suffering from a bleed on the brain after falling from a third-storey window, an injury that almost certainly would not have been fatal had he not had the bleeding condition.

Even with advances in medicine, the risks associated with haemophiliacs bleeding to death have always been considered great, leading some physicians to conclude that any treatment, no matter how potentially risky, would be better than none.

It is understood that Queen Victoria's gene was caused by spontaneous mutation. Of her children, one son, Leopold, had haemophilia, and two daughters, Alice and Beatrice, were carriers.

Beatrice's daughter married into the Spanish royal family and passed on the gene to the male heir to the throne, while Alice had a carrier daughter, Alix, who became Empress Alexandra on her marriage to Russia's Czar Nicholas in 1894. Their son, Alexei, who was born in 1904, was treated for haemophilia by the mysterious and self-professed holy man Grigori Rasputin. Alexei's haemophilia was so severe that trivial injuries, such as a bruise, a nosebleed or a cut, were potentially life-threatening. He led a difficult life before being executed by the Bolsheviks during the Russian Revolution in 1918.

If Alexei had survived a few more decades, he might have benefited from the discovery of blood plasma. Often described as 'liquid gold' due to its amber colour, plasma was easier to transport and lasted longer than whole blood transfusions. It saved countless lives, and certainly helped the Allied forces during the Second World War. When a soldier is critically wounded, blood loss is extremely dangerous. In addition to the loss of oxygen-carrying red blood cells, the greatest concern is the loss of fluids, which results in low blood pressure. By transfusing casualties with plasma, blood volume is maintained and blood pressure remains at a normal level, preventing shock.

Because the red blood cells are removed from plasma, the need to match the blood type of the donor to the recipient is unnecessary. In addition, dried plasma can be stored for long periods of time without refrigeration and transported across great distances. Medics on the battlefield simply reconstituted the dried plasma by adding water before transfusion.

Dr Charles R. Drew, an American surgeon, developed the key techniques for preserving plasma in the US. The first African American to receive a Doctor of Science degree, Drew proved that plasma could be stored significantly longer than whole blood. He was headhunted by British officials during the Second World War to create a blood bank for soldiers and civilians. This became known as the 'Blood for Britain' programme and met the desperate need for blood to treat those wounded during the Blitz.[8] It was followed by a huge operation to recruit volunteers in America to give a pint of blood to aid the war effort, establishing the principle of blood donation. To encourage people to come forward, Drew first devised the use of bloodmobiles, trucks with refrigerators serving as donation centres. The American Red Cross participated in the scheme, collecting 13 million units of blood from 14.7 million donors by the end of the Second World War.[9]

Britain also did its bit for the war effort, setting up blood donation centres across the country. Bristol was at the epicentre of the donation programme and became the headquarters for the National Blood Transfusion scheme. At the start of the war, just 2,000 donors were registered; however, by 1944, when the system was running at peak efficiency, British soldiers wounded on D-Day received blood and plasma almost exclusively donated by Bristolians.[10]

After the war, the new miracle plasma was even more in demand, and more was needed for modern surgery and pioneering treatment, particularly for haemophiliacs and patients with von Willebrand disease, the most common hereditary blood-clotting disorder.

In the early 1960s, Dr Judith Graham Pool discovered a process of freezing and thawing plasma to get a layer of factor-rich plasma. A group of researchers at Stanford University, USA, discovered it had ten times the concentration of factor VIII, the missing coagulation factor in patients with haemophilia A. Cryoprecipitate, as it was known, was heralded as a wonder cure for haemophilia, as it was seen as the most effective way to stop bleeds. However, it could only be administered via transfusion in hospital, and because there was still only a small number of donors, it was always in short supply.

The real game-changer came with the development of factor concentrates. It was discovered that if cryoprecipitate was dissolved, treated chemically and subjected to a centrifugal process, it produced a crystalline powder, which had ten times the clotting power of cryoprecipitate. This became known as factor VIII concentrate because it mimicked the naturally occurring factor VIII coagulation factor.

The first plasma-derived factor VIII concentrate was approved in 1966, followed by a factor IX concentrate in 1970. Clotting factor could be freeze-dried into a powder that was easy to store, carry and transport. It meant that people with haemophilia could be treated more quickly and have their bleeds dealt with at home or at work, enabling them to lead more normal lives. When a cut or bruising led to bleeding, they could simply take a bottle containing factor VIII, or factor IX, out of the fridge, inject themselves with it and their blood would start clotting.

Seismic scientific discoveries often come hand in hand with potent commercial opportunities. Major pharmaceutical companies could smell the emergence of a significant new revenue stream. The creation of a booming global plasma trade in the 1960s marks the genesis of the contaminated blood scandal.

Sadly, haemophiliacs were to bear the brunt.

•

Dame Anita Roddick, who was infected with tainted blood products in 1971, is one of the earliest victims in the UK.

By then, the four pharmaceutical companies who manufactured plasma products for patients across the world – Baxter, Bayer, Armour and Alpha – had begun to engage in disturbing and unethical practices. As demand grew, these companies went to extreme lengths to find enough donors.

The first ominous warning of the tragedy that was about to unfold was chronicled in 1970 by Richard Titmuss, Britain's leading commentator on social policy at the time, in the book for which he is most remembered, *The Gift Relationship*. He demonstrated conclusively that the British system of voluntary blood donation was superior to the American paid-for system in two crucial respects. It avoided contamination of blood products, but it also reaffirmed, on a personal level, the collective duty of care to strangers on which the NHS was founded. The book stated: 'In the United States, Britain, and other modern societies the most dangerous of these hazards [resulting from the use of blood and blood products] is serum hepatitis. It is becoming a major public health problem throughout the world.' The book concluded that a private market in blood entails 'much greater risks to the recipient of disease, chronic disability and death'.[11]

Not a lot happens in the rural southern US state of Arkansas, best known for hosting the World Cheese Dip

Championship and the World Championship Duck Calling Contest. But inside the Arkansas Department of Corrections, looming among the cotton rows in this 'deepest of the Deep South' town, a global scandal was brewing.

In 1964, some pharmaceutical firms, including Baxter and Bayer, took the fatal decision to collect blood from prisoners in an apparent attempt to cut costs and boost profits. At the Cummins Unit, home to Arkansas' male death-row population, and the place where the country and western singer Johnny Cash once performed as part of a tour, inmates 'would regularly cross the prison hospital's threshold to give blood, lured by the prospect of receiving $7 a pint'. One commentator described it as a 'creepy ritual to behold', with 'platoons of prisoners lying supine on rows of cots, waiting for the needle-wielding prison orderly to puncture a vein and watch the clear bags fill with blood'.[12]

Administrators, more recently under the state governorship of Bill Clinton, then sold the blood, which could be traded on the international plasma market for $50 a pint, to brokers, who in turn shipped it to other states, and to Japan, Italy, Spain and Canada. Half the profits were funnelled back to the Arkansas Department of Corrections.[13]

Unfortunately, many of the prisoners were addicted to drugs and their blood contained several deadly diseases, including hepatitis – the same virus that eventually killed Roddick.

Dangerous blood being injected into the global blood supply did not seem to concern the Arkansas prison authorities. Years later, they were exposed for doctoring prisoners' medical records to remove any evidence that the inmates were carrying the deadly diseases.[14]

Bill Douglas, a former prisoner and hepatitis sufferer, described the regime in the Cummins Unit in Arkansas, where he regularly donated plasma. 'They didn't care if you had to crawl to get there so long as you were able to give blood,' he said. 'You were never checked. It was like a cattle chute. That's the way it was done.'[15]

Dr Edwin Barron, a medical administrator at the facility, was so disgusted by the practices there that he decided to resign. 'They did little or no screening of anybody,' he said. 'It was obvious to me . . . that this was a time bomb that had been planted here.'[16]

The pharmaceutical companies were raking it in and seemingly failed to share his concerns. One of those involved was the reincarnation of a company that already had form for prioritising profits over human lives.

Bayer is a chemical and pharmaceutical giant founded in Barmen, Germany. During the First World War, it manufactured chemical weapons including chlorine gas, which was used to horrendous effect in the trenches. Bayer later merged to form the massive German conglomerate Interessengemeinschaft Farben, or IG Farben for short. It became the largest company in Germany and the single largest donor to Adolf Hitler's election campaign.

During the Second World War, IG Farben used slave labour in many of its factories and mines. By 1944, more than 83,000 forced labourers and death-camp inmates had been put to work in the IG Farben camp at Auschwitz in Nazi-occupied Poland.

Auschwitz was a vast labour and death camp that consumed as much electricity as the entire city of Berlin, and is estimated to have cost more than one million lives. IG employee and SS major Dr Helmuth Vetter, stationed at Auschwitz, conducted human medical experiments by order of Bayer. He was convicted of war crimes in 1947 and was executed in 1949.

Years later, correspondence between the Auschwitz camp commander and Bayer was unearthed. It dealt with the sale of 150 female prisoners for experimental purposes and involved haggling over the price. One exchange noted: 'The experiments were performed. All test persons died. We will contact you shortly about a new shipment at the same price.'[17]

In 1946, the Nuremberg war crimes tribunal concluded that without IG Farben the Second World War would simply not have been possible. Telford Taylor, the chief prosecutor, warned: 'These companies, not the lunatic Nazi fanatics, are the main war criminals. If the guilt of these criminals is not brought to daylight and if they are not punished, they will pose a much greater threat to the future peace of the world than Hitler if he were still alive.' The indictment also warned that due to the activities of IG Farben, 'the life and happiness of all peoples in the world were adversely affected'.[18]

A few years after the conclusion of the war, in 1952, Bayer quietly re-formed out of the disgraced assets of IG Farben.

Back in Arkansas, problems with blood plasma supply were not solely down to the high-risk prison donors. Risks of infection also increased exponentially because of the decision by pharmaceutical companies and so-called blood fractionisers, which transform the blood into medicines for haemophiliacs, to mix blood provided from large groups in the manufacture of factor VIII products. Blood extracted from as many as 60,000 donors could be used for each batch, meaning one infected donor could contaminate each batch and then infect every patient who received it.

Many victims were later able to trace batch numbers of the blood products they received back to the Arkansas prison. The first to do that was Carol Anne Grayson. Her husband, Peter Longstaff, a haemophiliac, died aged forty-seven after being infected with HIV, hepatitis B and C, and vCJD. Grayson, who lives in Jesmond, Newcastle, told the *Northern Echo*: 'Batch numbers of treatment received by my husband Peter who had both viruses was tracked back via US lawyers to Arkansas State Penitentiary where prisoners sold their blood, which was used by the NHS. Blood was imported from the US putting profit before safety and sourced from high-risk donors [. . . violating] virtually every safety rule in the book.'[19]

In the UK in the early 1970s, another issue was emerging. With all the excitement around developments in blood plasma, the NHS was struggling to keep up with surging demand. The Department of Health and Social Security was facing regular criticism in the media for failing to meet the ongoing need for new blood products that could be more easily administered at home.

A small amount of domestically produced factor VIII concentrate was made at the Blood Products Laboratory (BPL) in Elstree, north London, and at a smaller plant, the Protein Fractionation Laboratory, in Oxford. But by 1972, clamour from patients – in particular haemophiliacs – led to increasing quantities of commercial factor VIII being imported to the UK from the United States.

Despite repeated promises from politicians that the UK

would become self-sufficient and produce enough home-grown factor concentrates, this was never achieved. The reasons for this have been the subject of intense debate over the decades; many blame the lack of a centralised funding model, and the absence of a central body with the executive power to direct and coordinate efforts.

The introduction of the imported factor concentrates caused quite a stir among the haemophilia community. At the time, nothing substantive was yet known about the dangerous donor and sourcing process, and many believed the treatment would be a gateway to a healthier and more normal life.

The *Yorkshire Post* and *The Sunday Times* both ran campaigns attacking the lack of the new blood plasma products in the early months of 1975. In one article in the *Yorkshire Post*, entitled 'Angry Doctors Speak Out', Dr Peter Jones, the head of the Newcastle Haemophilia Centre, is quoted extensively about the frustration he felt about the perceived undertreatment of his patients at a time when commercial concentrates were available.

He said: 'The answer lies in the reorganisation of the British Blood Transfusion Service. Personally, I am not prepared to wait for that reorganisation or for a British product to become available in sufficient quantities. When I see my patients growing up and suffering, I am convinced that home therapy is the only answer. The sooner a patient treats a bleed, the sooner it stops and the less concentrate it requires . . . [It] is the same old British story – no money to develop anything.'[20]

In its annual report for 1975–6, the Scottish National Blood Transfusion Service reflected the increased calls for the use of factor concentrates:

Of all the blood products available, the only one which has aroused an emotive response in the UK (Scotland is less vociferous) is the supply of factor VIII and its use in the treatment of haemophilia. Parliamentary questions, newspapers, wireless and television have all been used to publicise the demands of the pressure groups. Propaganda has been along two main lines – a demand for immediate implementation of home therapy regimes . . . and a philosophy that the haemophilia patient should lead a perfectly normal life.[21]

Few ordinary citizens knew at this stage that the miraculous and hugely popular new treatment carried hidden dangers. But the World Health Organization (WHO) did. In May 1975, it published Resolution 28.72 on the use and supply of blood and blood products, which expressed 'serious concern' at the international blood and plasma trade. One of its principal concerns was that there was a 'higher risk of transmitting diseases when blood products have been obtained from paid donors rather than from voluntary donors'. The WHO, therefore, recommended that its member states promote the development of national blood services based on the voluntary, non-remunerated donation of blood.[22]

This resolution from the WHO was one of the first warnings on record to be ignored. Sadly, it would not be the last.

The first significant crack in the façade came six months later, in December 1975. An investigation team from Granada's groundbreaking *World in Action* programme first exposed the murky world of the US plasma trade to a mainstream audience.[23] It sent a team of reporters to the

Hyland Donor Centre in San Jose, near San Francisco, one of twenty-four clinics in the US producing plasma products sent to treat haemophiliacs in the UK. The documentary focused on the fact that US donors were paid, which meant that blood banks became a magnet for those on the lowest rung of the socio-economic scale, desperate for their next fix. Such was the scale of the phenomenon among the country's down-and-outs, they even had their own phrase for donating: 'Ooze for booze.'

It didn't seem to matter to the company featured in the programme, the Hyland Division of Baxter Laboratories, that the blood they were selling on to foreign health services such as the NHS came from donors who were already infected with life-threatening forms of hepatitis.* The programme revealed that the health risks from US paid donors were thirteen times greater than from British volunteer donors because of their backgrounds.

The makers of the episode, entitled 'Blood Money', spent four weeks in the US observing clinical practices after an unprecedented outbreak of hepatitis among UK haemophiliacs appeared to be linked to a blood product called Hemofil, manufactured by Hyland. Hemofil, a synthetic form of factor VIII, contained blood plasma taken from paid donors, including America's drug addicts and alcoholics.

At least sixty cases of hepatitis linked to this treatment were identified in the UK at the time, including two that may have contributed to the patients' deaths. The outbreak was discovered by Dr John Craske, a consultant virologist at a Manchester hospital. His study on the surge in cases of hepatitis among patients at the Bournemouth haemophilia

* Hyland were approached for comment, but they did not respond.

centre who had used a commercial concentrate was published in the *Lancet* on 2 August 1975.

He told *World in Action*:

Checking amongst the incidence of hepatitis in the local
population shows that there was no abnormal incidence of hepatitis in the local community or amongst
the various patients affected, and it seemed therefore
that the most likely thing was the introduction of some
new product or something else associated with their
treatment.

We therefore checked the transfusion histories of
these patients, and it became apparent that this jaundice was associated with the administration of one
particular batch of a commercial concentrate . . . called
Hemofil, which had been introduced for use for the first
time at the end of 1973.[24]

Professor Ari Zuckerman, a leading British hepatitis
expert who accompanied the television crew, added: 'Well,
it's been recognised for a number of years now that bought
blood does carry a higher risk. And it's difficult to actually
pinpoint the reason, but it seems that individuals who are
willing to sell their blood are normally from a background
which appears to be rather poor socio-economically.'[25]

World in Action visited the Hyland Donor Centre in East
Baltimore, USA, in the heart of the city's red-light district.
The decision was taken to film outside the clinic after the TV
crew was denied access to the centre by the pharmaceutical
company. The reason given by the company was: 'unattractive outside situations, unattractive donors'.[26]

At 6a.m., the film crew filmed a queue of donors waiting
to give blood in freezing temperatures. The queue was largely

made up of unemployed African Americans. Some were homeless, while others said they were on parole or had recently left prison. The crowd was fractious, and the narrator suggested many of those present appeared to have been drinking alcohol. The camera panned in on one individual who was swigging from a bottle before sticking it underneath the band of his trousers and tucking his shirt over it to obscure the evidence. The narrator claimed the plasma industry was booming because of the recession America was suffering.

'Government rules say that any donor under the influence of alcohol is unsuitable, and centres tell donors not to drink twenty-four hours before selling plasma,' said the narrator. 'But many we saw did just that. Donors are allowed to sell half a litre of plasma twice a week. They usually get two pounds fifty for the first half litre and five pounds for the second.'[27]

For every litre of blood donated, Hyland was left with about half a litre of plasma. Up to 6,000 litres were 'pooled' before there was enough to extract the concentrated factor VIII, which could then be sold on for a profit.

Dr James Mosley, of the University of Southern California, told the programme there were risks from pooling thousands of donations to make Hemofil, as just one unit of blood carrying the disease could contaminate the entire batch. He said:

> If it's one in a thousand and you pool them, it's going to contaminate the other nine hundred and ninety-nine, and particularly if there is a concentration technique which not only concentrates the factor that you are interested in – the clotting factor – but also concentrates the virus.

Unfortunately, that happens to be true for the clotting factors – the virus is concentrated along with them. So even with the best donors, a large pool is a risk, and the larger the pool, the higher the risk.

Asked to assess the risk of getting hepatitis from a clotting factor concentrate, Dr Mosley said: 'Probably one hundred per cent if the individual is susceptible.'[28]

When journalists posed as donors at five Hyland centres, the checks to reduce the potential risk of high-risk donors giving blood were largely absent. The undercover reporters were shocked by their findings. No checks were made on false addresses, which would have excluded donors who were homeless. Drugs checks were also not always carried out, and physical examinations were not always done fully but were certified as such. Certain medical questions, such as those about their medical history, were also not asked, but were filled in on forms as having been answered satisfactorily.

According to the programme, Hyland had been warned thirteen times since November 1974 for breaking federal regulations at its plasma centres and processing plants. The same year, the US Bureau of Biologies was forced to close one centre temporarily.

Yet Hyland was not the only manufacturer of plasma to face these kinds of criticism from the programme. When *World in Action* spoke to Russell S. Tate, the manager of a centre owned by another unnamed supplier, he agreed that 'quite a few' alcoholics and drug addicts got through their screening processes to give blood. Asked if it was ethical to take blood from such people, Tate responded with a chuckle: 'American business. I don't know whether it is ethical or not, but up to this point in time, no one has found an acceptable substitute for human blood, and so we have to get it somehow.'[29]

The programme also revealed an explicit warning from Dr J. Garrott Allen, the US-based world-renowned hepatitis expert, in a letter to William Maycock, the then-head of the British Blood Transfusion Service. Dr Allen had written to Maycock saying:

> Commercial blood banking perpetuates the high-risk rates for hepatitis we encounter with their products and it also tempts these same firms to sell residual products. It does not take much commercial blood in a mixed combination to bring up an astounding attack rate from one that is relatively unnoticed; this is the basis of my concern about Britain purchasing commercial blood products from our country.

Like the WHO's warning, this stark letter was also ignored by the government – an action that would astound and disgust victims' families when it emerged years later.

World in Action interviewed Dr William Maycock, who denied he was complacent about the risks from imported concentrates from the US. He said: 'No, I don't think so. I think the quality of this material was controlled, both here and in America.' He added: 'Dr Allen's views are more his observations that had all been published and were well known to those concerned who were using this material.'[30]

Maycock's failure to sound the alarm would have devastating consequences. But others were not so dismissive. David Owen, a UK health minister at the time the programme aired, was concerned about its revelations when briefed by *World in Action*, but he said the UK was not in a position to refuse foreign donors as it was not then self-sufficient in plasma. Asked about the risk of viruses entering the blood supply, Owen told the programme: 'We'll never be absolutely certain, even when we produce it ourselves, so there is always some risk. There's a risk from any form of using blood from donors. But you have to balance the risk. At the moment, in this country, we have not got full production facilities of our own. I would much prefer it, and the sooner we've got our own, the better.'

He added: 'As soon as we've got our own, and we're self-sufficient, then comes the question of whether it is reasonable to any longer rely on provision from other countries, and I think that raises some profoundly important moral issues as well as the whole question of whether you're satisfied with their standards of safety.'[31]

British patients who were injected with imported factor concentrates from the US told the programme they were concerned about the terrible impact of the recent spikes in hepatitis uncovered by Dr Craske.

Keith Proud, a young, long-haired, bearded hippy wearing rose-tinted glasses who lived with his mother in Gateshead, revealed that he had been treating himself at home with Hemofil for the past two years, and had recently been diagnosed with hepatitis.

'It started off with backache, things like that, feeling pretty rotten, and a couple of days after that, I started to turn yellow, the whites of my eyes went yellow. I started vomiting and generally feeling pretty rough,' he told the programme. 'I couldn't eat anything. I was only drinking fluids.'

Asked whether he had since been put off using Hemofil, Proud said he was prepared to 'accept the risks'. He said the only time he had questioned whether it was worth it was when he was 'vomiting really badly', adding: 'But two days later, I had a bleeding in my elbow and I had no hesitation in going to the fridge, getting my Hemofil out, mixing it and injecting it, because I knew that would stop the bleed and the pain from that bleed was going to be so much worse than any of the pain I'd suffered with hepatitis.'

His mother told the programme: 'As much as I feared that Keith was really ill when he had hepatitis, he suffered far more when there was nothing at all.'[32]

Although Keith and his mother believed the risks associated with receiving the imported factor VIII outweighed the suffering he faced without the cutting-edge treatment, they could not have predicted the scandal that would soon engulf the haemophilia community. Yet by the time he had injected his first dose of Hemofil as a young twenty-something, the seeds of the impending disaster had already been sown. Despite the desperate hope that this new treatment would transform his life, and the lives of thousands of others like him, it instead did the reverse: it led him and a generation of young haemophiliacs to an early grave. Keith died in 1987. He was just thirty-seven years old.

*From left to right: Andrew Cussons,
Barry Briggs, Andrew Bruce, Norman Simmons and
Nick Sainsbury on a school trip to Canada, 1980.*

2

SCHOOL OF DEATH

1974–82

Nick Sainsbury woke up in his dormitory and turned to his best friend in the bed beside his. He immediately knew something was wrong. The boy's face had turned bright yellow overnight. In fact, his entire body was the colour of a banana.

The pair were only twelve at the time, and were in their second year at Lord Mayor Treloar College in Alton, Hampshire. They were still at a carefree age, unburdened by experience and doubt. Most events could be turned on their heads and transformed into humour. So it was in that spirit that Nick told his friend he looked like a 'Chinaman'. He was not intending to be racist, but, like many young boys, became swept up in the moment, and the two school friends collapsed into giggles.

They could not know, of course, that the unusual tone of the boy's skin was no laughing matter. It was an ominous indication of the horrors that were to come.

It was the autumn term of 1975 when Nick's friend developed jaundice – the year the Vietnam war ended and one of the very first blockbuster films, *Jaws*, was released on the big screen.

The boy was one of around fifteen students at the boarding school to suffer the same fate, in what was eventually diagnosed as a hepatitis B outbreak.

Hepatitis B is an infection of the liver caused by a virus that is spread through blood and body fluids. It often does not cause any obvious symptoms in adults and typically passes in a few months without treatment. However, in children it can persist for years, and may eventually cause long-term health problems, including liver damage, liver failure, liver cancer and death.

Ironically, it was the day of the routine school medical when Nick woke up to find his friend's eyes and skin tinged with yellow. The boys affected were told by the school's headmaster, Alec Macpherson, not to worry about their condition.

'The only explanation we were ever given was when the headmaster stood up at mealtime and said, "I understand that some of you are worried about this hepatitis that's been going round,"' Nick recalled. 'He said, "We've been told to ask you not to worry; there are two types of hepatitis, the fatal kind, serious, and the non-fatal, mild type, and you've got the mild type, so there's nothing to worry about." And that's all the information we were given.'[1]

But Nick could see the boys were affected for a long time afterwards. He was concerned to notice that school staff had started to sterilise the affected pupils' crockery and cutlery after every use, treating them rather like nineteenth-century lepers. It seemed a disproportionate response to a virus they were all being told was inconsequential, and Nick's suspicions began to grow.

'They had to hand their plates in to the canteen staff, and all their cutlery, crockery, it all had, I think, a red spot in the middle, and they had to hand that over in front of every-body [to be sterilised]. And I just thought that was awful,' he recalled decades later, when he was asked to recount the events from his school days.[2]

At first, however, Nick and his peers believed their teachers. 'We trusted what we were being told. We had no reason to believe anything else,' he told me in a telephone call from his home in Hull, decades after he had left the school. Months later, when the devastating *World in Action* programme was aired in December 1975, real doubts about what they had been told began creeping in. As we have seen, the programme lifted the lid on the dangers of the new wonder drug factor VIII, in particular Hemofil, a drug widely used at Lord Mayor Treloar College. Nick, who wore spectacles and was a slight redhead during his school days, remembered watching the programme with mounting concern. He had reason to be concerned: like his friend, Nick was one of a community of young haemophiliacs at Treloar's, as it later became known.

The school was founded in 1907, when the Lord Mayor of the City of London, Sir William Purdie Treloar, set up a 'Cripples' Fund' as his mayoral appeal. His aim was to build a hospital and school outside the city for children with non-pulmonary tuberculosis. On 13 June of that year, he wrote in his diary that Her Majesty Queen Alexandra 'came to Mansion House to open the Queen's Fete in aid of my Cripples' Fund'.[3]

By 1908, Sir William had raised enough funds to open a school and hospital in Alton, a market town that dates back to the Domesday survey of 1086, in east Hampshire near the source of the River Wey.

Since opening, Treloar's steadily grew to become one

of England's leading care centres for disabled youngsters. A unique NHS centre was opened on the campus to much fanfare, ensuring that pupils could access the latest medical treatments while continuing their studies with minimal disruption.

From 1956 onwards, it also became home to a growing number of young haemophiliacs, who hoped this elite country refuge could offer them the best chance of a normal life. With a snooker room, swimming pool and archery field, the imposing manor house seemed like something out of a fairy tale, offering opportunities for child haemophiliacs that they previously could only have dreamed of.

But their dreams quickly turned into nightmares. Over the years, it slowly emerged that the cutting-edge treatments that were supposed to help them instead hid a deadly secret – one that would lead Treloar's to earn a terrifying reputation as the 'school of death'. According to Nick, the events at his old school are a 'tragedy within the tragedy of the contaminated blood scandal'.[4]

•

Nick was born in 1963. He was diagnosed as a severe haemophiliac after suffering a serious brain bleed when he was just two months old, which left him with coordination problems. He attended the primary school opposite his family home near Hull, but his debilitating condition meant that he missed an increasing number of lessons. 'I was never there because of bleeds on my left knee,' he said.[5]

Nick spent long periods of time in hospital, and was not able to enjoy the same experiences as his peers. Instead of climbing trees and playing conkers, he was wrapped up in cotton wool by his parents, who knew that every time he had an accident or a bleed, he would spend more time away from them in hospital.

During the latter part of his time at primary school, he spent eight weeks in traction in Oxford, at a specialist haemophilia centre. He then spent another six weeks in Hull Royal Infirmary in plaster. He also underwent a hare lip and cleft pallet operation, the wound from which bled profusely for several weeks. In total, he had missed more than eighteen months of lessons by the time he left primary school.

Increasingly frustrated by the limitations imposed on him, Nick mentioned the impact on his schooling during one of his routine appointments with Dr Charles Rizza, the director of the Oxford Haemophilia Centre, who suggested a place at Treloar's could provide an ideal solution. Nick and his mum went to visit the school. Although he didn't much fancy being so far away from home, he recognised that attending the school 'was the only way that . . . I would get an education and have the medical support that I needed on the site'.[6]

When Nick joined the school in September 1974, he was one of forty-two pupils suffering from haemophilia. He hoped it would be an adventure and looked forward to being around boys who shared his condition, so they could bond over their difficult common experiences and support each other through treatment.

But it was not to be. Nick struggled to remember many happy memories of his time at Treloar's, where he claimed to have been badly bullied.

'When I joined, in 1974, it was . . . a very harsh . . . regime,' he reflected. 'It wasn't very personal . . . Away from home sixty-six per cent of the year. It was a bit draconian, surnames used only. All of us hated that. It was cold, institutional, no warmth. Our housemasters tended to be ex-military and only a few years away from retirement, and I just don't think they could really cope or knew how to tackle issues like bullying.'[7] The Treloar Trust has since accepted that while the majority of accounts by former pupils have praised staff at the college for their supportive and compassionate approach to students, this was 'not universal'. The charity said in its evidence to the Infected Blood Inquiry that this was a 'matter of considerable regret'.[8]

Nick recalled having his ear split open by another pupil on one occasion. He was attacked from behind and his glasses were punched through his ear. The culprit was given a fifty pence fine. Such incidents were made all the more serious when injuries could lead to dangerous bleeds. 'I would think that bullying and fighting must have [accounted for the consumption of] an awful lot of factor VIII,' said Nick.[9] He claimed that his parents were not informed of the assault.

It was an early example of the way the school kept parents in the dark about seismic developments in their children's lives – and their treatment.

Until he started at Treloar's, Nick's bleeds were treated almost entirely with plasma and cryoprecipitate. The only exception he can remember was when he went on a holiday to France with his parents in 1974. They were given several doses of concentrates in case of emergency, which thankfully were not needed. Nick remembered receiving cryoprecipitate transfusions when he arrived at the school, but gradually he was switched to factor VIII.

Although Nick is unaware of when he had his first dose of factor concentrates, a letter in his medical records suggest he was selected for a clinical trial in his second year at the school – something of which he claims to have no recollection. The unsigned letter, dated December 1975, was unearthed years later by lawyers investigating the scandal. Apparently addressed to his parents, the letter starts 'Dear', but the recipient is then left blank. It states:

> In view of the problems of hepatitis in haemophilia, I have been asked by Dr Rosemary Biggs, of the Oxford Haemophilia Centre, to conduct a survey on this subject.
>
> Your son has been selected to receive only Kryobulin [a brand of factor VIII] when he requires transfusing. By limiting him to this type of factor VIII containing material it will be easier to trace the source should he contract hepatitis.[10]

The main purpose of clinical trials is to 'study' new medical products in people. It is vital for people who are considering participation in a clinical trial to understand their role, as a 'subject of research' and not as a patient. According to longstanding medical regulations, participants in clinical trials must understand that they may not benefit from the new treatments. They also need to know that they may be exposed to unknown risks, allowing them to make an informed decision about whether to volunteer.

Nick said he was never told about his involvement in clinical trials, and claimed his parents were not told or asked for their consent either. It would not be the last time that pupils at Treloar's were used as human guinea pigs. Years later, Nick, a former civil servant who was forced to retire early due to ill health, recalled that there was almost no communication between doctors, children and parents.

'There was nothing consensual,' he said. 'It always bothered me a bit that if you were very poorly in bed with a very bad bleed, they never just rang up your parents and said, "Just to let you know, he's in bed and we're going to keep an eye on him over the next few days."'[11]

During his six years at Treloar's, Nick said, he was occasionally treated prophylactically – in other words, given treatment to prevent bleeds, rather than respond to them. His blood was also routinely tested for mysterious viruses. Nick believes his parents were not informed about this prophylactic treatment, nor about the routine blood tests that he underwent – a belief that is shared among other pupils being treated at Treloar's at the same time. Such a practice today, where parental consent is required for everything, including routine vaccinations, is almost unthinkable.

'We were just an ordinary working-class family,' recalled Nick. 'I think they [his parents] would just think, he's getting his treatment, he's doing OK.'[12]

By 1976, significant amounts of commercial concentrates were already in use at Treloar's. In that year, documents show that 13,000 units of Koate, the Cutter product (made by Bayer), 488,594 units of Hemofil, the Hyland product (made by Baxter), and more than half a million – 558,867 – units of Kryobulin were used to treat pupils at the school.[13] One unit of factor VIII is the amount of factor VIII found in one millilitre of fresh plasma. To treat bleeding episodes among haemophiliacs, between fifty and 100 units per kilogram of body weight would typically be administered every twelve hours.

When first treated with the concentrates, Nick remembered, he was being alarmed by some of the labels on the bottles. He tried to raise his concerns with nurses.

'I did read the warning label on the bottle,' he recalled. 'It said, "Warning: this product cannot be guaranteed to be free from viral infection." And I said to one of the haemophilia nurses, "What does this mean, really?" She said, "Take no notice, it's just there for legal purposes. It's because it's from America." So, I thought nothing more of it.'[14]

Nick began self-administering factor VIII in 1979 after being incentivised to do so. He had booked to go on a school holiday of a lifetime to Canada, but was only allowed to travel if he learned how to inject himself. It was no mean feat for Nick, as the coordination problems he had suffered with almost from birth had not been resolved. But Annie, the school nurse, whom Nick adored, was on hand to teach the boys in groups of four.

Having eventually mastered the injections, Nick made the dream trip to Canada. He and his school friends stayed with a local family who had two sons with haemophilia. Their log cabin stood on the shores of Lake Ontario, one of the five great lakes of North America, which boasts a hundred beaches along its coastline.

For Nick, that blissful weekend stay in the Canadian forest is among the happiest memories of his life, and it engendered in him a lifelong love of travel. He still cherishes a memento from the trip: a photograph that was taken on his sixteenth birthday. In it, he proudly poses alongside his school friends Andrew Cussons, Barry Briggs, Andrew Bruce and Norman Simmons. Despite sparking happy memories, the image also churns up darker feelings. None of the gangly, awkward teenage boys beaming alongside Nick in the photo are alive today. Most died before their thirtieth birthdays. All had received contaminated blood products.

As Nick starkly told me: 'What happened was the effective genocide of a generation of haemophiliacs.'[15]

•

In January 1976, the year of Nick's Canada trip, the *World in Action* episode that had exposed the trade in contaminated blood products was still causing reverberations throughout the medical community. Many doctors were resolutely opposed to the importation of potentially dangerous blood products.

In a letter to the *British Medical Journal*, Professor John Cash warned that bringing imported factor VIII into Britain 'represents an unequivocal pathway by which the level of a potentially lethal virus into the whole community is being deliberately increased'.[16] A senior doctor at the Edinburgh and South East Scotland Blood Transfusion Centre, Cash also questioned whether the aspiration for the UK to become self-sufficient by producing enough home-grown factor concentrates was achievable on current spending plans. His intervention would prove prophetic. But, once again, he was ignored by the powers that be.

The intransigence of the UK Government is difficult to understand. Perversely, commercial imports were more expensive than UK products, since the price included payment to donors and profit for the companies. If Westminster and Whitehall had decided to shoulder the upfront costs of producing enough home-grown blood product, perhaps they would have saved money – and lives – in the long run.

In a rare newspaper interview on the contaminated blood scandal in 2015, Cash told me: 'One doesn't always want to be a prophet of doom, but I questioned whether we knew enough about what we were doing. The questions about this have to be addressed by those at the very top of government, ministers and civil servants. We were foot soldiers, given our instructions by officials in London, and it would be nice to know what was in their minds.'[17]

One person at the top of government also shared Cash's concerns. David Owen, the health minister in the Department of Health and Social Security (DHSS) from 1974 to 1976, was a fervent supporter of the UK becoming self-sufficient in blood products when in office. He was primarily worried about the danger of infection from imported commercial products, and also mindful of the cost of these products, which imposed a heavy and increasing financial burden on regional health authorities. Owen's views were shaped by his own experience as a doctor. He was admitted to Sidney Sussex, Cambridge, to study medicine in 1956, and qualified as a doctor in 1962, at which point he began working at St Thomas' Hospital. Owen was a neurology and psychiatric registrar, and helped carry out research into Parkinsonian trauma and neuropharmacology. His interest in medicine continued long after he became a Labour MP in 1966 and his views on Britain's blood supply were influenced by Richard Titmuss's 1970 book *The Gift Relationship*, which clearly spelled out the risks of importing American blood products.

On 22 January 1975, in a written parliamentary answer, Owen said:

> I believe it is vitally important that the National Health Service should become self-sufficient as soon as practicable in the production of factor VIII, including AHG concentrate.
>
> This will stop us being dependent on imports and make the best-known treatment readily available to

people suffering from haemophilia. I have, therefore, authorised the allocation of special finances to boost our own production with the objective of becoming self-sufficient over the next few years.[18]

In a further written parliamentary answer in March 1975, Owen stated that he wanted to allocate £500,000 for increasing production at Blood Products Laboratory (BPL), then a state-owned facility that oversaw the manufacture of human blood plasma products in the UK. However, these funds eventually ended up being used in local campaigns to persuade the public to donate more blood.

In contrast to the United States, where donors were paid for giving blood, the UK has a long history of asking volunteer donors to give blood. The main motivation is often altruism and the desire to make a difference.

The localised strategy was successful. Contemporaneous reports note that blood donations increased from 2.9 million units in 1975 to 11.8 million the next year. However, this welcome progress would prove irrelevant, as the BPL facility still did not have the capacity to process the increased volume of plasma. The scientists in charge, who were well-qualified in research, had little experience in large-scale manufacturing. There was also a serious shortage of space for new materials, or cold storage, and the manufacturing facilities were not upscaled to meet the new demand.

One of the key processes conducted at BPL was fractionation, which is the separation of plasma into proteins that are then isolated and purified before being processed into blood products.

In 1976, Dr Helen Dodsworth, a senior lecturer in haematology at St Mary's Hospital in London, sat on a committee that was convened to advise the DHSS on how much factor VIII concentrate was needed to treat the UK's haemophilia patients. She said they were told that in order to treat their patients adequately, it would be necessary to fractionate at least eighty per cent of the blood that was donated. She explained that the government had, at that point, decided that money was not available for extending the fractionation unit at Elstree. Jenny Willott, the Liberal Democrat MP for Cardiff Central, summarised the situation at the time: 'They are generating more blood donations but actually there is nothing that can be done with the blood. And it is going to waste because they have more than they can actually process.'[19]

The decision to let the BPL wither on the vine spelled disaster for the UK's haemophilia community, who became even more reliant on dangerous factor concentrates imported from America. Dodsworth put it succinctly when she reflected on the situation several years later: 'This is really why we found ourselves buying large quantities of factor VIII concentrate from America, and why we infected so many of our patients . . .'[20]

Tragically, government records indicate a solution that would have saved thousands of UK lives was much closer to home. In 1977, the DHSS explored sending blood from England to the Plasma Fractionation Laboratory in Liberton, Edinburgh, which had the capacity to process a substantial volume of life-saving blood products in excess of Scotland's need. It was hoped that the Scottish facilities would generate enough concentrate for use in England too. However, the option was never taken forward – for reasons that have never been made clear.

Professor Cash said the decision not to use Scotland's spare capacity to produce factor VIII for England was 'a grave error of judgement'. In a letter later unearthed using freedom of information laws, Cash wrote that Scotland had 'very substantial' spare capacity, adding: 'It was assumed by those of us on the shop floor that this experiment would expedite arrangements to give England and Wales assistance – but nothing materialised.' Cash also spoke of 'serious defects in the operational liaison' between the Scottish Home and Health Department and the DHSS. He had attempted to 'persuade on numerous occasions' those higher up of the need for joint working, but to no avail.[21]

In May 1979, Margaret Thatcher swept to power by defeating the Labour Government under James Callaghan, whose ineffectual handling of chaotic labour strikes led to his downfall. The incoming Conservative Government spent some time exploring the rescue of BPL and the potential involvement of commercial partners. But the prospect appears to have been rejected – yet again – on cost grounds, coupled with fears that commercial companies might wish to introduce payment for donors.

With inertia deepening, problems continued to escalate. In July 1979, the Medicines Inspectorate were shocked when visiting BPL. They reported: 'If this were a commercial operation, we would have no hesitation in recommending that manufacture should cease until the facility was upgraded to a minimum acceptable level.' Among their recommendations, the inspectorate advised that the buildings were never designed for the scale of production envisaged. They commented: 'Under no circumstances should production of any product be increased under the existing manufacturing conditions.'[22]

Additional problems relating to the safety of the products were also uncovered. A draft submission to ministers, prepared by an official and dated December 1979, included the sentence: 'Moreover products derived from paid donor plasma are known to carry a ten-fold increase in the risk of transmitting hepatitis over the risk from products derived from voluntary donations.'

The gravity of the crisis appeared to be worrying some people at the DHSS. But rather than change tack and prioritise patient safety, it seemed they decided the most suitable course of action was to downplay the risks. A subsequent draft by a more senior official deleted the reference to a ten-fold increase, and substituted 'a greatly increased risk of hepatitis'.[23]

•

Back at Treloar's, alarm bells were beginning to ring within the close-knit circle of medics treating the haemophiliacs at the school.

The school had become a test bed for medical experiments, including the trial in 1976 that Nick Sainsbury had unknowingly been part of. Factor VIII concentrates were supplied by BPL to the school to be used in a prophylaxis trial.[24]

Dr Anthony Aronstam, a haematologist who became director of the Treloar's Haemophilia Centre in 1977, was excited about the potential for medical advancements at the school. At a meeting of the Wessex Regional Health Authority on 28 March 1979, he emphasised the 'necessity for research as the concentration of haemophiliacs found at Treloar's is unique within Britain'.[25]

However, he was also among the first doctors in the UK to see dangers lurking in the blood products used to treat his pupils. In May 1979, he was asked by the Public Health Laboratory (PHL) – the forerunner to the Health Protection Agency, which was then in charge of monitoring dangers to the population – to put children on a new trial, even if they were not currently suffering from serious illness. Incredibly, leaked letters show the government body was well aware that such a move might cause mild haemophiliacs to develop potentially fatal hepatitis – but decided to proceed anyway.

Dr Craske, who was then a consultant virologist at PHL, told Aronstam:

> You will be aware that the study of NHS factor VIII has been going for almost a year.
>
> I have not so far been notified of any cases of hepatitis in patients treated with the designated batches used in this study. Perhaps you could also let me know whether in actual fact you have had any cases after these batches.
>
> I would suggest that for the second year of the study some of this material should be used to treat mild haemophiliacs coming up for non-urgent operations such as tooth extraction. We have found from observations at Oxford this is the best way of finding out whether the material is associated with cases of hepatitis, as most patients treated under these circumstances will be as susceptible to non-A, non-B viruses in the transfused material.
>
> I am aware that you may prefer to use commercial concentrate for some patients in this class, but it would provide valuable information if you could use some of the material issued in the way I have suggested.[26]

The policy would have applied to outpatients using the clinic at Treloar's, rather than the boys boarding there.

In response, Aronstam was emphatic: 'We have not had any cases of hepatitis following NHS factor VIII. As far as your suggestion about transfusing mild haemophiliacs with this material is concerned, I totally disagree with this concept. I do not wish any of my mild haemophiliacs to develop hepatitis in any form and therefore adopt the policy of either using DDAVP or cryoprecipitate.'[27]

Craske's request is the first known example of mild haemophiliacs being used as guinea pigs for risky new treatments. Many of those who ended up on such trials were children.

While Aronstam's response on this occasion was firm, he has become a divisive figure among former Treloar's pupils. Some remain unsure whether he was their supporter or the architect of their demise. To this day, his former pupils debate whether he was following orders and trying to deliver the best in cutting-edge care, or if he was a knowing participant in the tragedy that was about to unfold in front of his own eyes.

The main bone of contention among his former patients is the prevalence of trials carried out on boys under his care. While Aronstam seems to have initially pushed back at some of the murkier government demands, there is little doubt that under his watch Treloar's became an epicentre of medical testing with no informed consent. Some of his boys are now engaged in a group legal action against the school, alleging a breach of a duty of care. At the time of writing this book, the school have maintained that liability rests with the NHS – something that continues to be disputed by the former pupils, who are expected to resume the case if the level of compensation awarded by the government follow-ing the findings of the Infected Blood Inquiry is not deemed commensurate with the suffering caused.

Among them is Gary Webster, who grew up in Lewisham, south-east London. Webster, who was diagnosed as a severe haemophiliac at six months old after a series of spontaneous bleeds, began boarding at Treloar's in 1975 when he was ten years old. I met Gary in a bar in central London, decades after he had left the school. Unlike Nick, Gary, who once had raven-black hair and is now greying with the passing of time, told me that he loved his time there.

'It was a marvellous place,' he recalled for the inquiry. 'Obviously, I didn't know anything about what I know now, but it was great. I mean, education was just like a normal education . . . and . . . you had to do prep in the evening afterwards. And then the social life was good, because you were with people with haemophilia, so you helped each other and things like that, and you got on with [people with] other disabilities as well. I mean, it was – honestly, it was a great time. And I think we all enjoyed it.'[28]

Gary was treated with cryoprecipitate until his second year at Treloar's when he was switched to Hemofil. He said: 'I remember them telling us about it. You know, it's this new, wonderful treatment. Don't get me wrong, you know, it was good, it worked, and it enabled us to have a fairly active life, far better.'[29]

But neither Gary nor his parents were told that during his time at Treloar's he was the subject of numerous medical experiments.

He has since been shown documents about his medica-tion, provided by the onsite NHS haemophilia centre, with the word 'trial' written on them. The first was in November 1978.

'I honestly don't remember having any information about going on trials research or anything like that,' he said. 'My parents never were informed of any of it . . . At the time we were just unaware, we just did as we were told.'[30]

Gary can't remember the trial itself. But one firm memory he does retain is the school being awash with gifts from the pharmaceutical companies involved, including watches, notebooks, kites and towels. He still has a blue teddy bear with the word 'Baxter' emblazoned upon it.

'I believe I was treated with factor VIII for research purposes,' he said. 'We, at Treloar's, were given factor VIII on a prophylactic basis, whether our haemophilia was mild or severe, every other day. I actually only needed treating for a bleed once or twice a month. It felt like we were being used as guinea pigs. It looks to me now that they were just filling us with factor VIII to see what happened.'[31]

Gary claimed that, years later, he went on a 'mission to destroy [him]self' when he discovered he had been handed a death sentence after receiving contaminated blood products while a pupil at the school. He tried to kill himself by driving a car into a brick wall. Now, he describes himself as an 'angry old man', and claims he has huge guilt about being one of only a handful of his school friends to survive.

He said: 'Losing . . . school friends who you've known since you were that high . . . It's just hard, because as I say, you lose all these people – why?'[32]

•

By the end of the 1970s, the thirst for profit among certain pharmaceutical companies had led them to plumb new depths.

In 1980, a Canadian company called Continental Pharma Cryosan was found to have sourced blood from Russian corpses and relabelled the product as originating from Scandinavian donors. The same company also bought out-of-date blood and plasma from desperate Haitian slum dwellers, which was relabelled for resale in Europe. Cryosan shipped huge quantities of plasma to Travenol in Belgium. Between 1980 and 1981, more than 11 million units of Travenol's Hemofil and Interhem factor VIII were imported into the United Kingdom. Following an investigation by Royal Canadian Mounted Police, Cryosan pleaded guilty and was fined. The human cost of this sinister endeavour remains unknown.

This shocking revelation alone should have been enough to turbocharge Britain's drive towards self-sufficiency. But instead, the policy appears to have been thrown into reverse, thanks to ongoing concerns about the conditions and lack of funding at BPL in Elstree.

This issue was explored in depth in another *World in Action* programme in December 1980.[33] The episode, entitled 'Blood Business', included an interview with David Owen, by now a former health minister, who acknowledged that no government had put enough money into BPL. He told the programme:

Well, I don't think we've invested enough. I thought then, on the best evidence that I had, I think it was £500,000 that we found, was going to be sufficient. But what has happened is that although we have increased, as I gather, at production, demand increased as well. I . . . ceased to be Minister of Health and went to the Foreign Office in 1976, but I think what has been needed is a steady investment, and not just into Blood Products Laboratory, but also into the regional blood transfusion services, which have been starved of money.

Dr Peter Jones, who ran the Newcastle Haemophilia Centre, said that the amount that should have been invested was 'something more in the region of twenty-five million pounds'.

The reporter's closing remarks were chilling: 'The Department says there's no money available. That means hospitals will spend millions more on imports, patients will risk the consequences of skid-row blood, and Britain will become increasingly dependent on the world blood market.'[34]

Shortly before the programme aired, the government announced a £21 million redevelopment programme at BPL in Elstree. The target time for completion was six years – a delay that campaigners claim undoubtedly cost lives.

By now, the alarm bells were even starting to ring in Whitehall. Memos show that officials had already been made aware of the risk of hepatitis in American blood products. One of the central figures in the government response to the contaminated blood scandal was Diana Walford, a former Liverpool doctor, who joined the civil service and rose to become the principal medical officer at the DHSS. There is strong evidence that she and other senior mandarins were aware of the dangers of imported blood products by the early 1980s, yet continued to reassure clinicians and the wider public that the risks were negligible.

In a letter in 1980, Walford said that it was important to prevent the contamination of 'UK material with imported hepatitis viruses', adding ominously that health officials were aware of 'post-transfusion hepatitis in the USA [which] can be rapidly fatal'.[35]

In January 1981, the concerns reached Parliament. George Young, a junior health minister, warned about the 'possible risks of hepatitis' from imported products, particularly from those made from plasma supplied by paid donors. His warning was only reported one month later, after a second outbreak of hepatitis B among ten pupils at Treloar's became public. They were all aged between nine and fourteen. The crisis at Treloar's was beginning to interest the national media. A report in the *Daily Telegraph* was published entitled '10 Sick After Factor 8 Doses'.

In the article, Dr Charles Rizza, the director of the Oxford Haemophilia Centre, is quoted admitting: 'There might be a greater degree of risk from commercial products.'[36] The article claimed that at the time of publishing, imports worth £10 million each year were coming into the UK.

Later the same year came another credible warning. A *British Medical Journal* editorial reported that a mysterious form of hepatitis known as 'non-A non-B' was the major cause of chronic liver disease in haemophiliac patients, and pointed to the dangers of large donor pool sizes. Once again, this warning had absolutely zero impact on fatal government blood policies.

•

While I was researching this book, one of the conclusions that was difficult to ignore is that haemophiliacs were used as unwitting human guinea pigs. Many of the victims of the contaminated blood scandal have similar memories to those shared by Nick Sainsbury and Gary Webster. They report being told they were on a new 'trial' without prior approval being sought from either themselves or their parents.

However, there does not appear to have ever been an official announcement of such trials by any medical institution in the UK. As the scandal developed over the decades that followed, fewer and fewer people were willing to talk about decision-making at the time, which means it is difficult to establish how and why such trials occurred.

Investigative journalists and campaigners were left searching through government archives, patient medical records and official papers to try to piece together what had happened. Some of these painstaking efforts eventually bore fruit.

One extraordinary reference uncovered by campaigner Carol Anne Grayson was located in correspondence from Professor Arthur Bloom, a Welsh doctor and one of the central villains of this piece. Bloom was one of Britain's leading haematologists, and his work was recognised across the world. He held positions including president of the British Society for Haematology, president of the British Society for Haemostasis and Thrombosis, and chairman of the Council of the International Society on Thrombosis and Haemostasis. During this period, he also acted as chairman of the UK Haemophilia Centre Directors. In short, his word carried significant weight.

In January 1982, Bloom wrote a letter that confirmed haemophiliacs were being experimented on. What makes it even worse is his bald admission that the patients were being intentionally infected with hepatitis, as the previous trial subjects – in this case, chimpanzees – were no longer sufficient to guarantee the 'quality control' demanded by factor VIII manufacturers.

Separate correspondence has also been unearthed that shows health chiefs were keen to conduct 'infectivity trials' on patients rather than chimpanzees, which would have been more expensive. Officials calculated it would cost £10,000 to conduct the trial on the animals for six months – a cost that they would not have to bear if humans were used.[37]

In the letter – which has become known as the 'cheaper than chimps letter' – Bloom wrote:

> Although initial production batches may have been tested for infectivity by injecting them into chimpanzees it is unlikely that the manufacturers will be able to guarantee this form of quality control for all future batches.
>
> It is therefore very important to find out by studies in human beings to what extent the infectivity of the various concentrates has been reduced.
>
> The most clearcut way of doing this is by administering those concentrates to patients not previously exposed to large pool concentrates.
>
> Those patients are few in number but a study along those lines is being carried out at Oxford to determine the infectivity of factor VIII concentrates produced by the Plasma Fractionation Laboratory, Oxford, and Blood Products Laboratory, Elstree.
>
> This study shows that it is possible to demonstrate infectivity effectively using quite small numbers of PUPs.[38]

The acronym PUPs meant 'previously untreated patients'. It is confirmation, if any were needed, that these people were being experimented on.

But that was perhaps not the most shocking news of all. An even more dangerous threat was soon to emerge: a threat that would spark fresh panic within the international medical community and the wider population. A killer new virus would soon ripple across the world, requiring a scrambled and hasty response. And once more, the poor haemophiliacs at Treloar's and beyond would be on the frontline of an emerging medical disaster, with fatal consequences for all involved.

Ade Goodyear, aged 17.

3

THE PLAGUE

1983–5

It was a bright, sunny afternoon when Ade Goodyear was told by his housemaster to go to the health centre. He was fifteen years old and had already been a pupil at Treloar's for six years. Ade, who was a severe haemophiliac and was regularly treated for his condition at the centre, initially thought nothing of the request. But it was a meeting that was to dramatically change the course of his life.

It was May 1985, the year Ronald Reagan was re-elected President of the United States and the Live Aid pop concert in Philadelphia and London raised more than £50 million for famine relief in Ethiopia.

Ade was among a group of five boys to be summoned to see the doctors that fateful afternoon. The centre had an open-door policy and the boys regularly wandered in and out for treatment. It was unusual, if not unheard of, for them to be seen as a group. During their school lunchbreak, the pupils were ushered into the doctor's office, a tiny space no bigger than twelve by twelve feet.

Sitting behind his desk was Dr Anthony Aronstam, the centre's respected director. He was accompanied by Dr Maneer Wassef, the resident haematologist, who endeared himself to the pupils by playing ping-pong with them in the evening after lessons. Unusually, Joyce Lovering, the head of physiotherapy, and two haemophilia nurses, Ann Hess and Jane Cartilage, were also present. With so many of them squeezed into the small room, the boys had no choice but to stand, which only added to their sense of alarm.

When the door was closed behind them – also something that had never happened before – the teenagers felt a terrible sense of foreboding, recognising almost immediately that this was going to be an afternoon none of them would ever forget.

Even before Aronstam opened his mouth to speak, one of the nurses began gently sobbing.

The boys, who were all haemophiliacs and had been receiving American factor VIII since their arrival at the school, looked at their feet and shuffled nervously.

Ade recalled: 'Aronstam and his team cautiously informed us . . . "You may have heard that the treatment that you've been given, the factor VIII, isn't as clean as it should be."

'We went quiet. "Yeah, we know," we replied. They talked to us about CNV, parvo virus, which is something that dogs get, apparently. They made it as comfortable as they could for fifteen minutes. It took them quite a while to get to the point, especially because we had to go back to school.'[1]

Eventually, Aronstam plucked up the courage to address the elephant in the room. With tears welling up in his eyes, he came 'straight out with it' as he told the pupils: 'Some of you here have been given HIV.'

Walking around the room, he lifted his left hand and

pointed to each boy and said: 'You have, you haven't, you have, you haven't, you have.'

This last 'you have' was directed at Ade, who was at the end of the line of boys closest to the door.

The boys were extremely disturbed. At the time, AIDS, which is the late stage of the HIV infection and occurs when the body's immune system is badly damaged by the virus, was sweeping across the world almost unencumbered.

One of Ade's friends immediately piped up: 'How long have we got?'

The response was chilling. 'As we know very little about HIV, we honestly can't say, but we think at this time around two to three years, but maybe more,' Aronstam told them. 'But we are going to do our absolute best for you.'[2]

'It felt surreal,' Ade recalled when we met decades later to discuss the impact of the tragedy on his life.

As he went on to tell the story of how he was first diagnosed, his warm and bubbly persona became more muted and his piercing green eyes clouded over with emotion. 'The doctors then went on to explain that it was something to do with T-cells. They hoped it was an antibody and we would have a resistance to it . . . they wanted us to understand as much as we could absorb.

'We were told not to tell anyone at school about our viral statuses as they did not want any more press interest at the school. It was a huge strain and drove a wedge between me and some other friends and . . . other peer groups who were not infected with HIV, but who had contracted hepatitis B and C.

'It was a frightening time and some of the haemophiliac boys were fighting because everyone was scared.

'We were sick and the world changed in a click for all of us that day in that room. Calm aligned with shock and confusion – yes, absolute confusion, like a spinning top out of control.'

As the boys left the room, they passed the next group of pupils heading into the office to be told of their tragic fate.

It is not known how many boys at Treloar's were informed about their HIV status that sunny afternoon, but Ade believes all those infected were told at around the same time. It turns out many of the boys, unbeknown to them, had been undergoing blood tests that had exposed the first worrying signs of the virus for some time.

Some of the boys immediately went off to telephone their parents and impart the devastating news, but Ade's relationship with his adopted mother had already begun to deteriorate by this point. He returned quietly to his lessons after spending a few moments outside with his school friends reflecting on their stolen futures in disbelief.

He told me: 'Walking out into the sunshine, after leaving the office, a numbness took hold . . . I remember looking at the sun and thinking, how many more days will I be seeing the sunshine for? We were children and we were bonded and we were going to die.

'Another friend said, "I think we're dead. We're fucking dead!" before heading to the horticulture department immediately next door to the centre and smashing a few potting shed windows in sheer anger at the situation. Personally, after the meeting, I was actually back in science class that afternoon.'

Ade, now a softly spoken singer-songwriter, is the only one of that group of five pupils to survive. The two pupils who were told they were not HIV positive later succumbed to deadly infections after receiving contaminated blood products, but the others had fallen victim to the new killer virus that was causing global panic. The HIV/AIDS pandemic swept through the West in the 1980s, but it had originated in Africa decades earlier.

•

Grethe Rask was overcome with tiredness as she prepared a chicken for Christmas Eve dinner in the tropical heat of her sub-Saharan surroundings. It was 1976, the year the first commercial Concorde flights took off and the Romanian gymnast Nadia Comaneci won three gold medals at the Montreal Olympic Games with seven perfect scores.

The overwhelming fatigue that had been plaguing Rask for the last two years eventually forced her to retreat to her bed. The Danish physician and surgeon was working in the Democratic Republic of the Congo, which would later become known as the 'Cradle of AIDS'. She had grown thin, suffered from swollen lymph nodes, had fungus in her mouth and complained of a shortness of breath. Her friend Ib Bygbjerg, a physician specialising in communicable diseases, had considered everything from tuberculosis to leukaemia to diabetes as the cause of her malaise, but was unable to find a diagnosis.

In the years to come, Rask, who had short dark hair and an infectious smile, would become a cause célèbre across the world when she was identified as one of the first non-Africans and the first heterosexual to die of AIDS-related causes.[3]

For years, the killer virus had been confined to Africa. The earliest evidence of the devastating AIDS pandemic has been traced back to the 1920s and the booming city of Kinshasa. It was in nearby southern Cameroon, a country lying at the juncture of western and Central Africa, that researchers believe that the HIV virus first jumped to humans from two colonies of chimpanzees. There are various theories about how this occurred. The most widely held view is that hunters became infected when they caught, butchered and ate chimps carrying the simian immunodeficiency virus (SIV), a virus strikingly similar to HIV.

Chimps, the scientists later discovered, hunt and eat two smaller species of monkeys – red-capped mangabeys and greater spot-nosed monkeys – that carry and infect the chimps with two strains of SIV. These two strains likely combined to form SIVcpz, which can spread between chimpanzees and humans.

HIV is a lentivirus, a strain of virus that tends to have a long incubation period and targets the body's immune system. It spreads by contact with bodily fluids, including semen, vaginal and anal fluids, usually through unprotected sex, sharing injections, blood transfusions and breastfeeding. The virus, which belongs to a group called retroviruses, attacks T-cells, a kind of white blood cell important in the immune system. It creates copies of itself inside these cells, gradually weakening the immune system.

HIV initially spread unnoticed, carried by people travelling along a snaking network of African rivers. It remained a regional infection until it entered Kinshasa, a former trading post that was developing into one of the fastest-growing megacities in the world. It was here that the first human epidemic began to grow.

Records show that by the 1940s, more than a million people a year passed through the city, which was the first navigable port on the Congo River, on the railways alone. Kinshasa had a relatively high proportion of men and, like many ports around the world, had a great demand for sex workers, which helped to spread the deadly disease. Some doctors may have also unwittingly disseminated the virus further, through the use of unsterilised needles at sexual health clinics.

At first, HIV was an infection confined to specific groups of people living along the railways and waterways, but the virus seemed to break out into the general population and spread around the world after the Democratic Republic of Congo achieved independence from Belgium in 1960.

This was the conclusion of an international team, led by Oxford University and University of Leuven scientists, that reconstructed the genetic history of the HIV-1 group M pandemic, the event that saw HIV spread across the African continent and around the world.[4] Researchers have since identified the AIDS virus in a blood sample drawn in 1959 from a man in Kinshasa, the oldest definite case of the infection in a human being. However, it is understood the virus may have been lying dormant in the African jungle for several years, or even decades, prior to that.

Grethe Rask, the Danish physician, first started working in the Democratic Republic of the Congo in 1964 before being recalled to Europe for training in stomach surgery and tropical illnesses.

She returned to the war-torn country in 1972, where she first worked at a small jungle hospital in the small village of Abumombasi. Conditions at the hospital where she worked were basic and she was often forced to work without surgical gloves. Disinfectant was also in short supply and the hospital had no disposable needles, so the same needle was often used multiple times to treat different patients. The meals were basic too, and the doctors were often treated to offerings of game meat by their grateful patients. One night it might be monkey, the next warthog or other exotic animals. Bats were not an uncommon delicacy.

By the time Rask moved to the Danish Red Cross Hospital in Kinshasa in 1975, she had already been suffering from the symptoms of a mystery illness for several years. After being forced to abandon her chicken dinner on Christmas Eve, Rask began to improve over New Year – although her lymph nodes remained swollen.

She was still working at the hospital in August 1976 when a terrifying plague broke out not far from Abumombasi, close to the jungle hospital where she had previously worked. People in the surrounding areas visited the hospital with a fever before they started bleeding out of their noses, eyes and virtually all the pores of their bodies. Most of them died within days, including thirty-nine nurses and two doctors. It was initially thought to be Marburg virus, a deadly disease first discovered in the German city less than a decade before. However, it turned out to be something far worse – a new virus named after a nearby river: Ebola.

Rask's proximity to the outbreak and her symptoms might have led some to the obvious conclusion that she was suffering from Ebola. But her symptoms and the longevity of her illness were not consistent with the virus, which can be transmitted through bodily contact.

What no one knew at the time was that Africa was playing host to an even more dangerous virus in the rainforest. Unlike Ebola, this virus would soon spread across the whole world, killing millions of people.

Rask was still under the weather the following year when she decided to take a rare holiday to South Africa. During the vacation, she struggled to breathe and was forced to rely on bottled oxygen. She decided to fly back to Denmark, where she underwent tests at Copenhagen's Rigshospitalet, the Danish national hospital.

The best specialists in the country gathered around her in a desperate bid to find out what she was suffering from. They tested for everything they could think of. In the end, the only conclusion the medics could agree on was that Rask was dying. She had contracted a number of opportunistic infections, such as Staphylococcus aureus (staph infection), candidiasis (yeast infection) and Pneumocystis iiroveci pneumonia (a fungal infection of the lungs). Bizarrely, the tests also showed she had a nearly non-existent T-cell count, leading to a severely depressed immune system.

Rask gave up. She decided to leave Copenhagen and spend her last days back home in Jutland, the large peninsula stretching northwards towards Scandinavia. Her good friend from her years in Africa, nurse Karen Strandby Thomsen, moved into Rask's little white-painted house outside Thisted to care for her.

On December 12 1977, Rask finally gave up her fight for life. The official cause of death was recorded as bacterial pneumonia and a staphylococci septicaemia. The woman who had dedicated her entire career to helping others died in a hospital bed. She was just forty-seven years old.

Rask's physician friend and colleague Ib Bygbjerg refused to give up. He wanted to find the answer to what was behind his friend's illness and demanded that further tests be carried out.

In 1984, following the advent of the AIDS crisis, Rask's blood was tested for HIV in Denmark. The test came back negative. Three years later, her blood was shipped to the United States, where it was tested with two different systems. Both tests were positive for HIV. Rask became known as one of the first victims of AIDS recorded outside Africa.[5] Ib Bygbjerg wrote in a letter to the *Lancet* that 'while working as a surgeon under primitive conditions, she [Rask] must have been heavily exposed to blood and excretions of African patients'.[6]

•

Gaetëan Dugas was born to fly. Adopted by a large family in the suburbs of Quebec City, he grew up next to the airport watching planes take off and wishing it was him soaring into the sky.

Dugas initially trained as a hairdresser. However, as soon as airlines lifted the ban on men doing the work of air stewardesses, he found his dream job and became one of Air Canada's new cadre of male flight attendants. Dugas was handsome, flamboyant and unapologetically promiscuous. With bleached blond hair framing his stunning features, he refashioned his uniform to make it skintight, and wore his sexuality on his sleeve. It was the late 1970s, an era when flying was still glamorous, and Dugas was 'surfing a jet stream of sexual liberation'.[7]

By the end of the decade, the Air Canada flight attendant with the alluring French accent and men in every airport had gained almost legendary standing among the airline crew and in the bath houses of New York and Los Angeles, which were frequented by homosexual men seeking sex. Those who knew the Canadian said he was convinced he would one day become a star.

Unfortunately, he did become famous. But for all the wrong reasons.

Dugas became the poster boy for the AIDS epidemic in

the West. In 1984, he became one of the 700,000 North Americans who would perish from an AIDS-related illness.

The virus had circulated for decades in Africa, but by the early 1980s, the developed world was waking up to this new and terrifying threat. The United States was the first Western nation to sound the alarm. In 1987, three years after his death, Dugas's face was plastered across the US and beyond. He was misidentified as 'Patient Zero' – the villain behind the AIDS epidemic. One infamous headline declared Dugas 'the monster who gave us AIDS'. Another dubbed him the 'Columbus of AIDS'.

In 1980, Dugas had been diagnosed with Kaposi's sarcoma – the skin cancer that would later become one of the most visible outward signs of AIDS. He was living in New York when he was interviewed by Bill Darrow, an investigator for the US Center of Disease Control and Prevention (CDC), who was studying a cluster study of men suffering with symptoms of HIV, the virus which, left untreated, can lead to AIDS.

Dugas estimated he'd had 750 sexual partners in the past three years, and gave Darrow a list of seventy-two contacts from his address book. He became known as patient fifty-seven in the study of forty linked cases. Dugas would later be incorrectly labelled 'patient zero' for his apparent connection to a cluster of the earliest cases of AIDS in the US. The mistake was made when Darrow published his report in March 1984 – the same month that Dugas died – and patient fifty-seven was named 'patient O'. The 'O' stood for 'out of California', but was misunderstood as 'patient zero', leading the media – and journalist Randy Shilts in his bestseller *And the Band Played On* – to falsely accuse Dugas of being the catalyst for the epidemic.

In fact, it is understood that HIV began its journey to the United States in the 1960s. It first spread from Africa to Haiti, and then to the Caribbean. It was most likely spread by one of the thousands of Haitian civil servants recruited by the United Nations to work in the former Belgian Congo after colonial rule collapsed. It has been claimed that a few cases in Haiti were multiplied by unsterile conditions at a private blood-collecting company, Hemo-Caribbean, that opened in 1971 and exported 1,600 gallons of plasma to the United States monthly. Plasma-clotting factors were used by American haemophiliacs, many of whom later died of AIDS. Werner Thill, a technical director for Hemo Caribbean, defended the operation at the time, which he said was of 'great benefit' to the Haitians involved: 'I don't think you can criticize what we are doing on ethical grounds. We are saving lives. We are providing a source of income in a country where the per capita income is no more than $75 a year.'[8]

Haiti was also a haven for sex tourism, another route the virus could have taken on its journey to the Caribbean and later the United States.

The first evidence of the virus's arrival in America was in 1969, when teenager Robert Rayford is thought to have become the country's first AIDS victim. The fifteen-year-old Black youth, who had never left the US, died of a mystery illness in St Louis, Missouri. Before his death, he was described as being weak and emaciated, rife with stubborn infections and riddled with Kaposi's sarcoma.[9] In hindsight, his symptoms bore all the hallmarks of HIV. Tests discovered a chlamydia infection, which had unusually spread throughout his body. He declined a rectal examination request by the hospital, and was described as 'uncommunicative and withdrawn'. Not much about Robert's personal life was disclosed, other than that he preferred to be called 'Bobbie' and that he was 'painfully shy, mentally slow, maybe even intellectually disabled'.[10]

It would be more than a decade before doctors started seeing similar cases among gay men in New York and California.

By then, the sexual revolution was in full swing, and HIV was silently spreading its way through homosexual communities across the United States. With it came the anti-gay backlash that accompanied the election of President Ronald Reagan, who famously turned a blind eye to the impending health crisis.

The first sign of looming disaster came when Ken Horne, a San Francisco resident and alleged gay sex worker, reported to the CDC that he was suffering with Kaposi's sarcoma in April 1980. He would later be identified as the first patient of the AIDS epidemic in the US. It was not long before news of the mystery virus hit the headlines. On 3 July 1981, the *New York Times* ran a story entitled: 'Rare cancer seen in 41 homosexuals'.

The article described how gay men were falling victim to the rare skin cancer in surprising numbers. Although the short report was buried at the back of the newspaper on page twenty, it was an important moment in the history of the AIDS pandemic, as it was the first time the virus had attracted mainstream media attention.

On the same day, the CDC published an article in its *Morbidity and Mortality Weekly Report* (MMWR) confirming that twenty-six gay men appeared to be suffering from the as yet unnamed virus. They were all reporting symptoms of Kaposi's sarcoma and Pneumocystis carinii pneumonia (PCP).

Three weeks earlier, the first ever published report about the mystery disease had appeared in New York City's own independent gay newspaper, the *New York Native*. Dr Lawrence Mass, who wrote a regular health column for the small weekly, had heard rumours of a new virus afflicting gay men in the city, but Mass was later assured by the CDC that there was no evidence of an emerging 'gay cancer'. He published an article entitled: 'Disease Rumours Largely Unfounded'.

But the CDC was wrong.

By late August 1981, the term 'gay cancer' had entered the public lexicon as panic began to spread among the country's homosexual community.

The latest issue of *MMWR* did nothing to allay concerns, as the number of known cases increased to 108: 107 of whom were male, and ninety-four per cent of whom were gay or bisexual. More shockingly, the report claimed that forty per cent of all patients to have presented themselves to doctors suffering from the virus's symptoms were already dead.

In December the same year, Bobbi Campbell, a gay San Francisco nurse, became the first patient with Kaposi's sarcoma to go public with his diagnosis. Calling himself the 'KS poster boy', Campbell wrote a newspaper column for the *San Francisco Sentinel*. He also posted photos of his skin lesions in the windows of local pharmacies, alerting the community to the disease and encouraging them to seek treatment. Campbell would be dead within three years.

By the end of 1981, there was a cumulative total of 337 cases of individuals with severe immune deficiency in the US: 321 adults and sixteen children. Of those cases, 130 were dead by New Year's Eve.

In January 1982, it became clear that the mystery

virus was spreading rapidly. Larry Kramer, the Academy Award-nominated playwright, author and film producer, founded the Gay Men's Health Crisis in New York to draw attention to what was happening amid fears that there were more questions than answers about a virus that still had no official name.

In May the same year, the *New York Times* published the first mention of the term GRID (Gay Related Immune Deficiency), which some researchers used to describe the new epidemic.

The term only deepened the erroneous public perception that the virus solely affected homosexual men. Later the same month, the *Los Angeles Times* published the first front-page story on AIDS in the mainstream media. The headline screamed: 'Mysterious Fever Now an Epidemic'.

The following month, the CDC finally made the link between a potentially sexually transmitted agent and the virus, promoting the first gay-activist group in San Francisco to publish a pamphlet on safe sex. The leaflet was distributed during the International Lesbian and Gay Freedom Day Parade.

However, it did not take long for scientists to realise that the virus was not the exclusive preserve of gay men.

In July 1982, the CDC published the first report of immunosuppression in patients with haemophilia who had no other known risk factors. The revelation led to GRID being renamed AIDS. The virus was defined as a 'disease at least moderately predictive of a deficient in a cell-mediated immunity, occurring in a person with no known cause for diminished resistance to that disease'.

By March 1983, however, scientists were still nowhere near finding the cause, leading to a blistering public attack by Kramer, who urged the community to get angry at the lack of government support for sick and dying gay men. His essay, published in the *New York Native*, traced the spread of the disease, the lack of a coordinated government response, and the apathy of the gay community, who seemed all too willing to bury their heads in the sand. The article was intended to frighten gay men and provoke them to protest against government indifference. Michael Specter, the leading journalist, later wrote in the *New Yorker*:

> It was a five-thousand-word screed that accused nearly everyone connected with health care in America – officials at the Centers for Disease Control, in Atlanta, researchers at the National Institutes of Health, in Washington D.C., doctors at Memorial Sloan-Kettering Cancer Center, in Manhattan, and local politicians (particularly New York Mayor Ed Koch) – of refusing to acknowledge the implications of the nascent AIDS epidemic.
>
> The article's harshest condemnation was directed at those gay men who seemed to think that if they ignored the new disease, it would simply go away.[11]

Tony Kushner, who later won the 1993 Pulitzer Prize for Drama for his play *Angels in America*, which was about the impact of AIDS in the US, said the essay 'changed my world', adding that Kramer had 'changed the world for all of us'.[12]

Within months, the US Congress passed the first bill that included funding specifically targeted for AIDS research and treatment. But the number of cases in the US continued to rise. Later that year, the American rock musician Bruce Wayne Campbell, known by his stage name Jobriath, became the first internationally acclaimed musician to die from the virus. Days later, German singer Klaus Nomi also succumbed to the illness.

As if the accelerating death toll was not troubling enough, by now it was becoming increasingly clear there was another disaster about to explode. AIDS had indisputably moved beyond homosexuals – and once again, it would be the struggling communities of haemophiliacs who would suffer. The virus had somehow found its way into the country's blood supply.

Although there were prior warnings about contaminated blood products, the first story to hit the mainstream press in the US was that of Ryan White, who was diagnosed with AIDS in December 1984.[13] He had become infected with the disease from contaminated blood products administered to him on a regular basis as part of his treatment for haemophilia. When his public school, Western Middle School in Russiaville, Indiana, found out about his condition, there was immediate pressure from parents and his teachers to ban him from the school premises. Due to the widespread fear of AIDS and a chronic lack of information, principal Ron Colby and the school board eventually agreed, which triggered a lawsuit from his family.

The disturbing story sent shockwaves through the haemophilia community around the world. Sadly, the stigma faced by AIDS sufferers, including haemophiliacs, was to become an all-too-familiar story.

The following year, the American scientist Robert Gallo identified the probable cause of AIDS, discovering that a retrovirus caused the illness, labelling the virus HTLV-III. This breakthrough followed the publication of two papers in the same issue of *Science* in May 1983 – one by Gallo and one by Luc Montagnier of the Pasteur Institute in Paris – both claiming to have identified a virus apparently linked to AIDS. While neither the US team nor the French team was certain of the link, their discoveries led to Gallo's subsequent breakthrough. The coincidence of both teams making the same original claim sparked a bitter dispute. The arguments continued for decades until it was agreed that Montagnier's team had discovered HIV, but its role in AIDS was first shown by Gallo.

While huge progress had been made in identifying the virus, it had come too late for those already infected.

One of the pivotal moments in the awareness campaign came with the death of Rock Hudson, who had played more than sixty leading roles in Hollywood movies. He died in October 1985, aged just fifty-nine. Hudson, who was friends with the US President, is understood to have helped change Reagan's view of the disease, which, until then, the White House had largely ignored. In fact, until that moment, the White House had actively sought to downplay the emerging health crisis, with Reagan's press secretary, Larry Speakes, and members of the media famously joking about the HIV/AIDS epidemic and laughing about one of the reporters potentially having it.[14]

By the time Reagan made his first significant intervention on AIDS the following year, the disease had already struck 36,058 Americans, of whom 20,849 had died. The virus had also spread to more than 100 countries.

One of them was Britain.

And it would be Ade and the scores of other pupils at the Hampshire school of Treloar's who would once again find themselves at the epicentre of a new crisis.

Ade Goodyear, aged 7.

4

GUINEA PIGS

1985

By the time he was diagnosed with AIDS at Treloar's in 1985, Ade Goodyear had already had a troubled childhood.

He was born Adrian Paul Shaw in 1971, the same year Anita Roddick was infected with hepatitis. Incessant bleeding as a baby led him to be diagnosed with haemophilia by the time he was six months old. His mother, Kay Wade, had three other sons from her first marriage, all of whom also had severe haemophilia. All of them have since died. Ade's brother Paul was the first to pass away, when he was just six months old. His other brothers, Gary and Jason, later died after receiving contaminated blood products.

Kay was already struggling with severe kidney disease by the time Ade was born. As a single mother, she struggled to cope, and he was swiftly taken into care. He was almost immediately fostered by a family in Purbrook, a village in Hampshire on the outskirts of Waterlooville, just north of Portsmouth.

Bernard and Margaret Goodyear had a long history of foster caring. Forty-two children had already passed through their household. Bernard was in the navy before gaining employment as a storekeeper in the ambulance service. Margaret was a nurse. They had five children of their own.

Ade was sent to a local primary school aged five, but his debilitating condition immediately set him apart. On his very first day, Ade recalled the headmaster pulled him up in front of the whole school during assembly to explain that he could not be caned or hurt due to his haemophilia. His peers were also warned not to hit him in case it caused a bleed. Ade was badly bullied from that moment onwards. Life became more difficult for the young boy when he was struck down with his first bout of hepatitis aged seven.

At the time, Ade, who had just been adopted by his foster parents, was being treated at St Mary's Hospital in Portsmouth. He believes he was infected after receiving his first ever batch of factor VIII concentrate to treat a bleed on his right ankle. Ade claims the effects of the treatment became immediately apparent. His arm blistered and he turned yellow within twelve hours of receiving the blood product.

'Dad was in the navy so he knew what hepatitis looked like,' Ade recalled decades later. 'When he saw me, Dad became quite distressed.' Ade remembered his dad having an angry conversation with one of his doctors. 'He questioned why I was fine when he dropped me off that morning at 7.30a.m., but I was yellow when he came to see [me at] 6.30p.m. the same night. He asked [the doctor]: "What have you done to my son, why does he look like that?" when he saw me turning all yellow and vomiting. He was simply told that factor VIII was revolutionary so not to worry . . . My dad was also told that "going yellow" was nothing to worry about, what was happening to me was "quite normal", that it would "eventually pass" and that it "would not come back".'[1]

Ade was reinfected with hepatitis when he was nine, and

again when he was eleven. The shocking developments had a dramatic effect on his father, who appeared to lose trust in the clinicians and institutions that were supposed support his sickly son. 'My adoptive mother said that my father was never the same after that,' he recalled.

Bernard had first become concerned about the treatment his son was receiving after being given an extraordinary piece of advice from a doctor some years earlier. The clinician had told him that 'in his professional opinion, it would be best just to let the children with haemophilia go as it was a terrible condition to live with'.[2] Ade claims the suggestion was repeated several times during his childhood.

The bullying of Ade reached a peak in the Easter term of 1980. He was nine years old when another kid smacked him hard on the elbow with an iron bar, immediately fracturing his arm in three places. The motivation behind the attack was simply to find out what happened to the haemophiliac when he bled. Ade's father lost patience with the school and sought refuge for his son at Treloar's following a recommendation from one of their doctors.

However, three weeks after the pair visited the school for Ade's induction, tragedy struck and his beloved father suffered a fatal heart attack. On the morning of Bernard's death, Ade had an eerie premonition of the dreadful event. 'I woke up at the exact moment that he died and jumped out of bed,' he told me. 'I remember it was exactly four minutes past seven, and I knew something terrible had happened but I didn't know what.' At 9.24a.m., Ade was told his father was dead.

The impact of his dad's death was devasting for the young boy. But it was also to have a seismic effect on his relationship with his adopted mother, Margaret, who blamed him for her husband's death. 'Mum used to tell me that he wanted me and she did not, and that the stress I caused him eventually also caused his death,' Ade said. 'That was when the abuse really started. He was always worried about me and I think she was envious of our relationship as she was a matriarchal and domineering type.'[3] Ade told me his mother was also sceptical about the concerns Ade had expressed about his treatment. After his first brush with hepatitis, Ade became increasingly worried about 'what was in the syringe', but his mother would insist: 'Doctors cure people, [they don't] harm them.' It was a conflict that would eventually lead to their relationship breaking down irretrievably.

Relieved to be leaving the heartbreak of his father's death behind him, Ade began his school career at Treloar's, which would become his home for the next nine years. Little did he realise at the time that he was jumping out of the frying pan and into the fire.

•

There was little sign of the tragedy ahead when Ade arrived in the idyllic Hampshire countryside at the start of Treloar's autumn term in 1980. 'It was like Hogwarts,' he told me. 'I was a bit homesick but compared to my home life, school was like a playground.'

Despite the traumas to come, Ade said he would never forget his first two weeks. 'I was never a very confident child, but I remember having this overwhelming feeling of yes, this is where I want to be.'

He told me being with other haemophiliacs was a 'good thing', explaining: 'From the minute I put my head down on the pillow in the first dormitory with five other lads, three of [whom] were haemophiliacs, in the five-bed dorm, I just thought . . . let's do this.

'We would support each other, and heartfelt friendships were formed based on our youthful understanding of the condition . . . We were a solid bunch, and it was a completely unique and immersive school experience, if not a little daunting being away from our families at such tender ages . . . We shared dormitories, fell in, fell out, fell over.'

Ade said it was initially comforting to live somewhere that 'understood bleeds' and taught the children how to 'self-infuse' blood products, which was a 'godsend'. He also enjoyed regular trips out of school and threw himself into the various clubs on offer, including chess, sailing, music and drama. Treloar's glittering reputation and declared commitment to supporting haemophiliacs meant the school was often visited by royals, pop stars and celebrities. Princess Diana even sprinkled some stardust during one trip. 'It was inspiring,' recalled Ade. 'Strong bonds were made beyond what we could ever hope for in our home lives, which sometimes drove wedges between us boys and our families.'

His initial experiences were so positive that Ade found the school staff even managed to inject dark humour into the debilitating conditions that plagued the children. Annie, one of the nurses, dubbed the haemophiliacs at the school her 'Golden Boys', as the plasma had a yellow tinge when it was administered. This was also an affectionate nod to the fact that some of the pupils, who suffered frequent bouts of hepatitis, would go yellow.

Ade told me the disturbing and frequent change in their colour was simply 'the norm': 'You just took the mick out of each other and supported each other in those periods. If only we knew what was lying in wait for us.'

With the increased frequency of hepatitis outbreaks at Treloar's, Ade said, it was an open secret that the blood products were riddled with viruses. Students were even provided with 'practical advice' on how to contain infection. They were told to dispose of their used needles and bedding neatly in a disposable bin marked 'hepatitis risk'.

As time went on, more and more of the children started to panic. Ade told me about one of his school friends being deeply concerned about Hemofil, the American factor VIII concentrate linked to hepatitis in the groundbreaking *World in Action* programme. He recalled: 'One lad said, "Don't take that shit mate, it's so infectious it will walk on the table on its own."'

The supply of deadly factor VIII to the schoolchildren was overseen by Dr Anthony Aronstam, the controversial haematologist who became director of the Treloar's Haemophilia Centre in 1977.

A thickset, balding, middle-aged man with a moustache, Aronstam's precise role in the contaminated blood scandal is difficult to nail down.

It is undeniable that the experienced medical practitioner contributed to the deaths of scores of children under his care. Yet, as we saw in Chapter 2, there is also evidence that Aronstam was suspicious about the blood products he was being asked to administer – and tried to raise the alarm. Ade recalled various moments when Aronstam appeared to push back against the Whitehall mandarins who cleared imported factor VIII for use in the UK, and also admonished the pharmaceutical companies producing the deadly blood products.

As early as 1980, Aronstam is understood to have attended a haematologist's conference in South America to discuss heat treatment and product safety. He is believed to have raised concerns about the need to heat-treat factor VIII in order to rid the products of viruses. Even before specific tests for hepatitis and HIV were available, factor concentrates could be made free of these viruses through heat treatment, a form of pasteurisation. This became routine in the mid-1980s once it was clear HIV was blood-borne. However, it is understood that Aronstam was ahead of his time, and had already begun investigating whether the heat treatment of the products he was administering to his increasingly sickly pupils would make a difference.

Ade was told about the conference by a former pupil at Treloar's who has since died. 'The issue became a problem within that conference because the Americans laughed him out [of] the room, because he really believed that factor VIII could be heat-treated and we were going to be safe,' Ade told the inquiry.

Sadly, Aronstam is no longer alive to give his version of events, but his instincts would prove sound. Several years after the devastating onset of the AIDS epidemic, the bigwigs of global public health policy would eventually recognise the urgent need to heat-treat blood products in order to minimise the risk from viruses such as hepatitis and HIV.

Back in 1980, Aronstam returned from the South American conference so concerned that he launched a mission to create his own makeshift heat-treatment regime.

Ade remembered: 'There was a mixing machine in the transfusion room. It made a heck of a noise, and they became, I would say, not obsessed but . . . really thinking about this mixing machine and how warm the water was, and they would always try and maintain twenty-eight degrees in that water and tell the nurses.

'By that point, Treloar's were providing all my home care out of the school's factor VIII. I was given a thermometer and told: 'You mustn't inject, Master Ade, you mustn't inject it below twenty-eight degrees,' so I believe, looking back on that, that's what happened. He was trying to do some kind of heat treatment.'[4]

Years after leaving the school, Ade recalled, he had an important conversation with Aronstam when he went back for treatment on an elbow bleed at the haemophilia centre at Treloar's. During a chat about the scandal that had since unfolded, Ade remembered Aronstam becoming 'quite exasperated and rather agitated'.

'He explained to me that the PHLS had "fucked him",' said Ade. The PHLS was the government's Public Health Laboratory, the forerunner to the Health Protection Agency, which was then in charge of monitoring dangers to the population.

Ade recalled: 'He said that he had done all he could and that he had done his best, but did not understand why they [the PHLS] did not listen to him and implement heat-treated blood products when he suggested they do so.'

Aronstam told him that 'by 1981 or 1982' the children should have 'all been on heat-treated products' and that the subsequent disaster that saw him lose his pupils one by one 'did not need to happen'.[5]

•

The UK Government was slow to respond to the developing AIDS crisis. An appalling inertia permeated Westminster and Whitehall.

John Eaddie was the first British AIDS victim – although he would not be identified as such until four decades later. He died at the Royal Brompton Hospital in Chelsea on 29 October 1981. The cause of death was recorded as pneumocystis pneumonia. He was forty-nine.

Eaddie had run a guesthouse in Bournemouth that was a safe haven for gay men to meet and drink in the 1970s and 1980s, a period of time when homosexuals were often vilified. When he died, Eaddie was surrounded by close friends and doctors who were baffled by his illness.

It wasn't long before his death was followed by that of Terry Higgins, who collapsed while at work at the Heaven nightclub in London. The former *Hansard* reporter, who had travelled to New York and Amsterdam in the late 1970s, died on 4 July 1982, at St Thomas' Hospital, London, of an AIDS-related pneumonia infection. He was thirty-seven.

Later that year, his friends established the Terrence Higgins Trust in his memory. Their intention was to prevent others from suffering the way he had, and to raise awareness and funds for research on this new illness. Early phone calls to the charity's helpline were filled with panic and fear, because so little was known about the causes of the virus.

At the start of the pandemic, the only advice they could give to people was: 'Don't have sex with Americans.'

By 1982, it was starting to become clear that the virus was not a 'gay plague' – the derogatory term seized upon by the often-homophobic British media – as reports emerged from the United States about women and children being infected.

The first clear signs that the country was sleepwalking into disaster came in September 1982 at a meeting of the UK Haemophilia Centre Directors' Organisation. Not only was it revealed that haemophiliacs were being infected by AIDS in the United States, there also appeared to be early suspicions that commercial blood products could be responsible.

According to minutes of the meeting, Dr John Craske, one of Britain's leading virologists, was tasked with examining reports of AIDS in three American haemophiliacs. The minutes state: 'It appeared that there might be the remote possibility that commercial blood products have been involved.'[6]

But it seems this wasn't followed up with monitoring of the situation, and so it became the first of many missed opportunities to deal with an escalating crisis that would go on to claim thousands of lives.

In the US, medics were further along in waking up to the health emergency. In January 1983, a series of articles appeared in the *New England Medical Journal* on haemophiliacs and AIDS. One recommended a return to the use of cryoprecipitate instead of factor concentrate because of the risk of AIDS – a clear signal that many clinicians were already cognisant of the developing crisis.

In the same month, an eminent group of UK Haemophilia Centre Directors, led by Professor Arthur Bloom, met with representatives from Immuno, a pharmaceutical company which manufactured and sold into the UK factor concentrates. At this meeting at the Excelsior Hotel at Heathrow Airport on 24 January 1983, the probable connection between factor concentrates and what later became known as HIV was discussed, including the latest report from the *New England Medical Journal*.

By March 1983, alarm bells were getting louder still when evidence presented by the CDC in the US showed that AIDS was being transmitted by factor VIII.

The Americans tried to tip off their counterparts in the UK. What followed is difficult to comprehend. Once again, Professor Arthur Bloom, who as we saw in Chapter 2 had authorised secret medical trials on his haemophiliac patients without their consent, was at the centre of the controversy.

Bruce Evatt, the head of the CDC, wrote to Bloom, chairman of the UK Haemophilia Centre Directors' Organisation, in March 1983. In the letter, Evatt declared: 'We presently have 13 confirmed haemophiliac patients with AIDS in the US . . . The incidence rate has been increasing in haemophiliacs . . . All have received factor VIII concentrates . . . I suspect it is a matter of time before you begin to see cases in the United Kingdom.'[7]

The warning was prophetic. Within a matter of weeks, there were reports of the first case of AIDS in a British haemophiliac.

Kevin Slater, from Cwmbran, was just twenty when he was diagnosed with the virus in April 1983. He had been treated for haemophilia with American factor VIII. He died two years after his diagnosis, aged just twenty-two.

Incredibly, Kevin was a patient of Bloom's. Notes from a meeting about his case include quotes from the illustrious Welsh professor, who described Slater as suffering from 'mild' AIDS.[8]

Despite first-hand knowledge of the case, Bloom inexplicably went on to diminish the scale of risk facing the wider community. In May 1983, he issued a note to all haemophiliac patients in the UK, which was distributed by the Haemophilia Society. The note warned of the 'unduly alarmist' press reports on AIDS, and stressed that the cause remained 'quite unknown'. Bloom went on to claim that 'it has not been proven to result from transmission of a specific infective agent in blood products', and said it would be 'counterproductive to alter our treatment programmes'.[9]

It was the second major missed opportunity to stop an escalating tragedy.

Bloom's refusal to sound the alarm across the UK is difficult to fathom. One possible explanation comes from the availability of haemophiliacs as human guinea pigs for the pharmaceutical companies.

In 1982, Bloom's eminent colleague Dr Charles Rizza had organised a meeting at the Blood Products Laboratory (BPL), then a state-owned facility that oversaw the manufacture of human blood plasma products in the UK. A note of the meeting records the need to coordinate clinical trials. It mentions the participants complaining of the 'random approach' being adopted by the pharmaceutical companies, an approach that 'has many severe disadvantages for the NHS and gives little or no payback to the UK in return for the opportunistic and non-contractual use of the special potential of the UK Haemophilia Service as a collective entity'.[10]

Documents show that Bloom was in close contact with various firms who lobbied him to buy their dangerous products for use in the UK. There are snippets within the files that suggest some sort of commercial relationship. In one letter to the American blood plasma firm Speywood, Bloom thanked the company for 'their most generous help' in 'assisting' a congress in Tel Aviv, Israel. In another, Speywood admitted to funding factor VIII research at Bloom's Cardiff centre. The firm also briefed another UK doctor that the latest batch was 'developed in consultation with . . . Bloom'.

In one letter to Bloom, Speywood complained that the company was 'a bit short of sales at the moment', and asked him to buy more products for his Cardiff centre. 'Anything which you can do to help will be greatly appreciated,' said the letter.

Documents show that Bloom was also offered a 'research fellowship' by Armour, another pharmaceutical company. In the end, he agreed that they should 'make a contribution to the Haemophilia Society for the express purpose of funding research'.

In March 1983 – the same month Evatt of the US CDC warned Bloom of the escalating AIDS crisis – the Welsh doctor and his counterpart Dr Rizza established new protocols in clinical trials across the UK. Patients would be monitored and the results – potentially highly lucrative for the drugs firms – would be sent back to Rizza's Oxford centre. Also in the same month, Rizza wrote to another doctor to reveal that '3 drug companies have been in touch with me in the past 3 weeks pushing strongly to formalise studies of their different presentations in mildly affected haemophiliacs'. He added: 'I think it will be necessary to use infrequently or previously untransfused haemophiliacs.'[11]

Not everyone was blind to the crisis. As is so often the case, investigative journalists ended up leading the campaign towards truth and justice, even as they were subjected to obfuscation and smear by the so-called experts charged with protecting the public.

On 1 May 1983, an article by Susan Douglas appeared in the *Mail on Sunday* referring to 'killer' blood from high-risk donors and the danger of AIDS. Douglas, who was at the time the paper's medical correspondent, had spoken to doctors up and down the country about 'concerns within the medical community' that patients were being treated with blood that was suspected of carrying a risk of the then unknown virus. Her article referred to two haemophiliacs who were dying of AIDS.

Dr Peter Jones, a close associate of Bloom's who ran the Newcastle Haemophilia Centre, reported the article to the Press Council, then the official press watchdog, who eventually ruled that the article was 'extravagant' and 'alarmist'.

The Haemophilia Society, which would eventually lose half of its committee members to AIDS, also threatened legal action. They criticised the media for 'dramatising the AIDS problem', and stressed that without the imported factor VIII, the quality of life for those who required the product would have been 'much poorer'.[12]

Douglas has since said she discovered a 'conspiracy of silence' about the risk of AIDS from blood products. She believes Dr Jones's complaint was an example of the establishment closing ranks.[13]

Despite being contested, the *Mail on Sunday* report sparked alarm among some of the keener observers at Westminster. Hugh Rossi, a minister in the DHSS, told an anxious constituent: 'It is an extremely worrying situation, particularly as I read in the weekend press that the disease is now being transmitted in blood plasma which has been imported from the United States.'[14]

One of the few experts to swim against the tide was Dr Spence Galbraith, the director of the Communicable Disease Surveillance Centre. Described by the *British Medical Journal* as 'one of the giants of his generation in public health', Galbraith had developed an interest in infectious diseases during the 1950s while serving as a medic in the British Army deployed in Egypt. He would eventually rise to the very top of public health policy in the UK, developing 'surveillance systems' that the *BMJ* believed were 'regarded as among the best in the world'.[15]

Galbraith cut his teeth by studying the work of John Snow, a British doctor regarded as the godfather of modern epidemiology. In 1854, Snow famously became greatly concerned that a cholera outbreak that killed 616 people was spread after the Broad Street pump in Soho, central London, had become contaminated with sewage. Snow worked around the clock to track down information from hospital and public records on when the outbreak began and whether the victims drank water from the Broad Street pump. He traced hundreds of cases of cholera to nearby schools, restaurants, businesses and pubs.

More than 125 years later, as the AIDS epidemic began to sweep through the haemophilia community in the UK, Snow's disciple Galbraith felt his spider sense tingling.

He disagreed with the laissez-faire attitude displayed towards the safety of haemophiliacs. In a letter to the DHSS in May 1983, he warned that imported US blood products should be withdrawn following the discovery of fourteen cases of haemophiliacs contracting AIDS after receiving factor VIII concentrate.

Dr Galbraith wrote: 'I have reviewed the literature and come to the conclusion that all blood products made from blood donated in the US after 1978 should be withdrawn from use until the risk of AIDS transmission by these products has been clarified.'[16]

Weeks later, he gave expert evidence at a meeting of a subcommittee of the Committee on Safety of Medicines (CSM), where his advice was considered but ultimately rejected.

Galbraith was not the only expert to voice concerns at the meeting. The subcommittee, chaired by Dr (later Sir) Joseph

Smith, also received a scientific paper on AIDS that warned of a potential 'ticking time bomb for haemophiliacs'.[17]

This was the third missed opportunity that could have helped change the course of history.

Sir Joseph has since defended the decision. He said it was taken amid concerns about the supply of blood products, recalling:

> The subcommittee faced the difficult decision of weighing the relatively uncertain risk of contamination from imported blood products against the serious risk of harm to patients with haemophilia should there be a shortage of the products. The conclusions reached were considered and agreed by the CSM.
>
> At that time the need for blood products for the treatment of haemophilia patients far outstripped the supply of the material produced in the UK.

Yet again, Sir Joseph blamed the calamitous failure to achieve self-sufficiency in the UK. 'The subcommittee wanted the UK to produce enough material as soon as possible so that import would no longer be required,' he added.[18]

Worse was to follow. During the same month that Dr Galbraith's recommendations were rejected in Whitehall, the United States finally got its act together. The US Food and Drug Administration (FDA) introduced tighter restrictions on blood donors with the overall aim of reducing the possibility of AIDS transmission. This included the approval of new heat-treated products.

Unfortunately for haemophiliacs in the UK, this meant that the unscrupulous pharmaceutical companies began dumping surplus contaminated American concentrate on the UK, whose policymakers were still listening to experts like Bloom and Diana Walford in the DHSS. Once again, concerns from medics on the frontline appear to have been ignored. A DHSS circular from May 1983 reveals fears among haemophilia centre directors that the 'more "dangerous" material may be dumped in the UK'.[19]

To counteract these concerns, Bloom recommended that imported factor VIII meet the new FDA standards. However, there were already large stocks of potentially fatal factor VIII in the UK, ready to be distributed. With concerns mounting, Britain quickly tried to play catch-up with the US by beginning the process of getting new heat-treated products approved – but the implementation of this vital, life-saving practice would be kicked into the long grass yet again. This time, it was the pharmaceutical companies who held up progress. They argued that further clinical trials of heat-treated products were needed before they could be shared with the public.

Once again, the conduct of the trials simply beggars belief. Documents from the DHSS show that haemophilia directors concluded that any 'meaningful trial' could only be conducted in patients who had not previously been treated with factor VIII, including newly diagnosed or mild haemophiliacs.

The clinicians knowingly appeared to ignore their Hippocratic oath to 'do no harm'. The papers show they knew that 'such a trial could pose ethical problems' because it had already been recommended that these patients should only receive blood products produced by the NHS.[20]

And so it was that even more innocent children who had thus far escaped infection would pay with their lives.

Increasingly, campaigners believe doctors making these decisions broke the Nuremberg Code, which governs the research ethics for human experimentation. The Nuremberg Code was created following the 1945–6 Nuremberg Trials and forbids medical experimentation on humans without their consent.

As we have seen, another concern constantly placed above patient safety was cost. As the new heat-treated blood products became increasingly sought after, another branch of the UK state piped up to urge caution. A letter from the Blood Transfusion Service to the DHSS stated: 'If demands are made for its use by either haemophilia directors or possibly the patients themselves, if they hear or read about it, it will play havoc with the RHA's [regional health authority] finances.'[21]

In its reply, the DHSS stated: 'Your comments about the potentially major financial consequences for health authorities . . . could be used to support the argument for . . . properly controlled clinical trials before such material is introduced into this country.'[22] Fears around patient safety, preventing infection or saving lives were as far away as ever.

Even when safer heat-treated products were finally introduced, NHS doctors were allowed to choose whether they wanted to use them. Many decided to continue using up older contaminated supplies first. Hundreds more people must have died as a result.

One possible motive for the behaviour of Bloom and others is contained in the minutes of a meeting held on 13 July 1983, by the CSM. The papers show that those present knew that 'patients who repeatedly receive blood-clotting factor concentrates appear to be at risk' of AIDS. They also knew that the risks were highest if the blood products came 'from the blood of homosexual and IV drug users in areas of high incidence – e.g. New York and California', and for those who repeatedly received high doses of the blood plasma products.

Despite these frank admissions, the committee ruled that the risk of contracting AIDS had to be balanced against the 'life-saving' benefits of their use to haemophiliacs. They also argued that withdrawing the blood products was 'not feasible on the grounds of supply'. It appeared that the committee, while acknowledging the HIV risk, believed withdrawing the blood products would pose a more immediate danger to haemophiliacs.[23]

With warning after warning missed, the seeds of mistrust within the haemophilia community were being sown.

In October 1983, a Haemophilia Centre Directors' Organisation meeting noted that patients were refusing to accept commercial factor VIII because of the AIDS scare. One participant suggested that patients should revert to using cryoprecipitate. Bloom overruled the idea, erroneously claiming, in defiance of all the information that had emerged thus far, that there was 'no evidence that the commercial concentrates were the cause of AIDS'.[24]

This outrageous assertion proffered by Bloom and others in the DHSS was starting to be questioned by trade unions. In October 1983, Clive Jenkins of the Association of Scientific, Technical and Managerial Staffs wrote to complain about comments made by Lord Glenarthur, then the parliamentary undersecretary of state for Health and Social Security:

You say that there is no conclusive evidence that AIDS is transmitted through blood products. I would argue that the evidence is very strong. There are now about

20 American haemophiliacs with AIDS, and this figure is likely to underestimate the risk because of the apparently long incubation period.

I also draw your attention to a paper prepared jointly by DHSS staff and the HSE, which was submitted to a recent meeting of the Advisory Committee on Dangerous Pathogens. This paper states quite specifically that 'there is now strong circumstantial evidence that AIDS may be transmitted by blood products'. I am tempted to ask you what you would consider to be conclusive evidence, particularly in the circumstances where the agent or agents for AIDS are as yet unidentified?[25]

In his evidence to the Infected Blood Inquiry, Glenarthur admitted there was a 'tension' between the statement that there was 'no conclusive proof' of transmission of AIDS by blood products and other evidence of risk to haemophiliacs from blood products. '[My] understanding would have been that the wording of all statements about risk in this case was carefully considered by both scientific/clinical and policy officials in DHSS,' he said. 'They were the experts, helpfully providing advice to ministers who did not have the necessary detailed knowledge. To reiterate, we never denied the risk of transmission, but acknowledged its possibility. We had to balance it against the counter-risk of serious injury to haemophiliacs who would suffer from not being able to accept treatment with blood products.'[26]

•

One month later, the public health crisis that had thus far played out largely behind closed doors finally burst into the public consciousness.

The *Guardian* newspaper published a report headlined: 'US blood caused AIDS'. It revealed that the first British haemophiliac had died of AIDS, citing a study in the *Lancet* that stated: 'The British haemophiliac who died from AIDS almost certainly caught the disease from contaminated supplies of the blood-clotting agent factor VIII, imported from the US.'

Following the article, a note from an unnamed civil servant asked Dr Diana Walford, the principal medical officer in the DHSS: 'Is it OK for us to continue to say there is no conclusive proof that the disease has been transmitted by American blood products?' Dr Walford responded in a handwritten note: 'Thanks. Yes, it is OK.'[27]

In that same week, Ken Clarke, a junior health minister who would later rise to many of the great offices of state, including Chancellor of the Exchequer, Home Secretary and Justice Secretary, was asked a parliamentary question in response to the *Guardian* article. Clarke reassured MPs that there was 'no conclusive evidence that [AIDS] is transmitted by blood products'.[28]

Given the evidence available to ministers and the DHSS at that moment in time, the answers provided by Walford and Clarke are staggering and make heavy weather of the word 'conclusive'.

To recap: more than one year earlier in September 1982, a Haemophilia Centre Directors' Organisation meeting heard claims that haemophiliacs in the USA were suffering from AIDS that might be linked to commercial blood products; in January 1983 came articles in the *New England Journal of Medicine* recommending that cryoprecipitate rather than concentrate be used because of the risk of AIDS; in March that year, Evatt of the CDC specifically warned Bloom of the risks; Bloom's own patient Kevin Slater then contracted AIDS after being administered factor VIII; the eminent epidemiologist Spence Galbraith raised serious concerns; and the DHSS had taken to referring privately to imported factor VIII as 'dangerous material'.

Clarke has always defended his use of the phrase 'no conclusive proof'. He later said the written parliamentary answer to Edwina Currie, MP, 'wasn't drafted by a minister'.

'I can't remember who did it, but obviously somebody decided that that was the best most accurate line to take,' he said. 'It was repeatedly used by every minister. We kept repeating that because that was [the] scientific advice we had, until it was perfectly clear to the medics that there was in fact sufficient proof . . . we weren't playing down that possibility.

'It seems to me . . . it's a perfectly accurate description of where medical opinion was at that time. That's presumably why the haemophilia doctors were still using factor VIII.'[29]

Years later, after thousands had died, Walford performed a U-turn, admitting that a better phrase to use would have been 'blood products are a likely cause of transmission of AIDS', as it was the 'mainstream view' in the DHSS at that time.[30] However, she went on to defend her actions, telling the Infected Blood Inquiry: 'Of course I now know about AIDS and its terrible consequences – but I still believe that, at that time, the hazards were unproven of transmission and basically what one knew was that the severe haemophiliacs desperately needed factor VIII or factor IX.'[31]

Clarke did bring himself to admit that had he seen the letter from Dr Galbraith recommending the recall of American factor VIII, he would have 'saved thousands of lives'.

He described the letter as 'pretty startling', adding he was 'amazed to read a document which is so perspicacious'.[32]

Following Clarke's public reassurance in November 1983, the damage continued to spread.

In March 1984, documents show that Rizza and Bloom were still organising clinical trials of commercial factor VIII that they freely recognised carried a 'putative risk of trans-mission of AIDS'.[33] In a letter to haemophilia doctors across the UK, Rizza and Bloom advised the clinicians to 'draw up a list of patients in your centre who might be suitable for such a trial'.[34]

In 1985, the FDA in the US banned medical use of blood from high-risk groups, including prisoners. However, exports were allowed to continue – and, incredibly, the NHS continued to buy it.

It was still believed among some within the UK medical community that haemophilia itself – and the risk of a fatal head bleed – was more dangerous than a deadly virus. This is a theory that some experts maintain to this day, given that before the advance in treatment the life expectancy of haemophiliacs was not much more than forty.

The cavalier attitude regarding informed patient consent continued. By late 1984, the medical profession realised they had committed grave errors and some leading figures decided not to tell the patients of their potentially fatal diagnoses.

Minutes from the meeting of the Haemophilia Centre Directors' Organisation on 10 December 1984 show Dr Peter Kernoff, head of the haemophilia centre at the Royal Free Hospital in London, commenting that as an astonishing seventy per cent of haemophiliacs were now HIV positive, it may be considered irrelevant if they were told.[35] Presumably, they didn't need to be informed about their HIV status because their life expectancy was already so much lower than those without the bleeding disorder.

By 1985, the true scale of the scandal was starting to become clear. Once again, it seemed the threat to life was just not the top priority for civil servants.

Memos exchanged within the DHSS in March of that year discussed the extent to which HIV infection would be likely to spread through the community. An official called Michael Lloyd warned that about a third of Britain's haemophiliacs were 'sero-positive', meaning they had antibodies linked to the virus that later came to be called HIV. Around eight per cent each year would develop AIDS, which would ultimately equate to forty per cent of all haemophiliacs.

The figures shocked the message's recipient, John James, who calculated that up to 1,200 of the 5,000 haemophiliacs in the country could develop AIDS. He wrote:

> Frightening figures. But figures which also suggest that, however dispassionate the analysis, steps to prevent the remainder of the haemophiliac population becoming sero-positive are likely to have a strong cost-benefit plus in terms of lives saved.
>
> Of course, the maintenance of the life of a haemophiliac is itself expensive, and I am very much afraid that those who are already doomed will generate savings which more than cover the cost of testing blood donations.[36]

Could it really be that James and others in the DHSS thought the AIDS epidemic would rid Whitehall of the financial burden of ongoing support to suffering haemophiliacs?

Whatever the truth of the matter, one of those already 'doomed' was certainly Ade Goodyear.

•

Ade's fate was sealed when he became one of fifty Treloar's boys to take part in a clinical trial run by Speywood.

Despite repeatedly raising concerns about imported blood products, Dr Anthony Aronstam selected dozens of pupils for the eight-month trial in September 1982. Ade was among the guinea pigs chosen – a decision he believes handed him and his school friends an almost certain death sentence. His mother was never asked for her consent.

During the trial, Ade and his friends suffered several adverse reactions and mysterious rashes. Decades after leaving Treloar's, Ade said his awareness of Aronstam's involvement in the trial has created 'a perplexing tear in the timeline of my knowledge base'.

He spoke to me of his ambivalence towards Aronstam, who at times had been a hero to the young schoolboys. 'To this day, I do not understand why Aronstam was involved with such a risky trial . . . especially after attending the 1980 conference regarding his then commitment to heat treatment and safer supplies for us,' he reflected. 'Why the change of tack? It was the polar opposite of who Aronstam was as a doctor and who I thought he was as a person.'

He added: 'I do not know if it was wilful blindness or whether he was being guided at the time to undertake such a project with us children and young teens without due regard for our medical wellbeing.'

Ade went on to forge a successful career in the music industry, working with some of the most famous bands on the planet, including Bucks Fizz, The Human League and

Status Quo. But he saw one of his dreams fade when he was prevented from joining Peter Gabriel's 1993 Secret World Tour after being warned that he would be denied entry to some countries because of his HIV diagnosis – the origin of which he believes lies with Speywood.

Ade told me every boy on the trial went on to develop HIV. 'We didn't attend the school to be tested on without our or our guardians' consent in trials – we were simply there to learn. During the trial, there didn't appear to be a shortage of either Scottish or English factor VIII, for that matter. They had three fridges and on the top shelf was the Scottish factor VIII, as this was deemed the safest, then the English factor VIII on the next shelf down, and at the bottom, the American factor VIII. We had previously been told to start at the top with the Scottish factor VIII.'

He was later told by one of the haemophilia nurses that it was 'one batch' that infected the pupils. 'I believe the Speywood "Hemofil" plasma to be the missing link in how I contracted the virus at the school,' Ade said.

After Christmas 1982, the boys returned to Treloar's after the school holidays to find the treatment centre had undergone a massive extension. Some of the pupils, including Ade, have since wondered whether any of the pharmaceutical companies were responsible for funding the dramatic upgrade, which came at roughly the same time as the trial.[*]

---

[*] In asking Treloar's whether pharmaceutical companies paid them and/or provided funds for the extension in exchange for testing on pupils, they said: 'As we are waiting for the report of the Inquiry, and we have been notified of possible legal action against Treloar's following this, we are unable to comment at this time beyond the statements already made to the Inquiry. Our thoughts of course remain with the victims and those affected by this tragedy.'

During the following year, 1983, a number of American pharmaceutical companies continued to visit Treloar's in an attempt to peddle their new wares. By this time, Aronstam appears to have had a change of heart. Ade recalled being in the new treatment centre one lunchtime when Aronstam walked two American pharmaceutical representatives out of the building, robustly informing them: 'Don't come selling your shit to me again.'[37]

By then, the damage had been done and news about the impending tragedy was already leaking out.

With the AIDS crisis growing almost daily, staff at the school were told to remove newspapers from the library in an attempt to shield the boys from the scandal. But on 1 May 1983, a member of staff slipped up and left a copy of the *Mail on Sunday* in the TV room, which contained the seminal story by Sue Douglas referred to earlier in this chapter. The headline screamed 'Hospitals use killer blood', and the story alleged that blood imported from the US by the NHS could be threatening the lives of thousands of British people. 'A sexually transmitted killer disease, which has struck more than 1,300 Americans, is present in contaminated blood used in transfusions and operations,' said the article. 'Experts revealed exclusively to the *Mail on Sunday* that two men in hospital in London and Cardiff are suspected to be suffering from the disease after routine transfusions for haemophilia.'

The alarming story was immediately shared widely around the school. Ade recalled that a friend picked up the paper, saying, 'What does this mean? That's us. It says haemophiliacs.'

However, Ade claimed the pupils were too young to kick up much of a fuss. 'You weren't going to ask, not at that age,' he said. 'Again, we were compliant. We were children, so you don't go to your doctors and say . . . is there anything wrong?'[38]

Within the first week of the summer holidays in 1983, however, Ade started to realise just how much trouble he and his friends might be in when he became 'extremely poorly'.

'It started with a dreadful and debilitating earache and a gland behind my left ear that became rather enlarged,' he recalled. 'My eyes became yellow, every gland went up. I had vomiting and diarrhoea and many spikes in temperature with sweats. These were the first signs that something was not right.'

Ade said his mother took him repeatedly to the GP, but was told it was likely to be glandular fever. 'I spent most of that summer on the sofa.'

When he returned to Treloar's that autumn, Ade found a note on his bed telling him that he had to present himself at the sick bay. He was then restricted in isolation for three weeks and told he had contracted hepatitis again. He told me there were times during those weeks when he thought he might die. 'I said my prayers in the dorm many times.'

Ade was not the only one who had fallen sick. His friend Richard, who was on the same trial, had become very pale and gaunt. He had lost a lot of weight and was unusually withdrawn.

'I instinctively remember thinking something [was] very wrong,' Ade recalled. 'I looked at him and I thought, you're going to die. I knew he was. I knew he was going to die, and we were really tight. He wasn't at the school very long but we bonded quick. He was a bit of a loner, but we bonded. So, I saw him before he went to the medical centre. I said, "Richard, have a look at your eyes. Oh, they're a bit dark"

– you know, the normal banter where you talk as kids. And he said, "Oh, I'm in trouble. I'm in some trouble. I'm not very well," and he looked skeletal . . . He died. We believed he was the first one to die of AIDS and that was confirmed later on by a member of his family.'[39]

Richard never returned from the October half-term. His death was later casually announced at a school assembly.

At this point, Ade and a few others started asking about what had happened and why.

'We were told not to worry until more information was known, and that we would be looked after. We had no reason to doubt this at the time as we were young, but little did we know that his immune system had just crashed.'

Not long afterwards, Ade remembered, one of the pupils had confronted one of the nurses about the American factor VIII product being administered to another school friend.

'What are you giving him that for? It's got AIDS in it,' the boy had said.

The nurse had responded, 'Oh, don't be silly. What else can we give him?'

Ade recalled, 'And then I said something along the lines of, "There's British in the fridge, isn't there? Why not give him British?" And then we were asked to leave the transfusion room.'[40]

The boy in question only received three shots of factor VIII in his life. After Richard, he was the next to die.

•

Alec Macpherson was the headmaster at Treloar's between 1974 and 1990, during which time the AIDS pandemic hit Britain.

In his first ever newspaper interview in June 2021,

Macpherson told me how the tragedy unfolded inside the 'School of Death'. Speaking almost three decades after his retirement, as he was forced to account for his role in the scandal, he said it was Dr Aronstam who first told him that some of his students had been infected after receiving contaminated blood products. Many of them died young, killed by the very treatment that was supposed to save their lives.

'It was a pretty massive shock to find that you had this in the school, among a group of pupils,' he recalled. 'And it was something that really none of us had much idea about. We didn't know about it. I mean, AIDS was something you thought was in Central Africa, and then you heard that the United States was troubled by it. We never expected to have it under our roof.'

He added: '[A] lot of staff were terrified that they were going to get it, and of course you had a lot of boy–girl relationships [that you] normally . . . have in any co-ed school. Fathers of daughters at the school were coming to see me. I mean, it was a massive problem.'[41]

'I was told there were problems with the blood we had been using and that some of the boys had become infected. I suppose that was the start of it . . . The vast majority did die. There are only a small number left, and nobody really knows how they managed to survive.'

Macpherson, who was forced to ban the boys from playing football because it caused too many dangerous bleeds, remembered the distress of his pupils when they learned of their illness.

'We had to tell them the truth. When we discovered that they were probably going to die prematurely . . . some of the older ones, they got very angry about it.

'[There was] anger there – you could see it . . . It was

very difficult – on the one hand, you had to keep the school rules, and you had to make them behave like normal, civilised human beings. On the other hand, you realised that they were very, very upset and very worried young men who knew that . . . their lives were going to be cut short.

'A group of them would go out at weekends and get drunk – come back drunk – and I remember once I was called by the police to the police station, and there was one of our boys lying in a cell being watched by a policeman. He was fifteen and completely unconscious. He was so drunk, he was lying on his side in the recovery position in a police cell. These were not the kind of problems you expect when you become a head teacher.'

Macpherson, who still lives in Hampshire, said there were many other problems he had not anticipated, including trying to stop his infected pupils from having sex with female students. 'There were incidents where a housemaster would come in to see me and say, "Look what I found in Johnny's locker" – you know, a pack of condoms. What should we do?'[42]

Macpherson said he thought the staff did everything they could to help the infected pupils, whom he described as having a 'rage inside them'. He also thought the doctors onsite did their best to keep the boys safe, although he also said he believed the school was at the 'sharp end of introducing better treatment for haemophilia and . . . experimenting . . . with the use of factor VIII'.[43]

He told me he found it 'hard to believe' doctors would not have acted straight away if they had known about the danger of contamination.'[I'd be] very surprised if that is true, and I would be pretty horrified and disgusted as well, as that's not how I would have wanted it dealt with.'

He said: 'Dr Aronstam was fighting the corner very hard . . . I didn't have anything to do with the medical side, but I was . . . very involved in all the meetings . . . discussing what to do. I think we did try and do something about publicity – but I don't really remember much about it now. I was really involved in the pastoral care side of things.

'Our main mission was to make the lives of our pupils as normal as possible despite the extraordinary circumstances we found ourselves in.'

Ade's fears about his health deepened in the summer of 1984. Aronstam invited Ade and a friend to join him and his wife for an afternoon by their swimming pool. It was an occasion Ade would never forget.

The pair were being treated to the outing after missing a number of school trips due to illness and treatment. Ade told me they spent a 'wonderful afternoon' with the Aronstam's family and his two springer spaniel dogs, sipping lemonade contentedly in the garden. But the intimacy of the occasion clearly pricked the doctor's conscience, and the sunny day took a dark turn.

Ade recalled: 'Towards the end of the day . . . I thought we would be helpful kids and we picked up the . . . lemonade tray to take it back to a small kitchen annexe that was on the back of his house.'

There, he caught Aronstam 'welled full of tears . . . and pushing his hands on the sink . . . rocking and we'd never seen that, just in pain, I think, emotionally in pain.' Ade's friend eventually summoned up the courage to ask the doctor what was wrong.

With his voice full of anguish, Aronstam replied: 'We've fucked up . . . We've messed up. It's all gone wrong.'

Confused, the boys pressed him again and asked: 'Are we going to be OK, Dr A? Are we all right? Are we OK?'

His response left the boys cold. 'We'll do our best,' Aronstam said. 'We're going to do our absolute best for you.'[44]

They were the exact words Aronstam would use almost one year later, in May 1985, when he finally gathered Ade and his four school friends together to tell them which of them had contracted HIV.

Even before Ade's formal diagnosis, his relationship with his adopted mother had deteriorated still further amid fears he had contracted the deadly 'gay plague'.

Ade said she told everyone on their street that he was HIV positive. 'It was almost as if she was wishing it on me so she could reject me yet further,' he recalled.[45]

When he went home for leave weekends and school holidays, he was taunted with daily chants of, 'Hey Ade, you got AIDS yet?' and 'Live AIDS coming.' Others shouted at his mother: 'We know what your son got: G.A.Y – Got AIDS Yet?'

'I was so isolated and alone. It would be heartbreaking if it was happening to someone else, let alone happening to me,' Ade said. 'I could no longer go out in the surrounding areas of Portsmouth. The newspapers were full of haemophiliacs, viruses, haemophiliacs, viruses – and so it went on. You didn't dare use the word haemophilia outside of Treloar's because of this.'[46]

About a year after he was formally diagnosed, Ade's relationship with his mother broke down entirely. He claimed she attacked him with a two-litre Coke bottle, accusing him of bringing 'shame on her'.[47]

Ade returned to care and was placed in a children's home in the summer of 1986. After ten months, he left care after two members of staff at Treloar's, Pat Salt and Maureen Leary, agreed to become his guardians and allowed him to stay with them during the school holidays. He remains close to both of them.

Ade was one of almost 100 boys at Treloar's to be infected with HIV and hepatitis during routine haemophilia treatment at the school. He is one of only sixteen who are still alive today. He puts his survival down to a near obsession with eating oranges. At one point, he was eating fourteen a day. Speaking about the viruses that have ravaged his body and the injustice he feels about being given life-threatening illnesses by a treatment that was supposed to enhance his life, Ade said: 'It significantly affected my emotional wellbeing during my teenage years and irrevocably altered my expectations, prospects and working life and dreams. I was always worried about letting people down by simply dying on them.'

Ade was eventually forced to give up his dream job in the music industry, which had paid between £400 and £600 a day. He now struggles to make ends meet by running a local disco for £150 a night, – £50 of which goes to paying his roadie, because he is too weak to carry the equipment himself. He lives in rented accommodation because he cannot get a mortgage due to the infection, and worries almost constantly about what will happen to his partner if he is not around. He is ashamed that he has been forced to live off the benefits system.

He said: 'I think, on almost a daily basis, "I'm still here, I'm still alive," and [I] question why often. I suffer from survivor guilt because I have outlived the prognosis I was given. I have also outlived my buddies and peers from Treloar's who were co-infected, and my biological half-brothers.'

He added: 'There are too many empty chairs in too many family homes up and down the country set against years of confused and blurred lines handed down by successive governments. It is a systemic tragedy.'[48]

Clair Walton.

5

UNTIL DEATH DO US PART

1985–9

It was a beautiful spring day when Clair married her child-hood sweetheart, Bryan. The couple could not have looked happier as they posed for their wedding photographs on 21 May 1983.

Although they were part of the 'biker scene', they ditched their leather jackets for more traditional wedding attire as they said 'I do' in front of dozens of their closest friends and family.

The effervescent bride, with her long dark hair cascading down her back, wore a traditional white wedding gown with high neckline and lace sleeves, while the groom, with his long dark locks and neatly groomed beard, looked the part in his dark morning suit, a white rose jauntily tucked in his buttonhole.

They could not have known then that their marriage vows to love each other in 'sickness and in health' and 'until death do us part' would soon have such resonance.

The pair had met five years earlier, when Clair was seventeen and Bryan was twenty.

In her evidence to the Infected Blood Inquiry, Clair recalled of her first love: 'He had a real love for life, a real zest for life. He had great aspirations for what he wanted to do with his life.'[1]

The couple got engaged on Clair's twenty-first birthday and threw a massive party to celebrate. They started to make plans for their future, buying their first home together close to their families in Leamington Spa, in Warwickshire. It was a three-bedroom semi-detached house with a 120-foot garden.

'It was a beautiful start to our life,' Clair remembered. 'This house was going to be the start of our future and our family.'[2]

But eighteen months into their married life, disaster struck. The couple received devasting news that would leave them living the rest of their lives together in sickness rather than health.

Bryan, who was a severe haemophiliac, was diagnosed with HIV and told he had only two or three more years left to live. He was twenty-six.

The petrol station manager had been a student at Treloar's. Like Ade, Bryan had been receiving factor VIII for years to treat his condition.

Clair recalled being handed a pair of surgical gloves to wear to protect herself from her husband as doctors imparted the life-changing news. The offer of gloves appears all the more bizarre on reflection, as the clinicians seem to have known about Bryan's diagnosis for some considerable time – a period during which the couple continued to have sex. Although the date given for Bryan's first positive test in his medical records was 15 June 1984, the couple were not told for another six months. They were also given little advice about how to manage the condition other than to use condoms if they were having sex.

Clair remembered it being a 'terrifying time'. She said: 'We were seeing . . . the coverage about AIDS and about the panic and, obviously, seeing reports on television, and it was incredibly frightening, incredibly frightening.

'We knew, really, that the best thing was to keep quiet, to be silent, because we were witnessing how other people with HIV were being stigmatised, how people were losing their jobs . . . so we really didn't know who we could talk to and who we could confide in.

'So, [news of the diagnosis] was kept very, very minimal, just parents and very, very close family.'[3]

The couple had recently moved to Devon so Clair could take up a new post as an archive conservator, but they immediately decided to move back to Leamington Spa.

'It was Bryan's choice,' reflected Clair. 'He said, "If I'm going to die, I want to be back with my family," and so this . . . career . . . move, this whole . . . life ahead of us was just bluntly cut short.'

Having already sold their first home in the historic spa town, they found a new house to buy and vowed to 'carry on' as best they could.

'It was on the edge of a village in Warwickshire and it was just a magical house,' said Clair. 'It just needed some work doing on it and we sort of threw ourselves into that for a while.'[4]

At the time, Bryan was showing no signs of illness, but his mental health was starting to deteriorate. The key turning point came when he tried to track down an old school friend from Treloar's whom he knew lived in the Oxford area.

Bryan was too late. His former schoolmate had just died of AIDS. He was yet another victim of the Treloar's tragedy.

'This had a massive effect,' recalled Clair. 'He went to

his funeral. I think that might have been something that triggered an awful lot in him when he saw that, because we didn't really mix with the haemophilia community at all. We were completely isolated.'[5]

Clair claimed Bryan became angry and withdrawn, and the couple temporarily separated. She was heartbroken. However, within a few months, they got back together, and their discussions once again turned to their future and what they wanted to achieve in the short time Bryan had left.

'It was really [a case of deciding] what . . . we wanted out of life, and our dreams . . . of having children were still there,' said Clair.

So, the couple went to discuss their plans to have a baby with the haemophilia unit in Coventry. Clair recalled that they were told: 'Well, that's not a very good idea, but if you want to go ahead, we'll monitor you.'

In hindsight, it would turn out to be catastrophically bad advice.

Clair now believes she was being used as a guinea pig to see if she would go on to develop HIV.

She told the inquiry, 'They were watching [to see] whether I would turn from HIV negative to HIV positive. That was it. There wasn't any advice . . . There was no discussion around ovulation, about whether either of us were . . . fertile in any way . . . or the dangers of it.'[6]

Clair underwent monthly tests that came back negative until June 1987. She had just been 'very ill' with flu-like symptoms for a week, which was most unusual for her. When her next test result came back from the hospital, it was 'inconclusive' and she was asked to take a second test. She spent the rest of the summer anxiously awaiting the results.

As Clair tried to bury her mounting panic, the couple decided to take an unplanned holiday to Santa Barbara in America.

'As we were flying across the Atlantic, I said to Bryan, "Actually, they never gave me the result back," and he said, "Oh yes, they did. You are positive. They told me."'[7]

In what would nowadays amount to a shocking breach of medical protocol, Bryan had recently been told about his wife's HIV status during one of his own medical appointments. He had not imparted the devastating news before their transatlantic trip. Clair has since confessed that she believes this was because he thought she may not have gone along with the trip, for which they surely were not insured, as HIV sufferers often had trouble taking out travel cover.

Whatever the truth of the situation, Clair claimed the moment of the shocking discovery was surreal. Her dream of a family life with Bryan had been shattered. She decided that she could no longer try for a baby with her husband, as she did not want to risk passing the potentially deadly virus to her child.

When they returned from holiday, Clair threw herself into her 'dream job': setting up an archive conservation unit for the Shakespeare Birthplace Trust. She recalled: 'It was like my baby, I think, looking back . . . that was my baby that I'd been denied.'[8]

Her professional life may have been flourishing, but the fallout from the trauma of her husband's illness and her own diagnosis was never far away.

By 1989, the effect of HIV on Bryan's battered immune system was starting to cause other serious health problems. He developed non-Hodgkin's lymphoma – a type of cancer that affects the lymphatic system, a network of vessels and glands that run throughout the body. He was initially treated with radiotherapy, but two years later, the cancer returned. Fearing that he did not have much longer to live, Bryan decided to go on a road trip. He bought a long-wheelbase Land Rover and took off on a trip to Iceland. Clair still has recordings of him talking about his exciting Icelandic adventure. She even flew out to Reykjavik to join him for a few weeks. However, when Bryan arrived home, he looked emaciated. It became clear that the long car drive had taken a toll. 'It was really the beginning of the end for him,' recalled Clair.[9]

She believes Bryan's health had been further damaged by him taking large quantities of experimental HIV drugs on the advice of his doctors. He was given Zidovudine (AZT), a drug that can cause toxic side effects in high doses. The drug was given lightning-speed approval in 1987. However, many HIV patients believe it was AZT, one of several antiretroviral agents used to treat the disease, that killed people rather than the AIDS it was meant to treat.

'[Bryan] hated it,' said Clair. 'He felt there was something not right about it, and I've since discovered he was given mega-doses at the time. I actually think that may well have contributed to the downfall of his health.'

With cancer again ravaging his body, Bryan was also given 'harrowing chemotherapy' at the John Radcliffe Hospital in Oxford.

As the end neared, Clair remembered hugging him in the kitchen of their home. 'He was worried for me . . . He also said, "I don't want to die. I'm too young." He said, "I've got so much I want to do," and he was at this point thirty-four years old . . . Then he said he was worried for me if he died . . . "What's going to happen to you?" And I just said, "It's

OK, I'll be all right," and I don't know whether I lied or whether . . . it was something he needed to hear . . . I think he needed permission . . . to die.'[10]

Her words seemed to have the desired effect. On 13 March 1993, Bryan passed away, surrounded by his loving family. He and Clair had enjoyed less than a decade of married life together. Clair recalled: 'That morning as I was helping him in the bed, there was a magpie that came to the window, and he went, "One for sorrow," and by that evening he had died and I was just numb. Somebody took me back in the car and I afterwards thought, "Oh my God." Afterwards I was [thinking], "Who's going to be there for me?"'[11]

The death of her husband felt like the end of the world. She could not know it at the time, but Bryan's passing would just be the start of her own personal tragedy.

•

The plight of the partners of the original victims became a major new front in the scandal. Clair's experiences are far from uncommon. Sue Threakall, one of the central campaigners who has led the fight for justice, also fell victim to the extraordinary behaviour of her husband's doctors.

In January 1985, her husband, Bob, a severe haemophiliac, had tested positive for HIV. But the clinicians decided not to tell him until the following summer, and in the intervening months, the couple continued trying for their second child. The delay could have had deadly consequences for Sue, who remains angry with the doctors who so thoughtlessly disregarded the potential threat to her life.

Sue met her future husband in 1977 after she left college. Ironically, the pair were both working together at the DHSS. Sue believes that was the year Bob was first given factor VIII concentrates. Before then, he had been reliant on cryopre-cipitate. 'He didn't want to transfer to it,' recalled Sue. 'He had a natural suspicion about it. I could never understand in my naiveté then why he was reluctant to treat a bleed and, apart from the fact he could never find a vein, he just didn't want to use the product. I said, "Well, for goodness sake, if it stops bleeding, why not just use it?" and he said, "Because you don't know what's in it."'[12]

The couple married in October 1981 at St Mary's Church, in Handsworth, Birmingham. After the ceremony, the bride and groom jumped over the cemetery wall to pose for photographs in Handsworth Park. They celebrated their special day with friends and family not long after Bob became infected with hepatitis B (after his death, it was revealed that he had also been infected with hepatitis C). Sue told me: 'He had been actively encouraged to treat himself at home, despite a lack of confidence and not really wanting to do it. Like every other haemophiliac I have spoken to over the years, he had never been told of the known risks. It had been heralded as the miracle treatment that would transform lives. Well, it certainly did that.'

Bob believed his marriage to Sue had been a second chance at family life after his first marriage fell apart, but Sue claims that the whole thing was 'ripped away' with the HIV diagnosis.

At the time they learned of Bob's diagnosis, the couple, who lived in Birmingham, had a two-year-old son, David, plus two sons from Bob's previous marriage, Paul and Mark.

'I am angered by the six-month delay in Bob being informed of his HIV status, as this was a delay that could have proved fatal to me, as it did to so many others,' said Sue.[13] It was only through luck that she was not infected.

Still desperate for another baby, Sue, who was a deputy headteacher at the time, investigated sperm-washing techniques to see if these might allow the couple to safely conceive a child.

She said: 'I was desperate for a second child, but obviously he'd already got three, so there wasn't the same yearning for another baby really. I wanted one so that David had a sibling closer to his own age . . . and I must admit I got a bit like a dog with a bone . . . because I'm not very good when people say, "You can't do that."'[14]

Sue wrote to Dr Charles Rizza, the director of the Oxford Haemophilia Centre – and another senior clinician who made a highly questionable decision. Rizza invited the couple to a meeting and gave them some surprising advice that contradicted what other experts had told them about safely conceiving a baby.

'He was kind of saying, well, if you want to go for it, yes, there's a risk, but – and then he went on to say that people don't like discussing their sex lives and there's . . . clearly a bigger risk with anal sex and people don't like to tell you if they've been indulging in anal sex. He was basically saying that the heterosexual transmissions were probably through anal sex, so as long as you don't do that, you should be OK.'[15]

Sue said the couple were not able to make an informed choice about pregnancy, partly because the medical knowledge was not there, but also because the bulk of Bob's treatment took place at a haemophilia unit rather than somewhere that specialised in HIV treatment.

Sue never gave up on her dream of having another baby, and even as her civil servant husband came close to the end of his life, the couple were still investigating artificial insemination using donor sperm. In fact, one of the last outings they went on together was to discuss their options at a Brook Advisory Centre after they were approved for NHS treatment.

Beyond Sue's desire to have another child, Bob's diagnosis put enormous strain on their family, particularly as his health began to deteriorate.

'We were very fortunate in that we had a close-knit circle of friends and a good social life . . . and good jobs and the people that we interacted with on a daily basis appeared to accept it, appeared to be supportive,' recalled Sue. 'But you see, you never know what's going on quietly in the background.'[16]

Her son was rarely invited to other children's birthday parties.

'He was a very, very quiet child, but still at the back of your mind you think is that because we were the AIDS family, and that's how we were known . . . People started dying: Rock Hudson . . . various other people, and it became more and more real and more and more scary . . . A letter to the *Birmingham Evening Mail* suggested that everyone with HIV should be instantly rounded up and put on an island – somewhere off the coast of Scotland I think was the preferred venue – and, you know, we were suddenly dealing with all this . . .'[17]

In particular, Bob began deteriorating after being put on large quantities of AZT, the drug that also had a deleterious effect on Clair's husband, Bryan.

'He wasn't too bad until he was put on AZT, and after that it was just catastrophic,' Sue said. 'It was like slipping off the side of a mountain. He got multiple infections. They were constant. It was tonsillitis or it was a urinary tract infection, or he'd have a chest infection or something would be wrong somewhere. He was never free of infection. He lost a tremendous amount of weight. He started looking like an AIDS victim.'[18]

Despite the pressures on his health, Bob continued to work as a DHSS executive officer until just months before he died. By now, Sue had been forced to give up the job she loved at Erdington Church of England Primary School in order to nurse her dying husband.

'I loved my job, loved the school and most of all loved the children,' she told me in an interview for the *Sunday Express*. 'Five years after Bob's HIV diagnosis, I realised there was no way I could cope with such a demanding job, Bob's deteriorating health, our six-year-old and my two stepsons. So, I went into supply teaching.'[19]

Bob took a turn for the worse in January 1991 and Sue insisted they take him into hospital.

She eventually got him on to the ward and the doctor turned around to her and said: 'Well, he doesn't look as bad as you made out he was on the phone.'

But it was already too late.

Sue recalled: 'They X-rayed his chest and did loads of bloods and everything, and all of a sudden there was all hell let loose. I got taken into a small room with three doctors, I think, and they were showing me the chest X-rays and clearly trying to tell me that Bob was dying, and I just wasn't having any of it. You know, it just wasn't going in. He said, "But . . . do you realise what we're trying to tell you? He has no or relatively no normal lung tissue left. It's all been destroyed."'[20]

By now, Bob was on 100 per cent oxygen and was still blue. His family knew it was only a matter of time before he would die, and they began to rally around him. As he neared the end, Sue made a promise to her husband that she would fight for justice.

'He weighed just five stone and died the kind of death you would not wish on a rabid dog,' she told me. 'His last words to me were, "Is everything sorted?" Meaning, would we be OK financially? I lied and told him we'd be fine, and a few minutes later he died.'[21]

As both Sue and Clair would find out, the contaminated blood scandal did not just have a devastating effect on its victims' health. The survivors would also suffer incredible financial difficulties as a result of callous government decision-making.

The horrors that were still to come meant that Sue continues to struggle with the belief that she failed to honour her deathbed promise to Bob. 'It is because of this I have never been back to where his ashes are scattered, and [I] never will until I can hold my head up high and say that now it is sorted,' she told me.[22]

Bob's death on 20 February 1991, at the age of forty-seven, shattered his family. His eldest son Paul described him as the glue that held the family together.

Thinking back on the hardest time of her life, Sue recalled: 'I was a mess, [an] absolute mess. I did try and go back to some teaching . . . Even now I will dream about children in a classroom two or three times a week, all the things that I used to love doing with them. I think I was good at my job but I could never get it back.

'I lost weight, I couldn't cope with being a mother any more. I couldn't cope with being a homemaker any more. It was just so difficult doing all that on my own . . . I loved being a mum. I adored it. When David came along, it was that unconditional love . . . and still is . . . I'd found something I could do, something I was good at. My own family background is quite dysfunctional . . . I never felt secure at home, but I did once I got my own home. But then it all just fell apart.'[23]

Summing up her feelings about the loss of her beloved husband, she told me: 'It was not just the loss of a son, husband and father, it was the loss of a good, ordinary man who trusted the advice he was given by doctors and who was terribly let down.'[24]

•

Responsibility for the contaminated blood scandal does not solely rest with the doctors who withheld diagnoses from patients for years, the government scientists who constantly misled the public about health risks, and the clinicians who performed secret, unauthorised and dangerous tests on hae-mophiliacs.

Ministers right at the top of government also share some of the blame. That is according to Norman Fowler, the health secretary at the peak of the AIDS crisis, who told me that the Thatcher government was too slow to warn the public of the impending health emergency.

Fowler told me about his memories from that period of his life in a telephone interview conducted after he took the decision to stand down as Lord Speaker in April 2021. He said he was quitting the role in order to be able to 'speak his mind' as an independent member of the House of Lords on the issues he had campaigned for, in particular LGBT rights in the UK and HIV and AIDS. Just weeks before, Fowler had backed calls for the UK's first ever national AIDS memorial, with the aim of fighting stigma and discrimination against those with HIV and AIDS.

Lord Fowler was appointed as health secretary by Margaret Thatcher, who was prime minister at the time, as part of a reshuffle to 'purge the wets' from her front bench. Incredibly, although he first took up his post in September 1981, he did not learn about the AIDS pandemic until 1985 – more than three years after Britain's first victim, John Eaddie, had died of the virus. He remained health secretary until 1987.

Despite warning after warning about the emergence of HIV, Fowler said he couldn't ever recall Thatcher showing any interest in the deadly virus that was spreading like wildfire across the planet. He also claimed she never got involved in concerns that the country's blood supply had been contaminated by HIV, putting Britain's entire haemophilia community at risk. It is telling that even in her own autobiography, Thatcher made no reference to AIDS, despite the fact that by the time she left office in 1990, more than one million people had been infected worldwide.

Thatcher was not alone in thinking she should steer well clear of the public health crisis. Her private secretary, Mark Addison, advised in writing that the then-prime minister should not attend the 1985 opening of the new £30 million Blood Products Laboratory (BPL) at Elstree. The long-neglected plant was finally ready to treat and screen blood before it entered the nation's supply. However, Addison advised Thatcher to 'stay clear of AIDS even when it is a question of opening laboratories to help innocent victims'.[25]

With such uninterest, prejudice and lack of knowledge at the heart of government, disinformation continued to swirl around the virus, including ideas about its causes and methods of transmission. As a result, victims and their families, including Clair Walton and Sue Threakall, were scandalously kept in the dark about how the virus was spread and the potential risk posed to them should they attempt to get pregnant. As late as October 1985, there was still a debate raging among the UK Haemophilia Centre Director's Organisation about how much information should be given to the victims and their partners. There was even a disagreement about whether to conduct a comprehensive patient questionnaire designed to study the prevalence of HIV among their wives and partners.

Some believed such a study would be 'insensitive' and 'cause great anxiety to the families'.[26] This was despite the fact that the risk of AIDS to the partners of haemophiliacs had been widely known for at least two years.

Fowler appeared to be one of the only voices in government who believed that knowledge was power in the fight against the virus. He took it upon himself to visit hospitals in San Francisco, where there were wards full of young men dying from the disease. Fowler was photographed shaking hands with an AIDS patient during the fact-finding trip. This was months before Princess Diana made headlines for doing the same at The Middlesex Hospital in London. Many were convinced at the time that the virus could be caught by physical contact, and Fowler was determined to expose the lie.

At the time of his visit to the US, British hospital wards were also starting to fill up with AIDS patients. But whereas America was now in the grip of a media frenzy, forcing its government to take action, the famously tenacious British press was relatively silent – save for a few rare exceptions and a handful of salacious scare stories. As a result, few of Fowler's ministerial colleagues appeared to be interested.

'I realised that we hadn't got a moment to lose,' Fowler told me in an interview. 'At the time, we had little knowledge of this disease and no drugs to treat it and so the only thing we could do was to try to persuade people and give them knowledge about how to avoid it.'

The health secretary was determined to get a grip on the issue even when it became clear that Thatcher was not a supporter of his campaign. 'It became quite clear that unless someone from the Cabinet . . . like myself took charge, we weren't going to make much progress,' he told me. 'It wasn't something that could be done at a minister of state level, it could only be done at a Cabinet level . . . because they were the people that you needed . . . on your side if you were going to change policy.'

One of the first battles he faced was trying to persuade colleagues to support an initiative to give clean needles to drug addicts to limit the spread of the blood-borne virus. But the stigma wrongly attached to the victims of the epidemic meant that his efforts went in vain.

'A whole range of people, including some of my colleagues, said that you can't give clean needles to addicts because it would be condoning crime,' he reflected. 'I think the difference between what happened then and what's happened with the Covid pandemic is that with Covid, virtually everyone was on the same side. When we came to the 1980s and when we came to gay people, homosexuality, drug use, people weren't on the same side.'

Prejudice became a significant issue for Fowler to overcome. He also lobbied ministers to support his calls for a national public information campaign to combat apathy within the political class, a hostile media and a public keen to look the other way. The message being perpetuated was that the spread of the disease was down to a deviant minority, and most prevalent among what was purportedly a sexually promiscuous homosexual community. This was not helped by outrageous remarks voiced by several prominent figures. James Anderton, the then-Chief Constable of Manchester Police, remarked that homosexuals, drug addicts and prostitutes who had HIV/AIDS were 'swirling in a human cesspit of their own making'. Lord Monkton, a hereditary peer, argued that those with HIV should be quarantined and kept away from the general public.

Woodrow Wyatt, the Tory grandee and friend of Thatcher, told the *News of the World* in his column: 'The start of AIDS was homosexual love making. Promiscuous women are vulnerable, making love to promiscuous bisexuals. They then pass on AIDS to normal men.'

Alfred Sherman, an influential political figure on the right who was also close to the prime minister, wrote to *The Times* saying that AIDS was a problem of 'undesirable minorities . . . mainly sodomites and drug abusers together with numbers of women who voluntarily associate with the sexual underworld.'

Fowler told me he encountered a 'vast amount of prejudice and attacks' from all who questioned his determination to educate the public about the deadly HIV virus. He recalled being lectured by the Chief Rabbi, who was concerned that efforts to spread a safe sex message were immoral. Thatcher herself, whose premiership was rooted in the importance of the heterosexual nuclear family, was also reticent about some of the more explicit messages being disseminated.

Asked whether he ever won her over, Fowler's response was emphatic:

The answer to that is no. I didn't win her over. But to give Margaret credit, she didn't explicitly interfere. She argued against quite a number of the things that I was doing. She argued against the language being used in advertisements. She argued against sending leaflets to every household. She vetoed the idea of having a ministerial broadcast. Those were big things that she did. She was sympathetic about the people who suffered. There was no question about that, but on the policy, I think she was nearer to those people who were saying that our campaigns were telling young people things that they didn't know about. Her fear was that once they did, they would go out and experiment, which never seemed likely to me.

Fowler recalled one New Year's Eve when he made a visit to Downing Street to persuade Thatcher to allow him to make a televised ministerial statement on the emerging AIDS crisis. The Cabinet and the opposition had already agreed to the proposal, but the prime minister had the ultimate veto.

It was seven at night and Margaret said, 'I'm not going out tonight, I'm too busy.' And so, we went off and we had a perfectly genial conversation. Except she said: 'There's no way, Norman, I'm going to allow this ministerial broadcast to take place.' And then she said: 'You mustn't just be known as the minister for AIDS.'

Now, I misinterpreted that as being a slight pat on the back and it was actually things were going well, and I was going on to new departments. Not a bit of it! What she really meant was, for goodness' sake, stop spending all this energy on AIDS and go on and do something more useful.

Eventually, Fowler succeeded in persuading the prime minister to set up a Cabinet committee on AIDS. But he still believes precious time was wasted that could have cost people's lives. 'We could have started the campaign a bit earlier,' he admitted. 'We had to go through the business of setting up a Cabinet committee devoted entirely to AIDS. We lost a bit of time there.'

Fowler also admitted the government was slow in changing its stance that there was 'no conclusive proof' HIV could be transmitted through blood products, the false message first delivered by Ken Clarke as a junior health minister in November 1983.

Fowler's plans were not only thwarted by Number 10. The Treasury was also loath to part with any money to spend on his campaign. Fowler has since described his battles with the Treasury over his health budget as the 'bloodiest battleground in British politics'.[27] The health secretary was preparing to mount a massive public awareness campaign but had been told in no uncertain terms that he would have to find the resources from inside his own department's budget. He told the inquiry: 'I remember very distinctly when we were going to send a leaflet round to all homes in the country, warning them about AIDS. We got this through the special committee on AIDS, and then right at the end the Chief Secretary said, "And of course I do have to say . . . all this is on the understanding that no extra resources will come from us."'[28]

This penny-pinching delayed public awareness of the risks posed by the deadly virus still further. Finally, five years after the first AIDS victim had died in the UK, the government found the funding. In 1986, Fowler and his team, which included Sir Donald Acheson, the then-chief medical officer, were given the green light to launch one of the country's largest ever public health campaigns.

It was a major victory for Fowler, who had taken on not only Thatcher and the civil servants, but also some in the medical establishment who were terrified of causing panic among the public.

Although at the time there was no cure on the horizon, education was regarded as the best way to stop the spread of the virus. Under the slogan 'AIDS: Don't Die of Ignorance', a mailshot was distributed to 23 million homes, giving the public clear facts about the virus and its transmission. Posters stated that AIDS was not prejudiced and could affect anyone, gay or straight, man or woman. The adverts also stressed that it could be spread via sexual intercourse with an infected person, regardless of their sexual orientation.

Controversially, clean needle exchanges were set up for drug users. But the most striking element of the campaign was the harrowing tombstone and iceberg TV adverts voiced by the actor John Hurt. The campaign was undoubtedly effective. A Gallup poll one year later showed that ninety-eight per cent of the public were now aware of how HIV was transmitted. The vast majority declared support for Fowler's campaign.

'I have heard it said that the advert was so scary it put a whole generation off having sex,' Fowler told me. 'Well, I don't think there is any evidence that it actually did! What I do know is that I get letters from time to time from people who say thank you – that it saved their life. In politics you don't get that kind of letter very often.'

•

As the scale of the tragedy around contaminated blood products became apparent, pressure began to mount on Margaret Thatcher to compensate the victims of what later became known as the biggest treatment disaster in NHS history.

But Norman Fowler claimed the demands were initially destined to fail because of opposition from both the prime minister and the Treasury. He claimed that ministers were worried that if they awarded special payments to haemophiliacs, it might set a precedent. He recalled:

> It was doomed to failure. There was no chance that I was going to get permission to do that, no chance whatsoever. The Treasury was against it, the prime minister would have been against it because she would have been told that it would have other effects.
>
> I can't think of anyone, with the exception of one or two Cabinet ministers, who might have had some sympathy. It was a hopeless case I'm afraid, because they took the view that if [this was] agreed to, the floodgates would have been opened.[29]

Fowler felt that he had largely expended his political capital with Number 10 and the Treasury by the time that he left the DHSS to become the new employment secretary in June 1987.

In response to demands for compensation, Baroness Trumpington, a health minister who had responsibility for blood and blood products at the time, was clear. She wrote in March 1986:

> The government have the deepest sympathy for the plight of haemophiliacs. However, there has never been a general state scheme to compensate those who suffer the unavoidable adverse effects which can in rare cases unhappily arise from some medical procedures.

Compensation is awarded by the courts in cases where negligence has been proved. It would, of course, be improper to prejudge any case which a haemophiliac might bring, but no suggestion has been made that the doctors treating haemophiliacs have acted negligently. Before the availability of heat-treated factor VIII, the possible risks of unheated factor VIII had to be weighed against the effects on the lives of haemophiliacs of ceasing to have treatment.

Trumpington displayed a chronic lack of understanding of the appalling mistakes of the 1970s and 1980s when she added: 'Doctors treating haemophiliacs were, we believe, careful in explaining these risks to their patients.'[30]

Yet within months of Fowler's departure from the DHSS, John Moore, the new health secretary, had surprisingly come up with a limited financial package to support the victims of the scandal. This volte-face came after pressure from the medical community and MPs, including Labour MPs Jack Ashley, Frank Field and Frank Dobson. There were also concerns that the Haemophilia Society was considering taking legal action against the NHS on behalf of its infected members. The Haemophilia Society had previously raised concerns about some of the scaremongering from the media in their coverage of the scandal, but now appeared to be taking up the baton against the government. The tragedy had begun to engulf the Haemophilia Society itself, with members of the charity's board discovering they had also been infected.

Peter Jones, director of the Newcastle Haemophilia Centre, who had defended so many indefensibles up to this point, also located his moral compass, outlining the case for compensation for haemophiliacs in a letter published in *The Times*. He wrote: '[HIV] has added an intolerable burden to the lives of many families with husbands or sons already incapacitated by haemophilia,' adding that he hoped 'time [would] be found to consider the special needs of these families'. Then he set out the difficulties that patients infected with AIDS were having obtaining life insurance and mortgages. He concluded his letter: 'I believe that these families form a well-defined group with a special call for state help. In the case of haemophilia, the government should argue neither precedent nor an open-ended commitment, because of the iatrogenic nature of infection and the small and finite numbers involved. It would be of great and immediate benefit if some form of no-fault compensation could be provided to them.'[31]

In August 1987, Tony Newton, a health minister, sent a finalised submission to Moore, which was entitled 'Compensation for Haemophiliacs with HIV infection'. In the report, Newton, who is understood to have been instrumental in changing government policy, said that there would be both public and parliamentary pressure to do something for the infected haemophiliacs after the summer recess. He warned that the campaign for something to be done could be expected 'to attract considerable support on all sides of the House'.

His submission argued that the infected haemophiliacs could be classed as a distinct group who should be awarded a 'one-off solution', and defended such action as a 'special case'. Newton identified two options that would not set a precedent once adopted. This included lump-sum payments totalling £10 million in order to provide 1,200 of the affected haemophiliacs with £8,300 each, or £3 million to be given to the Haemophilia Society to distribute as they saw fit. [32]

Many of those deeply involved in the haemophilia community recognised the paltry payments on offer would not be enough. Dr Aronstam told the BBC in 1987: 'It's enough for a nice holiday but it's not enough for very much else.' He added:

> We gave [HIV] to them. We were trying to treat them. We were trying to make them healthy and what we did is we added another catastrophe to the disaster they already lived in.
>
> It's been devastating for many people. They have had to go underground in many ways. They would be isolated at work, [and have] problems at school, problems getting mortgages, problems getting insurance. It's a devastating problem, apart from having to live with the fact that they may die.[33]

Moore, the health secretary, was initially opposed to the proposal but was sidelined by Thatcher, who put the progressive Newton in charge of the issue. It was an interesting decision by the prime minister, who up until this point had shown little inclination to support AIDS victims and haemophiliacs more broadly.

Thatcher eventually overruled the naysayers and bean counters. In November 1987, the Cabinet signed off on a proposal to award £10 million to the Haemophilia Society, who were tasked with setting up a trust to administer the funds. The Macfarlane Trust (MFT), which was one of five trusts eventually set up by the government to support the different groups affected by the tragedy, was established for this purpose. A further top-up of £24 million was made to the fund, which was used to provide £20,000 in ex-gratia payments to each haemophiliac infected two years later.

But government inertia and bureaucracy would once again perpetuate grave injustice.

On 9 October 1988, one year after the MFT was set up, *The Sunday Times* published an article entitled: 'AIDS victims dying before trust pays up'. It revealed that only £132,000 out of the £10 million scheme had been paid out to infected haemophiliacs. The largest one-off payment was for £3,000. The article also suggested that few haemophiliacs were expected to qualify for regular support from the trust. Sadly, these were not just teething problems. The main concerns raised by those desperately needing support were the ad hoc nature of the assistance and the overly bureaucratic processes employed by the trustees overseeing the scheme. The five trusts, including the MFT, were all eventually replaced by one scheme, the England Infected Blood Support Scheme (EIBS), following growing dissatisfaction among those they were supposed to help. The main criticism of the trusts was that in order to obtain support, those affected often had to provide financial proofs and statements, as well as medical records proving they were in need. Many complained they found the process highly demeaning and onerous. Some victims felt it was yet more trauma laid upon trauma, and were reduced to tears.

A report by the All-Party Parliamentary Group (APPG) on haemophilia and contaminated blood, an influential group of MPs, went on to criticise the MFT and its sister trusts for submitting victims to the 'worst form of modern-day begging'.[34]

•

The victims of this bureaucratic inertia felt insult had been piled on to injury. But they had suffered so much already at the hands of the state that it did not come as much surprise.

As soon as her husband was diagnosed with non-Hodgkin's lymphoma in 1989, it was not just the fear that she would soon become a young widow that kept Clair Walton awake at night. She also worried about keeping a roof over their heads as debts started to mount.

Bryan had been told he had at most eighteen months to live, and his failing health meant he was forced to give up work. Growing increasingly desperate about their dwindling finances, Clair called the Macfarlane Trust (MFT) from a phone box in the hospital where her seriously ill husband was being treated. She was put though to one of the scheme's administrators. In her evidence to the Infected Blood Inquiry, Clair recalled he was 'matter of fact' in his response and promised to visit the couple at home.

The administrator from the MFT would not make an appearance for several months, but eventually showed up on a dark winter's night in November 1991. Clair opened the door to him, hoping beyond hope that he would be the couple's salvation. But his response would shock them to the core and present Clair with a fait accompli that made her future even more uncertain.

His first remarks about the couple's home set the tone for the conversation. 'Rather large, isn't it?' he sneered as he poked around the two-up two-down detached house.

He then offered to help the couple by paying off their mortgage – but the killer caveat was that the MFT would require a piece of their home. The proposal was that the MFT would put a charge on their house and take a fifty-eight per cent stake in the equity of the property. That was not all.

If the house gained in value, the MFT would demand a percentage of that, too. The charity set up with the very purpose of supporting the victims of a state-manufactured scandal was now looking to make a profit from the loan.

Clair and Bryan were gobsmacked. But presented with only one option, they felt they had no choice but to agree.

Clair recalled: 'We were forced to make the application because there was no other option. Bryan was dying and we had very little money coming in. The Macfarlane Trust put a man who was dying of AIDS . . . under extreme duress to sign over our home to keep a roof over our heads.'[35]

To add insult to injury, the process was further delayed. The couple was forced to spend the next nine months wrangling with the trust over the valuation of their home before the agreement was finally drawn up in June 1990.

Clair reflected: 'I didn't agree that . . . the charity set up to support haemophiliacs and their spouses should be profiting from people dying. It made no sense to me and I didn't think it was legal . . . It certainly was immoral.'[36]

The noxious charge on Clair's home would cause problems long after Bryan's death in 1995. Two years later, the grieving widow decided to make a fresh start and move out of the house where she had nursed her dying husband. She explored buying something at a similar price in Stratford-upon-Avon, Warwickshire, the birthplace of William Shakespeare, but the MFT was not prepared to offer her the support that she needed. They told her in no uncertain terms that the 'repayment of the loan will be required upon the sale of the property'.

In a subsequent letter from the MFT about Clair to an undisclosed recipient – which has since been disclosed to Clair under data protection – they presented two alternative options. 'The first is we require repayment of the loan on the sale of the property and refuse a further loan. We could then attempt to arrange a mortgage with the Nationwide, although I suspect they would baulk at a four times salary multiple.' They then added callously: 'Given this woman's poor money management track record, this [presumably the refusal of a mortgage] would not be a bad thing.'[37]

The second option presented proposed the repayment of the loan on sale of the house, with Clair being offered a second loan on the new property. Clair refused the offer. This is something that the administrator from the MFT, who had appeared at her door several years earlier, then raised in a letter to the trustees of the charity, writing: 'I am afraid the lady [Clair Walton] wants to eat her cake and still have it. She conveniently forgets the rent-free living she has enjoyed for seven years. It is not true that our decision prevents her from moving. It may well prevent her from buying outright so that she can continue to live rent-free, but that is not really our concern.'

Clair claimed the letter highlights the 'contempt' the trust had for her. 'I was . . . grieving, living with HIV myself, traumatised and this is how they treat me,' she said. 'It was of their making. It's their . . . equity loan. It was the only option and so then they continued to beat me. It was like . . . a stick every time I tried to sort it out . . . It was an investment that they wanted to return.'[38]

Clair claimed at one point she was told by the MFT that she would have been 'thrown out on your ear' if it wasn't for the charity.

'It was a mess created by the Macfarlane Trust,' she said. 'Instead, with the Macfarlane Trust unwilling to help resolve the situation, I stayed in the house, trapped, for years after my husband died.'[39]

Eventually, after the MFT appointed a new chief executive, Clair was allowed to move to a new house in Wood Green, north London, but only if she accepted a continued charge on her home. The trust made a considerable profit on its loan from the sale of the house.

However, the excitement about her long-desired move to the capital, which she had sought to enable her to progress her blossoming career, would be short-lived. By now, Clair had developed what she describes as 'full-blown AIDS'. She was in and out of hospital. At one stage she became so emaciated she weighed just six stone. It is amazing, given the health issues Clair has encountered, that she has lived to tell the tale. However, when I first spoke to Clair over the telephone more than two decades after Bryan's death, she had the fighting spirit of someone in perfect health and was determined to right the wrongs she felt she had been forced to endure at the hands of the very trust set up to support her.

Eventually, Clair became so unwell she felt she needed further support and wanted to be close to her mother in Warwickshire, so she took the difficult decision to ask the MFT if she could move again. Once again, the charity proved resistant, warning her she was 'still in hock to the Trust to the tune of over £168,000'.[40] She was subsequently warned that the subsistence payments from the trust, which had been agreed by a social worker to help her meet the cost of her bills, would be withdrawn.

After challenging the decision, she received a personal letter from Martin Harvey, the chief executive of the charity, on the thirteenth anniversary of Bryan's death, confirming the decision. Clair was told her failure to have children was being held against her.

'I do suggest that you might give some consideration to the fact that you are but one of some hundreds of people who look to us for assistance, many of whom are less articulate than you, do not have the benefit of owning any property as you do, have dependent families which you do not, and whose health is much more compromised than your own,' wrote Harvey.

'You might as well have just punched me in the face,' Clair recalled. 'I didn't have children because my husband had died.'[41] Clair later received an apology from the trust, but the charge on her property remained.

Despite years of campaigning by her MP Nadhim Zahawi, a Conservative politician who later briefly became Chancellor of the Exchequer, it looked like she would forever be shackled to the MFT, which was eventually wound up. Her debt was transferred to the Terrence Higgins Trust, which initially filled her with 'horror'. However, Clair claimed that dealing with the Terrence Higgins Trust compared to the MFT was like day and night. 'I was met with . . . care and kindness, and people who seemed to really . . . understand that this was a woman [who] was petrified about what was happening to her, and they assured me that the chief executive would get in contact.'[42]

In 2019, within months of a review of her arrangements, Clair received a letter from the Terrence Higgins Trust, bringing her near-thirty-year battle for financial independence to an end:

> We've undertaken a review to consider the financial and
> emotional impact of the loan. We are grateful to you for

assisting with these enquiries . . . I am pleased to advise you that we have decided to accept the recommendations in the report and, therefore, your loan is being written off with immediate effect. We do not consider that you are currently or are likely to be in a position to repay the outstanding loans without causing financial and emotional hardship or distress, and writing off your loan clearly meets the charitable objectives of the Macfarlane Trust.[43]

•

Sue Threakall also fell victim to the Macfarlane Trust following the death of her husband, Bob. The former deputy headteacher had been forced to give up her job to nurse him and, when he died, the loss of their combined £40,000-a-year income created a huge black hole in the family's finances. Sue struggled to make ends meet and, still reeling from her husband's death, she turned to the Macfarlane Trust for support.

Her requests for help were not particularly productive. She was awarded a few minor one-off payments over several years before the support dried up.

'I think they were beginning to realise that as people were dying they weren't actually getting rid of the problem,' Sue recalled. 'They were inheriting a new one in terms of widows and children and they started to tighten up and it became very difficult. I always had a policy that if I did need some help, I would approach them, because after all, that's what they were set up to do, and I just tried to . . . encourage them to do their job.'[44]

Sue's persistent requests seemed to be held against her.

Her doggedness and determination to ensure she and her family received every bit of support they were entitled to in the wake of her husband's death appeared to rub people up the wrong way. She later learned from one of the charity's trustees that they used to reject her requests immediately as a matter of principle. She was also erroneously told that she had received more than any other widow – the same falsehood that was presented to Clair when she was struggling with her finances after her husband's death.

A decade after Bob passed away, Sue, along with a new partner, was forced to downsize. They moved to Devon, to run a post office in a village near Barnstable. When she arrived, the property was 'virtually falling down'. It cost her every penny she had, plus some she didn't, as she plundered her credit card to make it habitable.

Eventually, unable to keep her head above water, she asked the MFT for help again. After much persuasion, they agreed to give her a loan of £8,000 to help her pay off her debts. However, just like in Clair's story, this was secured against her property.

'I applied for a grant and they flatly refused, and this was at a point when I was paying the mortgage on credit cards and buying food on credit cards, and you get pushed into this corner and you have no choice,' she reflected. 'They offered it as a loan and I took it.'[45]

Initially, the charity wanted her to pay back the loan in instalments of £300 a month, but when it was made clear that was not possible, the MFT lowered the amount to £25 a month.

The charge remained on her property until the Terrence Higgins Trust eventually took over the debt years later and, as with Clair's case, decided to waive the loan on moral grounds.

At one stage, Sue recalled, she received a letter from the MFT calling in the debt. The charity claimed they had checked the Land Registry and seen that she had recently sold the property for more than £300,000, and now wanted their stake back. However, the charity had made a mistake and checked the records for the wrong house. The one they had found the records for was the property immediately over the road from where Sue lived.

'It was something that just completely floored me,' she told me during an emotional late-night phone call as she updated me on the recent horrors to befall her since the last time we had met. 'I got the letter and my stomach hit the floor. I was worried about what was going to happen [next], but I was also shaken by what had happened. What on earth were they doing checking the Land Registry in the first place? It seemed to me to be pretty underhand tactics.'

It wasn't the first or the last letter to confound Sue. As soon as the MFT found out she was living with a new partner, the shutters came down in a move that was almost certainly unlawful under the Equality Act.

'They suddenly decided they'd come up with a policy . . . that they do not give grants to women who have moved on, for example, finding a new partner,' Sue recalled. 'The only reason I found a new partner was because the old one had been murdered by the treatment.'[46]

When Sue challenged the decision, she was told by the MFT: 'Although there is no firm policy, the Trust takes the view that after ten years following bereavement and where a non-infected widow has the good fortune to establish another relationship, that individuals should be afforded every opportunity to move forward in the context of that relationship and enable the Trust to provide support to others in less fortunate circumstances.'[47]

Sue claimed she was turned down for almost every request, meaning that she was left wearing broken glasses for eighteen months. She was even turned down for travel expenses by England Infected Blood Support Scheme – the organisation that replaced the MFT – when she developed breast cancer and needed to make a 120-mile round trip to Exeter five days a week for treatment.

Sue, who has held various roles in the campaign group Tainted Blood, including chair, has witnessed outrageous treatment by the MFT towards other victims through her campaigning work. She was passed emails by Gareth Lewis, the previous chair of the group, that would eventually lead to an apology from the charity.

Gareth and his brother Hayden, both haemophiliacs from Cardiff, were infected with hepatitis C and HIV, and died within six months of each other. The brothers were referred to in emails by the MFT as the 'Welsh terrorists'.

In another instance, members of the contaminated blood community were referred to as the 'great unwashed', and in a third instance, a victim's new partner was described as 'his latest squeeze'.[48]

Sue cannot pinpoint the moment relations with the MFT broke down with some of the widows in particular, but believes it was partly driven by the Westminster government failing to come up with a fair payments system.

Until only relatively recently, the rights of affected widows and widowers in England were not recognised at all, even though the spouses of the deceased in Scotland received

£27,750 a year in ongoing payments. The decision created a divide within the community. Sue told me: 'I think one of the worst things they [MFT] did was to turn the men against a lot of the widows. They rightly or wrongly saw that there was a pot of money being divided between those who were actually poorly and infected and the widows. I had one man say to me, "Why don't you just go and get a job?" and at that point I had three, and then another one who told me that when he died, he knew his wife would be quite capable of going out and getting herself a job.'

Critics of the scheme claim it only recognised those who were physically ill, ignoring the emotional, as well as financial, impact on other members of the family, which was huge and lifelong. In many cases, families fell apart after the death of their loved one and suffered terrible financial hardship with the loss of an income, or benefits, depending on whether the deceased had been well enough to continue to work.

Sue, who is a no-nonsense warrior in the campaign for justice, has a soft edge and a heart of gold. Despite leading the fight on behalf of so many others as part of her work with Tainted Blood, she has lived with a permanent fear of losing her home to the bailiffs. The home that was her only place of sanctuary after Bob's death eventually became a constant source of anxiety and stress.

She told me: 'I used to have a perfect credit rating, a great career, a lovely home and a family. Now, because of what was done to us, my family is a mess.'

The Cornes family at Garry and Lee's wedding, 1991.
From left to right: Alan, Andy, Paul, Garry, Lee, Merle,
John and Roy.

6

SEVEN BROTHERS

1989–94

When Roy Cornes died of AIDS, few people, other than his immediate family, came to his funeral to pay their respects.

However, not long afterwards when the location of his grave at Birmingham's Lodge Hill Cemetery became widely known, people travelled from miles around to throw rocks at his headstone. Someone even emblazoned 'shit' on his grave.

The Birmingham City fan was just twenty-six when he died of the deadly disease in 1994. For the last two years of his short life, Roy had lived under a grim media spotlight after being accused in national newspapers of deliberately infecting several women with HIV. The first stories about him broke in June 1992, one year after Freddie Mercury, the lead singer of the legendary rock group Queen, died of AIDS. The panic about the rapidly spreading virus was still gripping the nation and growing by the day.

It was a tip-off from a mole to the *Birmingham Post* that first lit the fuse. The influential regional daily featured a front-page article with the sensationalist headline: 'AIDS Maniac on the Loose with a Mission to Kill'.

The newspaper revealed that the unnamed 'AIDS maniac' was 'deliberately infecting' women as some sort of unspecified revenge on society, apparently without scruple or remorse. One of his victims had allegedly already died. The revelation sent the tabloid press into meltdown. One headline screamed: 'AIDS time bomb'.

The story quickly spiralled into a national scandal centred on the mysterious AIDS-carrier with a 'grudge against the world'. Roy's name eventually emerged after reporters interviewed victims who accused him of infecting them with HIV. Once his identity was known, his face was plastered across the front page of every national newspaper. Roy was portrayed as a monster and legions of reporters were sent to Birmingham, where he lived with his family, to hunt him down.

Roy, a severe haemophiliac, was seventeen when, his family believe, he was infected with HIV via an innocuous blood transfusion as a schoolboy at Treloar's in 1985. His family claim that he was not told of his diagnosis for several years.

Impossibly young to receive such devastating news, he was also on the verge of becoming sexually active – but too immature, perhaps, to understand rules about safe sex. Like other HIV-positive haemophiliacs, he was offered counselling and was encouraged to lead a responsible sex life, using condoms. According to a woman who counselled Roy, there was nothing to suggest he was acting improperly.

As he left adolescence, Roy not only had good looks but more money than his friends after being awarded an ex-gratia payment by the government. In 1989, he received £20,000 from the controversial Macfarlane Trust, a payment that was given to all HIV-infected haemophiliacs who contracted the deadly disease after receiving contaminated blood products. Three years later, he received a second payment of £23,000. This may seem like a lot of money. However, these one-off payments were granted to victims like Roy who had been unfairly handed a life devoid of almost all employment opportunities. And a life that would also be severely curtailed in length.

Passing off the money as a redundancy payment, Roy went on a wild spending spree. He is said to have splashed out on cars, expensive presents and drinks for friends in the pub. His favourite hangout was The Lifford Curve, a flashy local pub full of lads in tight T-shirts and jeans, and girls in miniskirts and white stilettos.

Strangely, it seems to have been well known in the Kings Heath area that he was an HIV carrier. Yet still, it is said, women queued up to sleep with him.

'He had more friends than he knew what to do with; then as soon as the money ran out, they disappeared,' said his mother, Audrey, in one of the many newspaper interviews she gave in the wake of the scandal. 'It's terrible what's happened, because he's a good-hearted lad really. The money was the ruination of him.'[1]

Gina Allen was only sixteen when she met Roy. The pair had a brief, one-month affair. Allen's family knew nothing about him until after her death. They didn't even know that she had been infected with HIV.

Gina died aged twenty from a rare form of pneumonia associated with AIDS after collapsing and being rushed to Selly Oak Hospital. She was placed on a ventilator for ten days before finally passing away.

'She never regained consciousness. We didn't even have a chance to tell her that we loved her,' said Rose Allen, her grandmother. 'You cannot imagine how much of a shock it was to find out what she had died of. When they said AIDS, we couldn't believe it.'[2]

Gina was not the only woman to claim she was infected by Roy.

Lynette Russell met Roy after he briefly moved into a squat in Ladywood in 1989. The relationship lasted a few months. She became infected with HIV and later received a payout as part of a government settlement. Russell claimed that Roy did not tell her he was HIV positive and that he slept with other women during their relationship.

'I asked him if he would wear a condom, but he said there was no need and that he was safe,' Russell told the media. 'I believed him, especially when he said, "If you loved me you'd trust me."'[3]

She said she found out that Roy was HIV positive after returning from a three-month trip to her native Australia. She immediately contacted police, but they said there was nothing they could do. Roy angrily rejected her claims, telling the press: 'I knew her ages ago. But I used something when I had sex with her. She was obsessed with me.'[4]

Then a third woman came forward to tell the newspapers that she too had been infected with HIV by Roy.

But there was a twist. Tina Orme, who had lived with Roy for a year, also alleged that Roy was the father of her son, Daniel, who was also later diagnosed with HIV. 'I keep hoping that by the time it develops in his body, they will find a cure,' she said in an emotional interview. 'He is only an innocent baby. He deserves to have some life.'[5]

Roy subsequently left Orme and married another woman called Linda. Roy's mother Audrey claimed that Linda married him in full knowledge of his medical history.

They are both said to have been shocked upon learning of Allen's death.

'He is very upset. He could hardly breathe; he has chest pains,' said Audrey, who revealed the couple were being supported by social services during the media storm.[6]

It is understood that links between Roy and the three women set alarm bells ringing at South Birmingham Health Authority months before the first story about him emerged.

AIDS workers became concerned when women with HIV began to mention Roy's name when asked for contacts from whom they might have caught the virus. Mild disquiet turned to serious concern with the death of Gina. A fourth possible female victim, who has never been named, was also identified, but doctors did not know where she was, or even if she was still alive.

As months went by, knowledge of the cases leaked out to a wider circle of doctors. Concerns mounted, and eventually a case conference was called to discuss how Roy might be persuaded to modify his behaviour. It was the details from this conference that generated the *Birmingham Post*'s initial front-page scoop.

The health authority's reaction was to issue a statement confirming the story in broad terms while refusing to name anyone involved. However, a 'friend' of Roy's then rang the *Post*'s sister paper, the *Evening Mail*, and named him. Roy initially tried to deny the allegations, but within days he, his family and almost every other significant figure embroiled in the affair had sold their stories to the tabloid press.

Doubling down on their scoop, the *Birmingham Post* thundered: 'A man who has ignored all advice to behave is on the loose, as deadly as an IRA terrorist with a new store of Semtex.'[7]

Terry Page, the editor of the *Post*, said he did not think such words were too strong, saying:

> How many bodies do the health authority want piled up before they do something? This man is walking about like a grenade with the pin taken out. The South Birmingham Health Authority should have named him. That would have been the quickest and easiest way of solving this problem. Instead, the newspapers were left to walk a legal tightrope over naming the guy. I think it is incumbent upon newspapers to be brave, but it is not incumbent upon them to be society's whistle-blowers. The doctors knew what was happening. They may have a duty to their patients but they have a duty to the rest of society, too.

In fact, the medical establishment felt powerless. AIDS is not a 'notifiable disease'; if it were, they would have greater public health powers to deal with it.

'To be fair, this is probably the first time they have ever had to deal with a case where one person can medically kill another,' said Page. 'There is a clash between medical ethics and the public's right to know, and there are no guidelines.'[8]

The dilemma was discussed endlessly in Parliament during the summer of 1992, as MPs demanded the government introduce a new criminal offence to allow the prosecution of HIV positive men and women who recklessly, or deliberately, infect sexual partners. But Virginia Bottomley, the health secretary, ruled out a change in the law to bring Britain into line with some American states, where deliberate transmission of AIDS is an offence. Speaking to the annual conference of the National Association of Health Authorities and Trusts in Harrogate, she said she was 'not convinced' it would be appropriate to 'pursue legal redress or statutory measures'. Her statement followed a separate report on the case that she presented to other Cabinet ministers.

'The biggest public health risk we face is, without doubt, AIDS,' said the report. 'The recent case in south Birmingham has focused many people's minds on the sad truth that the heterosexual community cannot afford to ignore or underestimate the HIV/AIDS risk. We must continue our efforts to convince the heterosexual as well as the homosexual community that they are at risk from casual, unprotected sex.'[9]

Politicians, the press and the public were finally waking up to the fact that AIDS was far from a 'gay plague'. The fallout was not pretty.

Roy's sister, Merle, a teaching assistant from Worcestershire, remembered the media maelstrom engulfing her ailing brother. 'The stigma surrounding the family was almost unbearable,' she told me during a telephone interview almost three decades after the event, the first time she had spoken to the media. Merle is softly spoken and clearly still traumatised by the impact on her family. 'We became known as the AIDS family and were told we were scum. You would not believe the filth and abuse that was daubed on our front door. It was absolutely horrible. The reporters would turn up and they would try and goad us into saying something. We felt like we were under siege.'[10]

But the true focus of Merle's anger is Birmingham's Queen Elizabeth Hospital. She believes doctors failed to tell Roy exactly what was wrong, and how he could protect his partners from the virus. 'No one told him he couldn't have unprotected sex. He was young for his age and was a typical young lad who had his brain between his legs,' she said. 'I am not excusing what he did, but it wasn't done deliberately or out of revenge. Roy just wasn't like that.'[11]

Roy was a 'jack-the lad' who had an eye for the ladies. It was a mark of his youth that when the press first started hounding him, he thought he was a celebrity.

'He was a good-looking lad,' recalled his brother John. 'He had several girlfriends, several flings. Roy had infected a girl with HIV, and she died before he did. The press got hold of it. They came down on the family, not just to Roy, but to my mum's house, to the rest of my brothers' houses, to my house, and they ripped the family apart.'

He added: 'Roy especially did not know the impact of how it could be passed on as he was simply never told . . . The truth is, we did not know much about the disease itself, the risks or the dangers . . . To me, he was a young lad. I think his mind started going when he was told about HIV and everything got out of control.'[12]

The media circus around the family meant they were not even allowed to bury him in peace. When he died in June 1994, his death made headline news around the world.

'People came to the cemetery to throw stones,' reflected John. 'I remember there being a comment: "Hurray. He is dead."'[13]

•

The ad hoc ex-gratia payments made by the Macfarlane Trust were better than nothing. But they were nowhere near enough to make up for the suffering experienced by Roy Cornes, Clair Walton, Ade Goodyear and the other victims whose lives had been decimated by infected blood products waved through by a state well aware of the dangers.

The refusal of the UK Government to admit its responsibility led to a long battle to win proper legal compensation for haemophiliacs infected with HIV.

Allen White's life was already ebbing away when he joined the fight. He had been given the deadly disease in 1982 following treatment with factor VIII – just as he and his wife, Christine, awaited the arrival of their first child. The virus developed into full-blown AIDS.

When he shared his harrowing story with *The Sunday Times* in October 1989, the year of the Hillsborough disaster and the fall of the Berlin Wall, White had been given just eighteen months to live. His story was the one used to launch a groundbreaking campaign led by John Pavison and Margarette Driscoll, two *Sunday Times* journalists determined to use the newspaper's influence and illustrious campaigning history to win legal compensation for the victims of the contaminated blood scandal.

Seeking to follow in the footsteps of the *Sunday Times* reporters who had exposed the thalidomide scandal in the 1970s, Pavison and Driscoll became dedicated foot soldiers in the fight for justice for haemophiliacs whose lives had been doomed by the tainted blood injected into their veins.

In an emotional interview, White told the newspaper: 'I try not to be morbid, but every time I pick up a new bug I think "Will this be the one?" Just now, I am as ill as I have ever been. I try not to think about it, but I have to be realistic. I have to come to terms with the fact that I don't know how long I've got.'[14]

As it transpired, he didn't have very long at all. White died less than two years later, on 7 November 1991, leaving behind his wife and two young daughters, Sarah, eleven, and Naomi, nine. He was just thirty-eight years old.

Prior to his death, life for White and his family had spiralled into a daily struggle. He had lost his job as a computer systems designer, and his wife, who was training as a physiotherapist, had to become the family's main breadwinner. They were living on benefits of £73.46 per week, plus a £20 top-up from the Macfarlane Trust.

By the time White joined the legal battle for compensation, more than 100 of the 1,200 haemophiliacs who knew they had been infected with HIV had died, including twenty of those who had already started legal action. Like 600 other haemophiliacs accidentally infected with HIV, White joined a class action to sue the government and his regional health authority for negligence. At least another 400 were expected to join the lawsuit.

Most of the victims were infected with HIV by contaminated factor VIII imported from the United States in the early 1980s. Their lawyers' case was that the government had ignored persistent warnings that imported blood products were unsafe; that it failed to respond to evidence that these could be connected to the spread of AIDS; and that it did not act quickly enough to make them safe.

The lawyers also highlighted the failure of Britain to become self-sufficient in factor VIII, a pledge that had first been made by David Owen, a junior health minister, in 1976. Those acting for the victims also pointed to the fact that Britain had always managed to be self-sufficient in factor IX, a similar product used for the treatment of five per cent of haemophiliacs. Only 6.4 per cent of this group became infected with HIV, as opposed to the forty per cent of those treated with imported factor VIII.

The lawyers also claimed that a method of heat-treating clotting agents to mitigate the risk from viruses was available in America from 1982, and in West Germany from 1980, yet appeared to have been ignored in the UK.

While the nature of the HIV virus that caused AIDS was not then known, they argued that had this process been adopted, it would have killed the virus at source. Heat-treated products from America became available in late 1984, but in Britain it took another year for all NHS factor VIII to be heat-treated. In the interim, the government failed to encourage health authorities to use the new, safer American product, and made it clear no special funds would be available to meet the extra cost.

In the best traditions of investigative journalism, the allegations were made in an article entitled 'Blood money: the battle for justice'. It had a devastating effect, and immediately set hares running in Whitehall.

David Mellor, a minister for health between 1988 and 1989, said the issues being raised by *The Sunday Times* were ones that 'could not easily be pushed aside'.[15]

Within weeks of the launch of the *Sunday Times* campaign, the Labour MP Frank Field, who was also chairman of the Social Services Select Committee and vice-president of the Haemophilia Society, had galvanised 200 MPs to write to the paper in support.

Many also wrote to the then-health secretary. In 1989, that role was held by Ken Clarke, the former junior health minister who six years earlier had erroneously told MPs that there was 'no conclusive proof' that AIDS was transmitted by blood products. He was already a bête noire for the haemophilia community, and his decision to rule out legal compensation for the innocent victims of the scandal did nothing to improve relations.

However, as the weeks wore on, the adverse publicity

appeared to rattle Thatcher, Clarke's ultimate boss as prime minister. She agreed to meet a group of senior Conservatives who were lobbying on behalf of infected constituents. Speaking on the subject in the Commons in November 1989, Patrick Cormack, MP for South Staffordshire, who now sits in the Lords, said: 'The campaign will go on and we shall not go away. *The Sunday Times* will continue its thundering and we shall continue our thundering.'[16]

A few days later, Clarke announced a £24 million top-up to the Macfarlane Trust, on top of the £10 million pledged by the government two years before. But this did not amount to the sort of compensation needed to sustain the victims' modest livelihoods, and it was not enough to satisfy Andrew Neil, then a tenacious editor of *The Sunday Times*.

In a damning editorial, his newspaper welcomed the extra funding but also made it clear that the campaign for compensation would continue. It was claimed that the 'government's mercy' was 'so strained as to be morally reprehensible'.[17]

Pressure continued to mount. The government's defensive approach to the litigation started to divide opinion among ministers and senior civil servants. Mellor claims that he was becoming 'increasingly uneasy' about defending the litigation in the way proposed. He said the Department of Health was given 'shoddy' legal advice in 1989, when it was told it did not have a duty of care towards the victims and that responsibility lay with local health authorities.[18]

He was not the only one uncomfortable with the way the government was handling the lawsuit. Memos reveal that Sir Donald Acheson, the UK's chief medical officer between 1983 and 1991, told Clarke that the circumstances being faced by the infected haemophiliacs amounted to a 'unique tragedy' and advised him to provide financial support to the victims on 'humanitarian' grounds.

Acheson wrote:

The key feature . . . is that HIV infection in addition to almost inevitably causing a very unpleasant progressive illness and death results in a substantial proportion of cases in infection of the female sexual partner and also on average one quarter of the subsequently conceived children. In both wife and children, the infection will also prove fatal . . .

The tragedy goes beyond anything which has ever been described as a result of a therapeutic accident and is very likely indeed never to occur again. I hope there-fore, that for humanitarian reasons the government will find some way to make an ex-gratia settlement to the infected haemophiliacs in relation to this unique tragedy. I cannot personally see how this could be regarded as implying any responsibility for other accidents such as benzodiazepine dependence, cerebral palsy following obstetric misadventure, etc.[19]

Clarke cemented his 'chief villain' status with the victims by ignoring Acheson's advice, largely on the grounds of cost.

'I agreed broadly with the points he was making about the strength of the humanitarian needs and I shared the desire to help victims if we could,' Clarke recalled decades after the event, when being quizzed over his role in the scandal. 'But I did also have to remember all the other worthwhile claims for health expenditure, and my overall responsibility for public funds. Furthermore, I doubt that others who were pressing parallels with other claims or categories of medical accidents would have accepted the distinction he was trying to draw, between the haemophiliacs and such other cases.'[20]

Another memo reveals that concerns regarding the HIV litigation went right to the top of Downing Street. In 1989, Thatcher held a meeting with Clarke to discuss whether to provide financial compensation to victims. According to minutes of the meeting, an unidentified participant aired fears that if a payment was made, it would be 'desirable, as well as avoiding any acceptance of legal liability, to avoid conceding any moral obligation'.[21]

As the pressure mounted on the government, even the High Court Judge, Mr Justice Ognall, who was in charge of the case, was moved to make an extraordinary intervention, calling for compromise. In yet another laudable *Sunday Times* scoop in November 1990, the paper leaked a written statement from the judge, sent earlier that year to both the Department of Health and lawyers representing the haemophiliacs and their families, calling for both sides to give 'anxious consideration' to a settlement.

In an unprecedented move, Ognall, who a decade earlier had been responsible for leading the prosecution against Peter Sutcliffe, the Yorkshire Ripper, at the Old Bailey, said there was a moral dimension to the court case that made it unique.

> It is rare that I take an initiative of this kind in civil litigation before me. But the circumstances of these actions are such that I have no hesitation in doing so, and in much more specific terms than might normally be expected or considered appropriate.
>
> A government which takes upon itself the role of public provider of medical advice and clinical services

is in a very different position to any commercial organisation. It is clearly arguable that its duty to innocent citizens who suffer injury under the aegis of such treatment has a moral dimension to it which should distinguish its assessment of its position from the criteria to be adopted by other defendants of a corporate character.

Government owes a duty wider than to its shareholders or insurers. It should also mean that the public may be entitled to expect from government an appraisal of its position which is not confined solely to legal principles to be found in the law of negligence, or problems of proof. Compromise does not necessarily betoken any admission of blameworthiness. In any event, it might be argued that any perception by the public of fault in the defendants may well be significantly less than the opprobrium attached to any apparent unwillingness to temper the rigours of the law with the promptings of compassion.

Of the infected sufferers, the judge said:

All of them suffer or live in the shadow of a fatal condition for which there is presently no known cure. I am told that the evidence will suggest that 'incubation' may be as long as 15 years.

Many have already died, and in the nature of things, many more will die without knowing the outcome of this litigation. It seems, to me at least, that this factor should be treated as cardinally important. It also sets it apart from any other action in my own experience. At best those plaintiffs will die uncertain as to the outcome. At worst, they will be deprived of money to comfort their last days, or . . . [deprived of] the knowledge (for those with dependants) that they will enjoy a measure of financial security.[22]

Within days of the remarkable statement being leaked, without the judge's approval, Thatcher was ousted from Downing Street. She was replaced by her former chancellor John Major, who told allies that he was keen to settle the issue.

Within a fortnight of taking office, Major and his new health secretary, William Waldegrave, agreed to an out-of-court settlement with the victims worth a total of £42 million. Individual payments ranged from £20,000 for a child to £60,000 for a married man with three children.

However, the story did not end there. There was to be yet another outrageous sting in the tail for the 1,200 haemophiliacs who brought claims against the government. The state that had sanctioned the use of the deadly infected blood products that were now killing them seemed to have set a new trap.

As part of the settlement agreement, the victims were forced to sign away all future legal claims without knowing they had also been given a second deadly condition.

It was only after they had signed the legal waiver in 1991 that they were told they had also been infected with hepatitis C, a new virus that attacks the liver.[23]

The contract, sent out via patients' solicitors, stated: 'I undertake not to bring any proceedings against the Crown or any health service body now or at any time in the future in respect of the said infection of (blank space for name) by human-immuno deficiency virus or hepatitis virus.'

Scandalously, the Department of Health was aware in

1989 that some victims had hepatitis C, but did not inform them until after the contracts signing away all possible future claims had been finalised.[24] Tests had been carried out on patients' blood without their knowledge when they attended haemophilia clinics.

A letter sent by an official from the department in October 1989 stated: 'In the case of NANB hepatitis (hepatitis C), the majority of haemophiliacs became infected after frequent use of concentrate, more quickly if commercial rather than UK concentrate was used.' It added: 'The new hepatitis C antibody test has shown the majority of severe haemophiliacs to be positive.'[25]

Most patients only found out they had been infected with hepatitis C in 1994 and 1995, when the Department of Health carried out further testing and results were shared with doctors. Patients with both HIV and hepatitis C tend to die much more quickly than those with just one of the viruses.

This apparent stitch-up meant that the UK state had insulated itself financially from all potential future claims brought by hepatitis C victims, who would once again be forced to fend for themselves with little to no support.

Waldegrave has since said he has no recollection of the clause in the contract, but said the purpose of the settlement was to draw the litigation to a close, adding: 'I would not understand it to be unusual to include a term preventing further future litigation, or that non plaintiffs being given an ex-gratia payment would, in consideration of such a payment, also waive their future litigation rights.'[26]

However, Major, the prime minister, later conceded that it may have been the 'wrong' decision to exclude haemophiliacs infected with hepatitis C from compensation.[27]

The decision only fuelled the victims' deep-seated mistrust in the government, which many believe have presided over a decades-long cover-up. Jason Evans, whose father, Jonathan, died in 1993 after being infected with both hepatitis C and HIV, described the move as 'the greatest trick the Department of Health would ever pull on them'.[28]

•

The remarkable story of Roy Cornes, the Birmingham native whose sexual conquests sparked a nationwide manhunt, would soon take an even darker turn. The contaminated blood scandal would have a seismic effect on Roy's surviving relatives, for he was not the only haemophiliac in the family.

Roy was one of seven brothers; six suffered from the rare blood disorder. At the time, they were the biggest haemophiliac family in the UK. All were infected with viruses including HIV and hepatitis C after receiving factor VIII blood products that were supposed to save their lives.

In a photograph taken on his wedding day in 1991, Garry Cornes, Roy's brother, and his bride, Lee, smile broadly as they embrace, surrounded by Garry's sister and five of Garry's six brothers. Gordon, the eldest brother, was the only one absent that day, because he was being treated in hospital for a bleed.

Yet such is the trauma that has been wrought on the Cornes family that even this treasured family photo triggers haunting memories. The photo was shared with me decades after the happy occasion, when the family decided to tell their heartbreaking story for the first time.

Sadly, Lee and Garry never got their happy ending. Garry was the first of the brothers to die.

Known as the cheeky member of the family, Garry had

contracted HIV and hepatitis C. He died on Remembrance Sunday in 1992, just a year after he and Lee got married. He was twenty-six. Lee, who discovered she had contracted HIV when she was seven months pregnant with the couple's first child, died eight years later. Lee had desperately wanted a child, and they were told there was a fifty-fifty chance that she would get infected. The risk did not pay off – something that deeply affected Garry before he died. In footage filmed by Central Television before his death, Garry told the interviewer: 'I feel like a murderer. I am a murderer. I have killed her.'

John Cornes, the second-eldest brother and family spokesman, recalled Garry, the second-youngest brother, being diagnosed with HIV. 'I can remember Garry saying he's got to go to the hospital for so many tests,' he said. 'They [were] talking about HIV. None of us knew at the time what HIV was. All we kept thinking [was] it was some sort of cancer, which they would be able to cure and I can remember the day he came home. We all of us went over to the house and he was sobbing his heart out, and he actually said he thinks it looks as if he's going to die. That particular day was quite emotional, because we were all crying.'[29]

Garry's death rocked the family. By now, they knew Roy, the youngest brother, had also been infected with HIV. He had been diagnosed about a month after Garry.

As youngsters, the brothers had spent much of their childhoods in and out of hospital being treated for their haemophilia. After missing too much school, they were eventually transferred to Treloar's. The surviving members of the Cornes family believe this is where they were both infected.

Garry's son Chris was an orphan by the age of ten. Speaking to me on the telephone, Chris, who was nervous about sharing his story for the first time having suffered from the stigma attached to his family's story, told me that the impact of his parents' death 'shattered his life'. 'I'm surprised I am still here, to be honest,' he added.

Chris admitted he had contemplated suicide, but could not bear for his own children to be left without a father as he had been.

'I remember sitting on a motorbike and thinking about ways of ending it all,' he said. 'So, I called a helpline and they helped to calm me down. But sometimes the only thing that keeps me going is my partner and children.'

The account manager, who suffers from post-traumatic stress disorder, remembers his mother Lee clearly. 'She used to dote on me. It was as if she was trying to make up for the fact that she and Dad weren't going to be around very long.' He has fewer recollections of his father. 'I have almost no memories of him except for one vivid image of us together when he lay dying in bed.' Chris's life was turned upside down when his mother died. 'I was alone and angry, and felt like I had no one on my side,' he said.

Initially, he went to live with his maternal grandmother, but by the age of thirteen, he had moved in with his aunt and his half-brother, Robert. Aged sixteen, Chris decided to leave his aunt's home and fend for himself. 'I wasn't really able to cope with what had happened to me,' he said. 'I didn't speak to anyone about it until I was much older. I had to distance myself from the rest of the family because it was just too painful to be around them.'

He found employment and rented a flat, but by the age of eighteen he had lost his job, and his life began to unravel. He spent the next two years in and out of homeless hostels and had barely enough money for food and clothes. He was stabbed twice, including being blinded in his left eye.

'I had to become a man the moment my mum died, but I have never really recovered from the tragedy of losing both parents as a little boy,' he said. 'It completely ruined my life and I suffer every day as a result. My life has been a constant battle to feed myself and children, and I often struggle to function given the toll it has taken on my mental health.'[30]

John told me that he suffered a breakdown that 'wrecked his marriage' in the wake of Garry's death.

He threw himself into work to try to distract himself from the grief. But it was not only the loss of their beloved brother that was causing the family's anguish. They were also being hounded by the media after the accusations that Roy had deliberately infected four women with HIV.

The media storm around the family meant they were not even allowed to bury their brother in peace. John said: 'It was very bad at Garry's funeral, because Roy had been the centre of newspapers' attention . . . We had them hiding in the bushes and there were lots, at least fifty reporters in the bushes. It really infuriated us all, knowing they [were] taking pictures. They didn't ask permission or anything and all they wanted was just to get the grieving AIDS family.'[31]

It was even worse at Roy's funeral in 1994. 'It was an absolute nightmare,' Merle, his sister recalled. 'They were born eighteen months apart and they died eighteen months apart. We hadn't even recovered from Garry's death when Roy died. To lose one brother was devastating, but to lose two in such quick succession almost destroyed us.'[32]

It did not end there.

Another eighteen months after Roy's death, the eldest brother, Gordon, the comedian of the family, who had also been infected with HIV and hepatitis C, died. He was forty, and left behind four sons and a daughter. Gordon had been told he had HIV about a month after Roy's diagnosis. After he received the news, he started to deny he had the condition and said the test result had been a mistake.

'He was my older brother and he started realising the effects,' recalled John. 'I can remember . . . looking at Gordon and Roy at Garry's funeral, and then looking at Gordon at Roy's funeral. What's he going through? What mental state is his mind in, because he knows it's going to [be him next].'[33]

As we have seen, haemophilia is a genetic condition that usually affects men. Women can only be carriers, which led to a particularly unique type of hell for Audrey Cornes, the mother of the six afflicted brothers. She carried the genes that her boys inherited. Having watched her children die one after the other, having been ravaged by the AIDS virus, her guilt and distress were made worse by being made to grieve in the spotlight.

Audrey, a cleaner, was the family breadwinner. She was a strong woman and was said by her children to have the frame of Cissie and Ada, the weighty northern housewives created by the comic actors Les Dawson and Roy Barraclough. She would put on a tough outer shell to encourage her boys to be strong after they lost their father George to stomach cancer.

But after the death of her eldest son, the shell crumbled and she became thin and gaunt. She died in 2002 from what her surviving sons believe was a broken heart.

John said: 'After Gordon she started getting thinner and

thinner and gaunt . . . You know how you always say to your kids "I love you", and when you go, you give them a kiss. My mum became even more obsessive with kisses and phoning. If you didn't see her [one] day, she would be on the phone half a dozen times that day. She would phone up just to hear your voice.' He added: 'I think she would be alive if it wasn't for what happened, because she was a strong woman. The tragedy . . . ripped her heart out.'[34]

Audrey died of a massive heart attack. The last person she had spoken to had been her sister, and they had been telling dirty jokes. Even after all the tragedy in her life, the silver lining for her children was that she died laughing.

The next brother to die was Alan. He had not long been clear of hepatitis C, after undergoing a new treatment, when he suffered a stroke. The father of seven, who had his own gardening business, was fifty-eight when he died in November 2017. He is buried alongside Garry, Roy and Gordon in Birmingham's Lodge Hill Cemetery.

Merle, who admitted she suffers from survivor's guilt, said: 'It's been like we have had a curse on our family. My brother John and I sometimes laugh about who will be next to die. If we didn't laugh about it, we would cry.'

She added: 'The last thirty years have been like a living nightmare. I have watched my brothers die and saw them go from being strong men to virtual skeletons. I held their hand until the very end, when sometimes I would just wish they would hurry up and die. Sometimes it's still almost too much to bear. I look at my four grandchildren and it feels like it's the only thing that keeps me going.'[35]

Merle, who is now the matriarch of the family and dotes on her surviving brothers, does not like hospitals. She recently visited John, who was clear of hepatitis C but was suffering from cirrhosis of the liver, in a ward in Birmingham.

'It brings back terrible memories,' she said, breaking down in tears. 'It feels like every time I go to that hospital someone dies.'[36]

John, a car park manager who had five children, always believed he would be next. Although he eventually grew fond of his name, he was urged by his ex-wife to change the surname of his youngest two children to protect them against the abuse suffered by the family.

Even after seeing brother after brother die, John struggles to understand his own frailty. 'I hadn't realised how bad my liver is,' he said in an interview with me. 'There was one day when I just burst out crying because I kept thinking, "My God, I don't want to die." But I know I will be next. They have warned me that the next step is having a stent and then I will be at an increased risk of developing cancer.'[37]

He told the inquiry: 'I cry when I think of my nephews and my nieces that haven't got dads. Luckily, I am still here. I don't know how long I am going to be here for, but I will be a bugger to go . . .'[38]

His brother Andy, who is also clear of hepatitis C after receiving cutting-edge treatment for the condition, though he has some health complications, finds it difficult to talk about what has happened to him and his family.

'It sometimes gets too much for me,' he told me. 'It feels like I can't look forward. Not a day goes by when I don't think about what this family has lost.'[39]

Paul, the eldest surviving brother, said his earliest memories are of his brothers crying in pain and their father, George, urging them to be quiet.

As the only son not to suffer any illness, he said he has always felt like 'the outsider looking in'. Illness and viruses left him untouched, but he is not unscathed.

'It has had a domino effect that has left brothers, sisters, wives, partners and children trailing in its wake,' he said. 'This family has been ripped apart, and it's not finished yet.'[40]

© Dorricott family

Mike Dorricott.

7

SHREDDED

1994–2002

Mike Dorricott had taken his daughter to hospital to have her tonsils removed when a nurse suggested he might need some medical attention himself.

The successful businessman had been experiencing symptoms of fatigue and mentioned to one of the nurses that he was a mild haemophiliac. The nurse suggested that he book himself in for a check-up, because he had not been seen at a haemophilia centre in years.

Mike took her advice and arranged an appointment at Addenbrooke's Hospital in Cambridge. While at the clinic, the doctors took the opportunity to take some blood in order to check his inhibitor status, which is an immune system response to factor concentrates, and his viral status.

Mike, who was a married father of two, was told that as he had received blood products prior to 1985, he could have been exposed to hepatitis C. This was the first time Mike had heard he was at risk of the virus – despite the warnings that factor VIII had been contaminated with the deadly disease two decades before.

It was 1995, the year Barings Bank collapsed and Blackburn Rovers won their first and only Premier League title, when Mike received the bombshell news: the blood tests, which had been ordered almost by chance by his doctors, revealed he had hepatitis C.

And worse still, the condition, known as the 'the silent killer' because it can lie undetected for years, had already left him with severe cirrhosis of the liver.

Without a transplant, Mike, who was twenty-eight at the time, was warned that he was likely to be dead in a few years.

The discovery that Mike was a haemophiliac came when he was just three years old. He had fallen off a playground slide and bumped his head. The swelling refused to subside, and eventually his mother, Jennifer, took him to the doctors. As haemophilia ran in the family, Mike was referred to Halifax General Hospital in West Yorkshire to be tested. The test initially came back negative.

When the head wound failed to heal, however, he was seen by a second specialist at Huddersfield Royal Infirmary, where he was tested again. This time, he was diagnosed with haemophilia, although his family were told his condition was mild.

Mike was initially only treated with cryoprecipitate. Unlike Nick Sainsbury and Ade Goodyear, who were severe haemophiliacs and spent much of their childhood going in and out of hospital to be treated for various bleeds, Mike's mother can only remember one occasion when her son was treated for the condition in hospital. He was seven or eight at the time.

However, in November 1982, when Mike was fifteen, he was booked in for surgery at Huddersfield Royal Infirmary to have four wisdom teeth removed after they had become impacted.

The routine operation was meticulously arranged in coordination with one of the hospital's consultant haematologists, who had been put on standby to administer the cryoprecipitate.

However, instead of receiving cryoprecipitate to help his blood clot, Mike was – unbeknown to him at the time – given factor VIII, a devastating decision that would leave him with a 'life-shattering' condition.

His mother, Jennifer, recalled: 'There was no discussion; there was no dialogue; there was no consent . . . There was none of that. They just gave him what they gave him, and it just happened to be factor VIII.'[1]

Mike had liver function tests around the time of his operation, which came back normal. But by the following year, there were ominous signs when follow-up tests revealed he had elevated levels of liver enzymes.

After being diagnosed – more than a decade after being infected – Mike became a prominent member of the campaign group Tainted Blood and began to investigate the scandal. He and his family eventually became convinced that he was one of the previously untreated patients (PUPs), who had been identified by doctors as potential guinea pigs. His family found a document uploaded to the Tainted Blood website with a reference to PUPs, which usually meant children or mild to moderate haemophiliacs. Mike printed it out and scribbled: 'Was I one of these?'

He also printed another document from the same website, and scrawled next to it more emphatically: 'My first factor VIII December 1982. I was a PUP.'[2]

Mike's conclusion was that he had been given factor VIII without his consent or knowledge, and contrary to the original plan of his doctors. It appears he was one of the victims

of the terrible secret experiments conducted on mild haemophiliacs, supported by Britain's leading haematologists.
As we have seen, the medical establishment and the pharmaceutical companies were desperate to establish whether
the factor concentrates being administered to patients were
contaminated with deadly diseases.

Years later, his dogged inquiries led him to unearth
medical records dating back to the wisdom teeth operation
he underwent in November 1982. His suspicions deepened
when he read the paperwork.

A letter dated that month stated: 'The doctor proposes to
admit him to Huddersfield Royal Infirmary on 14 December
for extraction of these four teeth under general anaesthesia
the following day and will arrange this with [redacted],
Consultant Haematologist, in order that appropriate cryoprecipitate can be administered.'

By contrast, a note dated December 1982, a few days
later, stated that rather than receive the safer treatment of
cryoprecipitate, Mike in fact received 3,000 units of factor
VIII, followed by a second injection with a further 2,820
units.[3]

Could this scarcely believable medical deceit have
any relationship to the letter sent in January 1982 by the
all-powerful Professor Arthur Bloom, the world-renowned
doctor who wielded incredible influence over UK haemophilia policy during the early 1980s, and who also enjoyed
a cosy relationship with the pharmaceutical companies?

The infamous 'cheaper than chimps' letter (see page 72)
contained the admission that British patients were being
intentionally infected with hepatitis, as using chimpanzees
as the 'guinea pigs' was no longer sufficient to satisfy factor
VIII manufacturers.

Years later, Mike's mother said:

I believe that Michael [Mike] was tested without his or our consent. I believe that he was used as a guinea pig and that he was used as a Previously Untreated Patient when he was given factor VIII aged fifteen.

When my son had his wisdom teeth out, I knew that he would need something to cover the bleeding but nobody asked for our permission. There was no discussion, no dialogue and no consent when he was given factor VIII instead of cryoprecipitate. In those days, we trusted the doctors implicitly. We didn't expect them to do something different without telling us.[4]

David Birkenhead, the medical director of Calderdale and Huddersfield NHS Foundation Trust, accepts much of the evidence presented by Dorricott's family about his treatment, but told the Infected Blood Inquiry that he cannot 'comment on what was discussed in relation to the use of cryoprecipitate and not factor VIII'.[5]

Mike, a high-flying graduate, was working as a manager for the cereal company Weetabix at the time of his diagnosis. The straight-talking Yorkshireman later moved to the Surrey commuter belt after he became a managing director for United Biscuits, the makers of McVitie's biscuits, Jacob's Cream Crackers and Twiglets.

In January 1999, Mike had his first treatment for hepatitis C and was administered with the drugs interferon and ribavirin. Sadly, the treatment failed. By the following year, Mike had been placed on the liver transplant list.

He suffered three false alarms when he rushed to the hospital for an operation only to be told that the livers that had been sourced were unsuitable. Finally, Mike caught a break and completed a successful transplant in October 2000.

The operation gave Mike a new lease of life. He and his family learned to ski and scuba-dive. He even started sailing and paragliding. The life-threatening conditions that had plagued him for so long seemed a distant memory.

'There were some minor hitches in the next few years, which included a bit of re-plumbing, hernia repairs, MRSA and Clostridium difficile but nothing I couldn't get over,' he told me in an interview as he stepped up his campaign for justice.[6]

Unfortunately, Mike was hit with a new crisis in the summer of 2007, when a routine scan found cancer in his transplanted liver. He was put on the transplant list once again, and advised it would take four weeks to get a liver, as cancer patients were quite high on the list. Eight 'hellish' months later, he received the second transplant. The surgery went well, despite him suffering numerous infections, including sepsis, but the hepatitis C came back very aggressively. The virus was 'running riot' as he was heavily immuno-supressed to stop the rejection of his new liver. He was told to start combination therapy again – only the fourth person in the UK to undergo the treatment post-transplant – in the hope of clearing the virus. The course was to last seventy-two weeks, during which Mike suffered an almost constant run of infections.

His wife, Ann, recalled: 'The second course of treatment was really bad, really bad. He had the flu symptoms, he had aching joints. At one point I remember him saying he just feels like he's been hit by a bus.'[7]

The treatment also had a deleterious effect on Mike's mental health and his wife claimed he suffered volatile mood swings, which gave him a 'Jekyll and Hyde character' that was completely unlike him. 'He was not himself,' she reflected. 'He was very aggressive . . . It was like he had a rage in his eyes. It was as if he was possessed, and I was scared of him.'[8]

His older daughter, Sarah, added: 'He was a lovely, lovely man, and this treatment really altered his mind. It was . . . very difficult and it took its toll on all of us and especially him.'[9]

In 2008, Mike retired from his well-paid job on health grounds when he was just forty-two. He estimated the lifetime loss of earnings caused by the fallout from Bloom's secret experiments to be £2.25 million.

The loss of his financial status affected him deeply, especially after the family was forced to relocate from Surrey to Sedbergh, in Cumbria, where the cost of living was more affordable. 'I am now not in a position to be able to provide what I should have been able to do,' he complained, following the move. 'The reduction in income . . . has had huge implications [on things] like the payment of university fees, the provision of nicer things in life, the fact that my wife has had to go back to work full-time to make the books balance, to the fact that we have had to move from the south-east to a more cost-effective part of the country, leaving all of our friends behind.'[10]

But Mike was not one to be defeated, and in 2013 he represented the UK in the World Transplant Games. He came home victorious, having won double gold at golf.

It was a personal high for Mike. However, it was not long before he was to experience a new all-time low. His youngest daughter, Eleanor, recalled: 'When we were growing up, Mum and Dad gave us everything that we needed, and obviously tried to act like a normal family despite everything that was happening . . . but obviously there was that underlying aspect . . . of, you know, he's had two liver transplants, he was on borrowed time, he knew at some point something was going to happen and [things would] go downhill.'[11]

It was February 2014 when Mike, who by now had been cancer-free for five and a half years, underwent a routine scan.

He was devastated to discover that the cancer had returned again, and this time he was told it was terminal.

Ann recalled: 'I was at work at the time, and Mike phoned me and said: "I've just had my scan and it's not good," and he just said the cancer's come back and there's nothing they can do, and it's terminal.'

Eleanor added: 'All I remember was sitting on the top of the stairs and hearing the phone call that he was having with his doctor . . . and crying and then going downstairs and just talking to Dad about it, and him being really upset.'[12]

Mike was told he had around twelve months to live. Being a brave and courageous man, he decided that if he was going to die, he was going to go down fighting.

In a telephone interview with me for the *Sunday Express* in June 2014, not long after this diagnosis, Mike made an impassioned appeal to David Cameron, who was prime minister at the time, to compensate the victims of the scandal that would soon claim his life.

'This scandal has been going on for in excess of thirty years,' he told me. 'It is now time to bring this to an end and allow those still living to live what remains of their lives in peace without having to go cap in hand for financial support. Unfortunately, I will not be one of those.

'Being infected with hepatitis C as a direct result of

government policy has ruined my life. I have been living on borrowed time thanks to the donor families and doctors who have kept me alive.

'My time is now up, as the prognosis of terminal cancer [means] I won't get to see my children grow up into adulthood.' He added: 'My life has been ripped apart by a wholly avoidable situation. Mr Cameron, you can and should put this right.'[13]

Within a week of being told his fate, the dying father attended a meeting with Jeremy Hunt, the then-health secretary, alongside Jane Ellison, a junior health minister, and twenty civil servants. The purpose of the meeting was to discuss what a full and fair settlement for the victims of the contaminated blood scandal would look like.

By the time the meeting took place, Mike and Hunt had already met several times during the period the family had lived in Fareham, in Surrey, in Hunt's constituency. Mike, who got quite emotional during the course of the highly charged meeting, revealed that he had terminal liver cancer and was living on borrowed time as he again expressed fears that any settlement might come too late for him and his family.

Towards the end of the meeting, Hunt came over to Mike and his wife and shook their hands. He told them: 'Don't worry about this, we'll sort it.'

Sadly, it was not to be. Years later, Ann reflected: 'Since that meeting, he [Hunt] has not fulfilled his promise.'[14]

•

In 1995, just as Mike was being told about the seismic consequences of his routine wisdom teeth operation as a child, campaigners were opening up a new front in the fight for justice.

The government had recently launched a 'look back' exercise to identify who had been exposed to hepatitis C through contaminated blood products. The results of these tests confirmed what many in Whitehall and the medical community already knew: that the vast majority of severe haemophiliacs who had received factor VIII concentrates in the late 1970s and early 1980s had been infected with the deadly virus.

It was also confirmation of the betrayal suffered by those victims also infected with HIV who had been forced to sign a waiver in 1991 agreeing to forego future legal claims without knowing they had been given a second potentially fatal condition. As revealed in the last chapter, a letter sent by an official from the Department of Health, dated October 1989, confirmed that the department was aware that hepatitis C antibody tests had shown the 'majority of severe haemophiliacs to be positive'.

Stung by the injustice of another group of haemophiliacs suffering the effects of another deleterious condition being deprived of any financial support, a group of campaigning MPs again swung into action. The group was led by the Labour MP Alf Morris, who decades before had introduced groundbreaking legislation giving rights to disabled people for the first time.

He tabled a series of early day motions – a parliamentary tool used by backbenchers to draw attention to the most salient issues of the day – calling on John Major's government to introduce financial assistance to haemophiliacs infected with hepatitis C similar to that given to those who had been infected with HIV. At the time, it was claimed that fifty haemophiliacs infected with hepatitis C had already died. The motion gained widespread cross-party support.

Crucially, it was also signed by several of Labour's rising stars, who would go on to hold Cabinet posts in Tony Blair's government after he swept to power with a landslide victory in 1997. Among them was Alan Milburn, who would become health secretary between 1999 and 2003.

Sensing an opportunity, almost as soon as Milburn took up his role in the Department of Health, lawyers acting on behalf of the infected haemophiliacs wrote to him to demand he make good on his expressed desire to provide financial support for those afflicted by the condition. Graham Ross, a solicitor who had been involved in the earlier HIV litigation and was now representing a number of individuals infected with hepatitis C, implored Milburn in a letter dated 4 November 1999:

> There has been an Early Day Motion (which you have signed and [a] copy of which I attach) calling upon the then Conservative Government to provide compensation.
>
> In point of fact there are many present members of the Cabinet who also strongly believe that Government should set up a compensation scheme for those infected, including the motion's co-sponsor, Angela Eagle MP.
>
> I fully appreciate that even though, as a backbench MP, one sees the strength of the moral argument, that, on entering the Cabinet and, in your case, taking charge of the relevant Department of State, that you may then become aware of priorities and issues that perhaps could lead you to take a different view. However, I would imagine that the force of the argument in this political case is so strong that there would be considerable sympathy and support still remaining with all

those in Cabinet who supported the Early Day Motion, notwithstanding the wider perspective that you might now have from your present position in Government.

The letter went on:

It would be not only unhelpful but personally insulting to me to receive yet another variation of the stock negative response. Basically, what I am asking is that, as you personally signed the [Early Day Motion], that you consider taking true 'personal ownership' of this issue rather than, as has been the practice of your predecessors from both sides of the House, leaving it to be run by the Department itself. By that comment I do not mean to offend the civil servants who assist and advise you but [am] merely seeking to make the point that surely the strength of the moral issue involved screams out for a truly personal response. Anything less, and given the signing of the EDM by yourself and colleagues in Cabinet, would be deeply offensive to my clients.[15]

The letter, which Milburn claimed he did not see, fell on deaf ears.

By the turn of the century, the campaign by the Haemophilia Society and others to win financial support for those infected with hepatitis C was being met with continued inertia. The British state was still refusing to recognise the earth-shattering, life-changing consequences of the actions of its leading scientists and mandarins two decades earlier.

In the absence of progress, or indeed humanity, the victims were once again forced to take matters into their own hands. They launched legal proceedings in the High Court and the case was listed for October 2000.

With yet another embarrassing showdown looming over the government, Lord Hunt of Kings Heath, who was a junior health minister between 1998 and 2003, advised the government to settle the case out of court. In a note dated June 2000, he wrote: 'This note seeks your agreement to a proposed strategy for settling litigation brought against the National Blood Authority (NBA) by a group of people infected with hepatitis C (HCV) through blood transfusion between 1988 and 1991. The case is set for trial in October, and Counsel's advice is that at least some of the claimants are likely to succeed.'

However, Lord Hunt was alive to the far-reaching consequences of such a settlement. Once again, as was so often the case throughout this sorry affair, his primary concern was the state of the public finances rather than the lives and livelihoods of thousands of innocent people. 'I want to ensure that there is a clear and defendable distinction between settlement of this litigation and our continued refusal to compensate haemophiliacs infected with HCV through blood products on the basis of non-negligent harm,' he wrote.[16] In other words, they had the government bang to rights. But it would be preferable if financial compensation could quietly be limited to those victims who had brought a claim, rather than the wider community suffering a collective, decades-long nightmare.

Liam Donaldson, the chief medical officer between 1998 and 2010, was also concerned about the potential impact of a settlement. In the end, he too came down against it. Milburn claimed this was partly because of the 'costs to the NHS' – estimated at around £4 billion – and the 'consequences for the NHS as a whole'.[17]

And so in October 2000, the landmark case began at the High Court in London, with lawyers acting on behalf of 112 people infected with hepatitis C after receiving contaminated blood products. The claim for damages was brought against the National Blood Authority in England, and against the Velindre NHS Trust in Wales, both of whom were contesting the action.

Opening the trial, Michael Brooke, QC, acting for the claimants, told the judge that those bringing the case had been infected with hepatitis C in a 'wide range of circumstances' over the years since 1 March 1988. Those infected included mothers like Anita Roddick, who had received a transfusion after childbirth, patients who had undergone emergency and routine surgery, and those being treated for blood disorders, among them young children with leukaemia.

The case was the first group action to reach court under a little-used law, the Consumer Protection Act 1987. The act was brought in to implement a European directive on product liability, creating a system of 'strict liability' that makes producers and suppliers of defective products liable even if they were not negligent.

During the hearing, lawyers representing the victims had claimed that those who receive transfusions are entitled to expect them to be safe. The National Blood Authority and the Velindre NHS Trust argued that they had taken reasonable steps to avoid infection and should not be held liable.

The case concluded at the end of March 2001. Just as Lord Hunt had predicted ten months earlier, the claimants were victorious. Mr Justice Burton backed their claim for damages. He ruled that the NHS was aware of the risk of hepatitis C in blood transfusions, but did not introduce screening until September 1991, long after many other countries.

Six test cases of anonymous patients were argued before the judge, who awarded them compensation ranging from £10,000 to more than £210,000 each. They included a seven-year-old boy infected by a transfusion after a road accident, who suffered a serious psychiatric reaction to being told about his infection but had since cleared the virus from his blood naturally. A further case involved a woman in her fifties who caught the virus during routine surgery and saw it develop into cirrhosis, causing disability. She needed a liver transplant, which brought fresh complications. The judge said she could return to court should her condition deteriorate further.

With more cases due to be heard in the coming months, the government was under pressure to act. Once again, ministers resisted. And Alan Milburn, the health secretary who had backed the victims' campaign for compensation as a backbencher, became particularly alarmed when he heard the Scottish Government was considering a package of support for those infected with hepatitis C north of the border.

An expert group set up by the Scottish Executive had recommended that those infected with hepatitis C be awarded £10,000, with up to £90,000 more available to those suffering serious and long-term effects. It advised that those with HIV who had received financial support were comparable to those who were suffering with hepatitis C.

Malcolm Chisholm, Scotland's health minister between 2001 and 2004, backed the proposals but was told by Milburn, his Westminster counterpart, to 'tough it out' and resist the calls for compensation. An email sent in November

2002 from Milburn's private secretary includes the details of a phone conversation the health secretary had had with Chisholm. It states that Chisholm 'feels he has to offer something, probably around payments to people once they become seriously ill'. In response, Milburn 'was very clear that he thought this would be a grave mistake', according to the email. The Labour Cabinet minister is said to have warned that the UK would be financially 'scuppered and on a slippery slope to payments running into the millions'.[18]

Chisholm has since said he had to consider the UK Government's opinion on the matter due to doubts that the payments would fall within the remit of the Scottish Executive, explaining: 'While we hoped it was a devolved matter, we couldn't be absolutely sure about it. And indeed, the following month we changed the nature of our proposals because we were advised lump-sum payments [instead of monthly payments] were more likely to be regarded as within devolved powers'.[19]

The Scottish Executive proposed an ex-gratia payment scheme, which would have paid up to £50,000 to people infected with hepatitis C. However, the scheme never got off the ground. Instead, a UK-wide scheme was eventually launched two years later after yet another dramatic U-turn by the Westminster government. The change in government policy came within days of John Reid succeeding Milburn as health secretary in June 2003. He set up what later became known as the Skipton Fund, which ran until 2017. It awarded £20,000 to eligible applicants with chronic hepatitis C and a further £25,000 to those who developed more serious symptoms or conditions.

Decades later, John Reid, who at the time was the MP for Hamilton North and Bellshill (now Airdrie and Shotts),

explained the reason behind his decision to change government policy. He told the Infected Blood Inquiry:

> To put it simply, HIV sufferers had obviously gone
> through terrible traumas, pain, anxiety, and so on. But
> so had sufferers from hepatitis C . . . People did try
> to distinguish between those suffering from HIV and
> those suffering from hep C. [Those with] HIV tended
> to be younger, they died quicker, and so on and so
> forth, but to me, they were people suffering . . . maybe
> not identically, but suffering in the same sort of way.
> The anxiety, the fear, the deaths – and I didn't find the
> distinctions between HIV and hep C sufferers . . . it
> didn't persuade me that they were justified. Secondly,
> the cause of that suffering, for both of those groups of
> people, was the same route. It was infection through
> blood products or blood transfusions supplied by the
> state. And, thirdly, I wasn't persuaded by the argument
> that there is no legal liability. I didn't believe there was
> a legal liability but . . . in my view . . . the obligations
> of the state go beyond legal liability. There is a moral
> compulsion on the state to protect its people (the old
> phrase *salus populi*, which actually means 'the health
> of the people') and when an agency of the state, which
> is the National Health Service, by its conduct, whether
> culpable or otherwise, results in the suffering of a lot
> of people, I thought that they should be treated in a
> manner that was just.

Reid added:

Now, the Scots' Government had obviously come to
that conclusion. And . . . that's not the reason that I

accepted or adopted my position, because there were decisions taken by the Government in Scotland over a whole range of issues, over which I disagreed and supported the UK Government taking a different position. Nevertheless, it was the catalyst for prompting these discussions and making me think about it and bringing it to my attention . . . if you like, fresh eyes that had just come in, and the explanation being given about why [people with] HIV were getting financial assistance and people with hep C weren't. And I didn't find that persuasive, I'm afraid. And, you know, if the line is wrong, you change the line.[20]

•

The timing of the hepatitis C litigation coincided with strange goings-on inside Whitehall. Just as the haemophiliacs were preparing to launch their landmark legal challenge, government officials were shocked to discover that hundreds of key documents detailing government policy relating to the case had mysteriously disappeared. It emerged that the documents had been destroyed, in a clear breach of official protocols.

The discovery came as politicians, civil servants and drug company executives in other countries, including France, Italy, Canada and Japan, were starting to face prosecution for their equivalent role in the importation and administration of deadly blood products to an unsuspecting public. In the US, pharmaceutical companies that had supplied infected products were also paying out millions of dollars in out-of-court settlements.

The first sign that the documents were missing came in the autumn of 1999, when the Department of Health received a request from lawyers acting on behalf of those infected with hepatitis C for non-party disclosure of papers from the Advisory Committee on Virological Safety of Blood (ACVSB).

Officials working on behalf of the government began their trawl and contacted Dr Jeremy Metters, the retired deputy chief medical officer who had chaired the ACVSB. He quickly responded to say he did not have all the papers in his possession, as they had been passed to his successor. Days later, a memo was sent to Charles Lister, the head of blood policy, from Anita James in the Solicitors' Division, advising that the papers had been 'shredded because they represented an inconvenience'. 'If you can replicate them, I won't hold a post-mortem,' she added.[21]

A few days later, Lister updated James to tell her that at least one volume of papers from January 1987 to November 1991 could not be located. He continued his endeavours and started to send James the documents he had uncovered. However, she emailed Lister on 19 January 2000 to say there are still 'some gaps', adding: 'We know Dr Metters' files have gone and I think he had a lot more than just the minutes of the Committee meetings. There must be some Finance Division papers and briefings to ministers. What I find surprising is the fact that we had ring binder after ring binder on HIV but there is so little on HCV. I wonder why this is?'[22]

A month later, Lister received confirmation that a number of the registered files containing ACVSB papers had been sent for destruction 'to the great embarrassment' of the department. In the case of Dr Metters' files, the documents were destroyed by his secretary because the procedures around the disclosure of documents relating to BSE, or mad cow disease, as it was once known, had 'caused her great difficulty'.[23]

An internal audit was launched to try to get to the bottom of the other missing papers. It reported back in April 2000 and concluded that the 'arbitrary and unjustified decision, most likely taken by an inexperienced member of staff, was responsible for the destruction of a series of files containing the minutes and background papers of the ACVSB'.

The report added: 'We believe that the destruction of these files would have been prevented had the person marking files for destruction been aware of their importance.'

In relation specifically to the destruction of the files, the authors found that: 'From the dockets it seems clear that a two-stage process led to the destruction of the files. In February and March 1993, the files were closed, retained in the section marked for review every five years from the date of the last document on each file. This part of the process followed normally accepted procedures. Before any of the files reached their specified review date, however, in July 1993, the files were marked for destruction.'[24]

This was not the only time that relevant departmental paperwork had gone missing. The same had happened during the earlier HIV litigation, when victims had been forced to sign waivers giving up their legal rights if they suffered any further medical conditions associated with the contaminated blood they received. After the case concluded, folders thought to contain the documents which had been removed were returned to the department. But in January 2005, the department received a request under the Freedom of Information Act for some of these records, and it emerged that they had gone missing again.

In May 2006, the resulting publicity led to a firm of solicitors acting for claimants in the litigation returning photocopies of 610 documents with which they had been provided. This appeared to result in searches within the department for files that had not been registered, suggesting that their content had not been previously recorded. As a result, a further 4,629 documents were discovered. These were in addition to the copies returned by the solicitors.

No sooner had Lister resolved, albeit unsatisfactorily, the issue of the missing papers than another problem arose in the autumn of 2001. This time, it concerned the ministerial papers relating to David Owen's time as a health minister in the 1970s, when he had committed the UK to becoming self-sufficient in blood products in order to avoid dangerous imports.

Lister had been tasked with helping to draw together the relevant paperwork to allow the government to respond to a parliamentary question by Lord Morris, who was then president of the Haemophilia Society, about comments made at the time by David Owen about the failure to implement his policy of self-sufficiency.

As previously discussed, Owen had announced in 1975 that within eighteen months, the UK would no longer need to import blood products from countries where donors were paid. After discovering that the policy had not been implemented, Owen had said that this was one of the reasons that patients had gone on to become infected with HIV and hepatitis C.

This has always been a key factor in the litigation, given the claims that the government's failure in policy had directly led to more people becoming infected and ultimately dying. Lister recalled: 'In the course of my team preparing this briefing for Lord Hunt on Lord Morris, I recall reviewing contemporary documents on file to establish the sequence of events set out in the briefing pack for the Parliamentary Question. I had expected to find the submissions sent to Lord Owen at the time he was Minister of Health and to his successor Roland Moyle but frustratingly these were missing from the file record.'[25]

In a subsequent email, he wrote: 'Unfortunately, none of the key submissions to ministers about self-sufficiency from the 70s/early 80s appear to have survived. Our search of relevant surviving files from the time failed to find any. One explanation for this is that the papers marked for public interest immunity during the discovery process of the HIV litigation have since been destroyed.'

He added: 'The fact that we can no longer find any of these documents – so can't say what ministers did or didn't know about the state of play on self-sufficiency – just plays into the hands of the conspiracy theorists.'

In hindsight, Lister believes the explanation for the missing documents was to be found in 'poor administration and not a deliberate attempt to conceal evidence'. He claims: 'My view at the time was that the quality of departmental record keeping was fairly poor and that decisions on closing and reviewing files were often left to junior staff, as seems to have happened with the ACVSB papers. The impetus was often about making space in offices, getting rid of filing cabinets etc. This reinforces my belief – then and now – that missing documents were due to poor administration rather than any conspiracy to hide materials.'[26]

To have lost one set of files relating to a legally contentious issue might have been considered careless, but to lose two sets of files seems more than just a coincidence, particularly given that Owen's private ministerial papers had already been pulped. When Owen learned in 1987 that the objective of the UK reaching self-sufficiency in blood products had not been achieved, he sought access to the papers relating to his period as minister, which the Ministerial Code entitled him to do.

He was astonished to be told that the papers had been destroyed 'under the ten-year rule', a convention that few in Whitehall knew of at the time – or, indeed, know of now – as it has no basis in law.

Owen's files were not the only minister's papers to go missing. In October 2004, Patrick Jenkin, who was the health secretary between 1979 and 1981, was asked to attend a meeting of the All-Party Group on Hepatitis. It was suggested to him that he might ask to see the papers that were presented to him during his period in office. Accordingly, he wrote to Lord Warner, a junior health minister, requesting certain papers. In his reply, Lord Warner stated that officials had carried out a search, but could find no trace of the papers described. Lord Jenkin pursued the matter by making an appointment to see Sir Nigel Crisp, the permanent secretary. On 10 March 2005, Lord Warner wrote further to Lord Jenkin, explaining that he had not meant to convey that the department held no records on the treatment of haemophilia patients and blood safety, and offering to discuss the papers required.[27]

The meeting took place the following month, and Sir Nigel apologised for the original reply. However, Lord Jenkin left that meeting with the clear impression that all the files relating to the issue of contaminated blood products had been destroyed, and that this had been done 'with intent, in order to draw a line under the disaster'. In response to a later parliamentary question about the missing documents, Lord Warner said: 'We regret the papers were destroyed in error, which was, I think, explained to the noble Lord in a meeting with the former Permanent Secretary to the Department of Health. I think that it has been explained to him on a number of occasions that there was no deliberate attempt to destroy past papers. We understand that many of the papers were unfortunately destroyed but I have to say that that did not take place under this government.'[28]

Campaigners, including Jason Evans, whose father died after being infected with HIV through contaminated blood, believe the destruction timeline raises serious questions about whether there was a deliberate cover-up. Evans has since painstakingly charted the destruction of files and matched them up against key developments in the criminal cases being pursued in other countries. He told me that his research revealed some 'eyebrow-raising coincidences between key events and destruction, or attempted destruction of evidence'. His discoveries appear to suggest that as high-profile court cases linked the scandal blew up around the world, British officials were quietly shredding documents which might have included potentially incriminating evidence.

In Britain, no individual has even been held responsible for the contaminated blood scandal, but the same is not true of other countries, where politicians and civil servants have been sent to jail. One of the first cases in Europe to reach court was in France, where, in October 1992, three former health officials were convicted on charges of distributing tainted blood that resulted in the infection of more than 1,250 haemophiliacs with HIV. Of those, twenty-three had already died. The case caused outrage in France after an official investigation showed that senior health officials had ordered the continued use of the blood-clotting factor that haemophiliacs need, even though they knew it to be contaminated, at a time when procedures to detect and eliminate the virus were already available. The court sentenced Michel Garretta, former head of the French National Blood Transfusion Centre, to four years in prison, and his deputy, Jean-Pierre Allain, the former head of research and development at the French National Blood Transfusion Centre and later director of the East Anglian Regional Blood Transfusion Service, to four years, two of them suspended. The two men, both doctors, were ordered to pay the equivalent of $1.8 million in compensation to the victims with AIDS and their families.

Both officials were found guilty on charges of 'fraudulent description of goods', which carries a maximum penalty of four years. Upon his release from prison, Allain resumed his role as a professor of transfusion medicine at the University of Cambridge.

Jacques Roux, a former health official at the French Justice Ministry, received a four-year suspended sentence for 'failure to assist a person in danger', and Robert Netter, another official, was acquitted of the same charge. The leader of France's ruling socialist party, Laurent Fabius, asked to be indicted for his role in the scandal in order to clear his name, but in February 1993 it was ruled that he could not be prosecuted due to a three-year statute of limitations on the crime, which was alleged to have occurred in 1985.

Three days after the case against Fabius collapsed, the Labour MP Alf Morris tabled a parliamentary question that asked the British government what representations they had received about providing compensation for the UK victims who were infected with hepatitis C. On the same day as the question was tabled, the ACVSB files were closed, sent to storage and marked for a review in five years' time. The documents would never again see the light of day. One of the volumes was destroyed in September 1994 – just days after it was reported that fresh charges would be brought against Fabius, and two other former French ministers, including complicity in poisoning haemophiliacs. Fabius asked for his own immunity to be lifted so he could stand trial and was eventually acquitted in 1999.

More UK Government documents were destroyed in October 1997, just a week after the Canadian Red Cross lost a civil lawsuit. For the first time, a Canadian Court had ruled that people had been infected with HIV as a result of the Red Cross's failure to screen out gay blood donors in the 1980s. Some payouts exceeded $1 million per victim.

When giving evidence about the scandal to an earlier independent inquiry in 2007, Lord Owen said that the destruction of documents in the Department of Health 'did coincide with it being a world scandal and well known in this country'. He said that while he was against conspiracy theories, 'the more you look at France, the more you begin to see people who were fearful of a legal process going on in this country'.[29]

•

Lord Owen is still angry. His fury, almost fifty years after his tenure at the Department of Health and Social Security (DHSS), has its roots in a decision by anonymous ministers and officials to abandon one of the flagship policies he announced to help clean up Britain's dirty blood supply.

When we met in his immaculate townhouse on the banks of the River Thames in London's now fashionable East End,

Lord Owen told me about the campaign he led – eventually in vain – to prevent what has since become known as the greatest disaster in NHS history. Despite his great age of eighty-four, Lord Owen, with his piercing blue eyes and tousled grey hair, was still surprisingly well versed in the arguments as we began our first ever interview in the front room on the second floor of his home.

Before we got down into the weeds of our discussion, Lord Owen's wife was kind enough to furnish us with a plate of home-made biscuits to keep us going. Although it was the first time Lord Owen and I had ever met, we had had numerous telephone conversations over the years about the contaminated blood scandal. Compared to Lord Owen, I am a relative rookie when it comes to my involvement in the scandal; he has been battling the establishment over the issue – from both the inside and the outside – for almost half a century.

It was long before he became a health minister in July 1974 that Owen first became aware of the risks of contaminated blood products originating from plasma extracted from paid donors after reading Richard Titmuss's book *The Gift Relationship* (see page 34). The book was to leave a lasting impression on Owen when he came to take up his post four years later in the DHSS under Barbara Castle.

Owen, who rose to prominence as one of the so-called 'Gang of Four' when he left the Labour Party to found the Social Democratic Party in 1981, told me: 'It was an amazing book . . . You couldn't put that book down and not say to yourself: this can't go on. We can't go on getting blood from skid row with all the dangers of contamination. Even though we couldn't yet detect hepatitis, there [were] obviously going to be other bugs around that were going to be equally dangerous.'

Owen's concerns were at the forefront of his mind when he was invited to take part in the groundbreaking *World in Action* documentary 'Blood Money' (see Chapter 1). Owen was initially advised by officials not to appear in the programme. But already concerned by the issues the programme was to raise, he defied orders and consented to give an interview.

He recalled: 'When the advice was not to accept *World in Action*'s invitation to go on the programme, I thought long and hard about it, and I thought, well, there's nothing to hide about this. It's out there. There's no secret. And people ought to be involved in this moral dilemma.' He added: 'It was a very important educative exercise for the general public. And everybody at that stage would probably know somebody who had haemophilia. I mean, it was common . . . if *World in Action* had ever had any hint in 1976 that we weren't fulfilling the commitment, they'd have done another programme.'

As we saw in Chapter 2, Owen said he wanted to see Britain become self-sufficient in plasma 'as soon as possible' and had set out the government's strategy for achieving this earlier the same year. However, the policy appears to have been abandoned around 1977 – although no official notice was ever given to Parliament. This was tacitly acknowledged in 1983 when Ken Clarke, the health secretary at the time, announced the redevelopment of BPL, which when completed would be of a 'size capable of making England and Wales sufficient in blood products'. This should have already been the case had the policy been upheld. Instead, it was an ambition that has never been achieved.

Owen, who left government before discovering that the policy had been quietly dropped, continues to be disgusted by the failure of successive governments to deliver on the policy. 'I made the commitment to self-sufficiency in a statement to the House of Commons, and it is absolutely intolerable in a democracy that you can make a statement to the House of Commons and then not correct it if you're not doing it,' he fumed.

'I remember being quite shocked to discover that they didn't have self-sufficiency . . . I don't think that my successors quite understood the gravity of what they were sitting on top of . . . like [a] sort of Vesuvius; it could at any moment blow up! And it was bound to involve other things. I mean, we all knew, we couldn't find the hepatitis virus at that stage, but we all knew that there was a danger there were other things also lurking in there.'

Owen does not know for sure why the policy was abandoned but believes changes in the governance of the Department of Health may have played a role. He blames the erosion of what he calls the 'dual hierarchy', where 'parallel medical and civil service' divisions operated in the department. However, as referenced in an article by Sally Sheard, a health policy analyst and historian, this had started to disappear as soon as Margaret Thatcher became prime minister in 1979.

Sheard wrote: 'The Whitehall efficiency reviews from 1979 onwards culminated in 1994 in the merger of the parallel medical and civil service reporting hierarchies in the Department of Health, effectively reducing the chief medical officer's ability to call upon the support of medical civil servants, at a time of increasing new health threats such as AIDS and MRSA.'[30]

Owen reflected: 'The more I think about it, the Department of Health . . . began to be run in a sort of different way, from civil service principles. I don't know what went wrong with it. I think Thatcher did huge, huge, unknowing damage, when she removed the doctors from the Department of Health.' He added: 'I think there was a deliberate attempt to sort of play it long. And I think that the permanent undersecretary, or a senior deputy undersecretary, should have said to the grouping: Look, we are on record as saying we're doing this. We can't just not do it.'

Owen believes that had Britain succeeded in achieving self-sufficiency, the British haemophilia community would have been protected against the AIDS crisis that would later engulf the world. 'It was AIDS that was the real scandal,' he said. 'If we had got the handling of this correct and they'd held out for self-sufficiency into the eighties, we would not have made the mistakes that we did over HIV. And I'm absolutely convinced of that. I think that the destruction of a proper policy for dealing with HIV has its origins in the way they moved away from self-sufficiency. And they did it deliberately. They made a conscious choice: it was going to cost too much money and the people who made those decisions, I think, were not understanding enough – let's be charitable to them – about the implications of this. But there [were] much, much deeper issues [with] having a blood supply of such corrupt origins – and for me, it will always come back to that.'

He added: 'They were setting themselves up for failure to deal with HIV with the diminution of the authority of doctors and the destruction of the dual hierarchy. There was a philosophical reduction in rationality.'

Owen was so enraged when he discovered what had happened that he complained to the ombudsman on behalf of a constituent in 1988, when he was the MP for Plymouth and Devonport. He said health officials should have admitted to subsequent ministers that the target of self-sufficiency could not be met without more money. But the commissioner would not investigate, saying that parliamentary answers Owen had given in 1975 did not suggest the risk of contamination had been a major factor.

'They put up every single possible argument against me,' he told me. 'It was absolutely ludicrous.'

Owen said that in 1988 he had been unable to give evidence of his personal view that the source of donors was unreliable because his private office papers had 'for some inexplicable reason been pulped'.

He recalled: 'In 1979 when we left government, they asked me what I wanted to do with my papers, and I said, well, they can be left and I'll take them later . . . But then when we asked to have my papers from the department, they told me they'd all been scrubbed, and I was told there was this ten-year rule . . . Well, if there is that rule, it ought to be damn well changed. Otherwise . . . there's no historic record of the health service in the way that all the other departments have, which are put in the National Archives.'

Owen has no idea why his papers were shredded, but suspects his letter to the ombudsman may have 'stirred the pot'. He told me: 'I think that there was a very real worry . . . And I think it was probably a slow process – starting off when they were looking at this . . . some people must have known that they were not fulfilling the commitment that I had made to Parliament.' He added: 'Well, there are two theories in life, aren't there? Conspiracy or cock-up. And I've always been a great supporter of cock-up. But there have been moments when . . . I can probably get a bit paranoid.'

•

Sadly, for Mike Dorricott, the decision to abandon David Owen's commitment to self-sufficiency exposed him to the dangers of factor VIII. Whether cock-up or conspiracy, he was one of the human casualties of the decision, which was to have real life-and-death consequences for thousands of patients.

Mick and Caroline Mason.

8

A CHANCE ENCOUNTER

2001–10

The stigma forced upon victims of the contaminated blood scandal was unbearable.

Mick Mason spent his entire adult life trying to hide his hepatitis C and HIV status from even his closest friends and acquaintances. But in February 2001, aged thirty-four, Mick felt the treatment of victims by successive UK governments had become so outrageous that he had little choice but to act. He nominated himself to manage public relations for the Birchgrove Group, an organisation set up support haemophiliacs infected with deadly diseases after receiving contaminated blood products.

No one was more surprised by his decision to take on this public-facing role than him. His mission was to draw attention to the plight of the group's members in the press and drum up support for a campaign to win a fair settlement for the victims of the contaminated blood scandal. Mick, who lived in Solihull, in the West Midlands, summoned up the courage to call every newspaper he could think of in a desperate attempt to secure media coverage. His overtures went unanswered. He was starting to worry whether he would ever get anywhere when he picked up the phone to make yet another call. This one was to the *Sunday Mercury*, a weekly regional newspaper covering the West Midlands, with a history of campaigning investigations. His call – known in the trade as a 'ring in' – was eventually routed through to me, the most junior reporter on the newspaper. I'd joined the team just a month earlier.

It would be a conversation that would change both of our lives forever.

Mick's call had come in to the news desk in the *Sunday Mercury*'s open-plan office in Colmore Circus, in the centre of Birmingham, which was shared with its sister titles, the *Birmingham Post* and the *Evening Mail*. I was twenty-one years old and had returned to my home city after university to try to establish a career as a newspaper reporter.

Only weeks earlier, I had completed a preliminary course at Trinity Mirror's training centre in Newcastle, having graduated the previous summer with a postgraduate diploma in newspaper studies at Cardiff University's much-celebrated School of Journalism.

To say that I was green is an understatement.

I had barely got my foot through the newsroom door when Mick told me his devastating story. At first, I thought he was a conspiracy theorist.

Journalism is a trade. Junior reporters make lots of silly mistakes, and learning through 'on the job' experience is vital. At the time, it was not unusual for rookie reporters to be put through their paces by mischievous news editors keen to test out the judgement of their often-hapless trainees.

I thought I had been passed Mick's scarcely believable story as some sort of Machiavellian test by my boss.

Mick told me he was a haemophiliac who had been infected by the NHS with hepatitis B and C, and HIV, after receiving blood products that carried the diseases. A death sentence had been passed on him as a teenager. Added to this, he had recently learned that he might also have caught vCJD after receiving blood from a donor who later died of the human form of mad cow disease.

Mick's first ever newspaper interview – and one of my first ever published stories – appeared in the *Sunday Mercury* on 25 February 2001 under the headline: 'I'm not taking any more risks'.

It was a story that would sow the seeds for what would become my career-long fight for justice on behalf of a group of people who were badly failed by the state.

Mick told me that he was going on a treatment strike if the government did not provide him with recombinant factor VIII – a safer but more expensive treatment that is largely synthetic. At the time, penny-pinching ministers had only authorised its use for haemophiliacs under the age of sixteen, or those who were new sufferers, despite its common usage in Scotland and Wales. Mick told me: 'I have taken all my factor VIII back to the hospital and refused treatment. It means that if I get cut, I will bleed continually. I am bleeding internally at the moment in my elbow joint and I am in excruciating pain. But I am not prepared to take any more risks.'[1]

Mick believed the least the government could do was to provide him with new safer blood products, which carried a lower risk of infecting him with yet another potentially deadly disease. He told me: 'Their attitude was "They've got a deadly virus, what's the point of throwing good money after bad?"'

The government eventually relented, and Mick received the new treatment. It was a small victory for him after a life that had been plagued from a young age by the dirty blood he had received. But it was not enough to make up for the suffering that he and thousands of other haemophiliacs had endured.

What Mick really wanted was a public inquiry to blow apart a situation that had seen a generation of people with bleeding disorders left dying from deadly diseases without apologies, without answers, and without access to any form of redress.

'I want the government to launch a public inquiry so we can discover the whole truth,' Mick said. 'It is an absolute scandal that this was allowed to happen when there are so many checks that could have been made.'[2]

Mick was diagnosed as a haemophiliac when he was eighteen months old. Unusually, he was the first member of his family to be diagnosed with the condition. Like other youngsters with haemophilia, he was often absent from school due to being treated for bleeds in hospital. At first, he attended a special school, before being integrated into a mainstream school. On frequent visits to Birmingham Children's Hospital, Mick met other youngsters suffering from the same condition, including the Cornes brothers. When he was around eight years old, he was switched from cryoprecipitate to factor VIII and taught to administer it at home. The decision enabled Mick to temporarily live a more normal life, but disaster was soon to follow.

When he turned eighteen, he received a letter that would turn his life upside down. His local hospital had sent Mick a diet sheet advising him on the best things for people infected with HIV to eat. The other side of the sheet detailed the symptoms of AIDS.

Mick was shocked and immediately called his consultant to find out why he had been sent such material. He spoke to a nurse, who said she couldn't speak to him over the phone, and he was given an appointment for the next day.

Panicking, he then called his GP and asked if he knew anything about the diet sheet and why he had been sent it. Mick recalled the extraordinary two-minute conversation with his GP when he first learned that he had HIV. 'He said, "I'm really sorry. We have known for eighteen months. We thought you had been told."'

The next day, Mick visited his consultant. 'It was one of those conversations you never forget. He sat down and we had what was literally a thirty-second conversation. He told me that he was really sorry, but that I had HIV and hepatitis B, and had probably only got six months left to live. He told me that I needed to go out and enjoy myself but not have sex. That was the end of the conversation, and I just got up and left.'

Mick has since discovered that he was infected in 1983. Although he does not know the exact blood that caused the infection, his medical records show that ninety-five per cent of the products used to treat him up to that point were American-produced factor VIII.

'I remember being in hospital a few times after they had received the test result, for things like chest infections, and they never said anything to me,' he told me.

It was the peak of the AIDS crisis when Mick learned of his disturbing fate. He spent the next few years in almost complete isolation. He remembers being depressed and sleeping a lot, while desperately trying not to focus on the death sentence that had been handed to him. Being in the vanguard of an emerging public health crisis, he received an appointment letter advising him not to discuss his HIV status in the waiting room because it would scare other patients.

'It was an upsetting time,' he said. 'There were often times when I would see other patients who you just knew you weren't going to see the next month, because they looked so ill. Over the next four or five years, most of the other haemophiliacs I had known from my days being treated at the Children's Hospital had died.'

For years, Mick told no one of his illness – not even his divorced parents. His mother had her own health issues, and his father was ex-RAF and someone whose 'emotions don't come to the surface easily'.

'I just felt so isolated,' recalled Mick. 'I didn't talk to anybody. I told my best friend quite a few years afterwards and made him promise not to tell anyone else. He was the only person I told for years, and we never really talked about it. Given the stigma, I didn't want anyone to think I was gay, a sex worker or a drug addict.'

Mick was still coming to terms with his illness when he met Caroline, the 'love of his life', four years after being diagnosed. Realising almost immediately that he had fallen madly in love, Mick, who was then working as a panel-beater, knew it was only a matter of time before he would have to tell her the news. However, he was beaten to it by his best friend Mark, who could see the couple were getting close and did not want either of them to get hurt.

'As soon as I heard him say the word "haemophilia", I started panicking. I was already falling in love . . . and I could guess what was coming,' recalled Caroline. 'At first, I felt really angry that someone so special could be hit by something so awful. But soon my anger turned to devastation . . .[3]

When the couple first met, the hysteria around AIDS had reached fever pitch and Caroline believed the sensible thing to do was to forget him. She said: 'My mind was racing – could I share a cup with him? Could I kiss him without worrying? How would we have sex? What would my parents say? My head was telling me not to get involved but, emotionally, I was already too close.'[4]

Caroline, then a mortgage broker, decided to get as much information on the illness as possible so she could make an informed decision. She picked up lots of advice leaflets from her doctor and phoned the National AIDS helpline. They answered a lot of the questions she had been worrying about.

A week later, Caroline forgot her fears and kissed Mick for the first time. 'It was wonderful,' she said. 'I knew that if I didn't give the relationship a chance, I'd regret it for the rest of my life.

'On the physical side, we took things really slowly and only kissed for the first couple of months. I insisted on taking things steadily because I was scared. I'm sure he thought I was quite cold because I made excuses not to go any further. But I wasn't prepared to get more intimate until he admitted he was HIV positive.

'I gave him plenty of opportunities to talk about his illness. I even brought up the problem of haemophiliacs and infected blood. But he kept changing the subject.'[5]

Two months after their relationship began, Caroline could contain herself no longer. As she drove him home one evening, she blurted out: 'I know.'

At first, Mick laughed and pretended he didn't understand but things quicky escalated and he stormed out of the car, leaving Caroline in floods of tears and wondering if this would be the end of their fleeting relationship. As Mick's anger dissipated, he and Caroline met up again and talked all night about how they could make their relationship work.

Five months after getting together, the couple got engaged and bought a house together. They married the following August.

'We got married quickly because it always felt as if we were living with a time bomb,' Caroline said. 'We had a wonderful day. It was a proper white wedding with all the trimmings. I wanted to do it properly. That day, neither of us spoke about HIV, and I don't even think we thought about it. It was a purely happy day.

'For our honeymoon, we went to Florida for two weeks. We really splashed out because at the back of our minds, there was that nagging knowledge that we didn't know how long Mick would be around for.'[6]

Mick added: 'Every birthday and Christmas, we believed it could be my last. I was constantly living my life around my CD4 count [an indicator of the strength of the immune system]. In the house, we talked about the infections openly, but outside in public, I always had to consciously watch what I was saying . . . It's hard to make friends when you are keeping a large part of your life secret.'

As time passed, Caroline encouraged Mick to start speaking to other haemophiliacs who had been infected with HIV. After facing discrimination at her own workplace after telling colleagues about her husband's condition, she urged him to attend one of the weekends held by the Birchgrove

Group in Manchester. It was during this weekend that Mick performed his 180-degree U-turn and decided to offer himself up as the organisation's media spokesman.

He recalled: 'That was when things really started to change for me, because for the first time, I discovered there were other people that I could really talk to.'

Unbelievably for someone who had kept his condition secret for so long, it even led him to start talking publicly about his condition to a certain young journalist working for the *Sunday Mercury*.

But despite Mick's burgeoning media career and newfound inner peace, there were still bumps in the road ahead.

Disaster struck in 2003 – three years after the couple had wed and two years after he first called me. Mick suffered a brain haemorrhage while on holiday in the Canary Island of Fuerteventura and was taken to hospital. Sadly, the stigma that had swirled around him in the UK had followed Mick to the island. His HIV status meant he was left untreated for forty-eight hours before doctors eventually decided to airlift him to a hospital on the larger island of Grand Canaria.

By the time Mick arrived in an air ambulance, it was touch and go as to whether he was going to survive. He managed to pull through, but the near-death experience led the couple to re-evaluate their decision not to have children. They had previously ruled out unprotected sex for fear of transmitting the virus but, soon after the events in the Canary Islands, the couple joined a semen-washing programme to explore the possibility of having their own children. The treatment involves removing the matter around the sperm that carries the virus. However, tests revealed a nasty side-effect of his HIV drugs. Mick's sperm had been destroyed, so the couple decided to look into IVF.

At around this time Mick, received a small lump sum for being infected with hepatitis C. 'We spent most of that giving it back to the NHS trying to have kids,' he said. Sadly, it did not work, and Mick said the 'whole process was very traumatic'.

In 2010, he and Caroline adopted twin girls, Natalie and Nicole, who were twenty-two months old at the time they came into the couple's lives. Mick said the experience of being a parent 'changed his life'.

Yet the joy of being a father was tempered by the additional stresses that came with being a victim of the contaminated blood scandal. At one point, Mick's illness left him unable to work, and Caroline was forced to cash in her life insurance to support the family. It left with Mick with nagging concerns about the future should the worst happen.

'The main concern I have is what will happen to my wife and children if I drop down dead,' he said. 'I do not feel financially stable, as if anything happened to me then my wife and kids could be out on the streets . . . It's upsetting not to be able to afford a holiday once a year. Sometimes I feel as though I need to escape from everything.'

Despite his concerns, Mick has forged a successful career as a counsellor. He rose through the ranks to become a regional manager for the Terrence Higgins Trust, the charity that supports people with HIV, before becoming the chief executive of a charity providing counselling and support for young people. Mick, who now lives in Leicestershire, believes that unlike other infected haemophiliacs who have put their lives on hold for the last forty years because they expected to die, he made a conscious decision to live.

'They thought they were going to die, so they never had children, they never had a career,' he reflected. 'Whereas

I think, certainly when I met Caroline, which was several years after my diagnosis, I remember getting up and thinking: I'm still alive, I need to do something with my life.'

He added: 'I often think we're the luckiest unlucky people.'[7]

•

The injustice of Mick Mason's plight left a lasting impression on me. As a young journalist just starting out in my career in 2001, I found it incomprehensible that so few column inches had been dedicated to such a scandal – one that was continuing to unfold before my own eyes. As I followed up on the first initial story, I found many others like Mick who had struggled for decades to discover how and why they had been infected.

Having dipped my little toe into the exhilarating world of campaigning and investigative journalism at the *Sunday Mercury*, I came to the conclusion that all roads lead to Westminster, the only place where scandals of this magnitude could be uncovered.

Since studying politics at the University of York, I had always had a fascination with the lobby, a group of journalists given privileged access to politicians in the Palace of Westminster, and had long hoped that this would be where I would eventually find a home. However, my journalism tutors had always warned me that competition to win a place in the lobby was fierce – and for those not coming from a national newspaper role, it was nigh on impossible.

With that in mind, I began scouring job adverts to see if there was anything suitable. As luck would have it, in the summer of 2004, a job was advertised for a parliamentary correspondent for Northcliffe Newspapers Group, the regional arm of the *Daily Mail* group. The position involved covering politics for six different regional dailies, including the *Hull Daily Mail*, the *Grimsby Telegraph*, the *Scunthorpe Telegraph*, the *Lincolnshire Echo* and the *South Wales Evening Post*. Sensing an opportunity, I applied for the role. In September that year, on the day pro-fox hunting activists stormed into the House of Commons chamber to oppose a new bill, I entered Parliament for the first time to start my new lobby career. It was a baptism of fire.

I remember going through security on the parliamentary estate on my first day and feeling like a fish out of water. I had been transported from a life in a newsroom in Birmingham, covering murders and court cases, to the hallowed halls of Westminster, where I had been handed the keys to what at first appeared to be an exclusive, male-dominated private members' club. It was both daunting and exhilarating to think that I could roam freely and rub shoulders with government ministers and MPs whom I had only ever seen before on the television.

The following year, not long after Tony Blair became the longest-serving Labour prime minister in history, exceeding the combined record of Harold Wilson's two spells in power, I covered my first general election. It was called on 5 April 2005, and exactly a month later, Blair was returned to power for a third term, but with a greatly reduced majority of sixty-six seats.

Of the 119 new arrivals in the House of Commons, forty were Labour. They included Diana Johnson, the new MP for Hull North. She and I became acquainted because of my work for the *Hull Daily Mail*. Neither of us knew it at the time, but we would eventually form a successful partnership that would pile increasing pressure on ministers to address the contaminated blood scandal. Johnson would eventually be heralded as a hero of the campaign and be made a baroness for her role in fighting for justice for the victims.

However, in the aftermath of the 2005 general election, there was another hero waiting in the wings to try to ambush the government over the issue. Alf Morris, president of the Haemophilia Society, had been made a life peer by the Labour Party in 1997. Morris had been growing increasingly frustrated by the inertia with which his demands for a public inquiry into the contaminated blood scandal were met by successive governments. He was buoyed by his success in 2004 when he established an independent inquiry into Gulf War syndrome, financed by £60,000 of private philanthropic donations. It concluded that the damage to veterans' health was 'indisputable' and that compensation should be paid.

Once more showing his skills as a parliamentary tactician, Morris now set up his own independent inquiry to look into the UK's use of dangerous imported factor VIII. His inquiry, which was established in 2007, was also funded by private individuals and charitable trusts. It was chaired by Labour's respected former solicitor-general, Lord Archer of Sandwell.

The Archer Inquiry was a private inquiry. It was not established or funded by the government and it had no statutory power or official status. Its terms of reference were to 'investigate the circumstances surrounding the supply to patients of contaminated NHS blood and blood products; its consequences for the haemophilia community and others afflicted, and further steps to address both their problems and needs and those of bereaved families'.

On the eve of the inquiry in April 2007, BBC's *Newsnight* aired disturbing new claims that British doctors had ignored warnings about using haemophiliacs to test out new blood products.

Newsnight disclosed that many haemophiliacs became infected from supplies of the clotting agent from abroad, and much of the plasma came from prison inmates in the US, who were allowed to sell their blood even though there were questions about their health.

The programme also revealed that official documents had 'mysteriously disappeared', although the government claimed some were shredded and others had not been released on grounds of commercial confidentiality.

It appeared the timing of the inquiry was felicitous. Opening the inquiry, Lord Archer said: 'Our purpose is to unravel the facts, so far as we are able, and to point to lessons that may be learned.'[8]

Not long after the Archer Inquiry got underway, the Scottish Nationalist Party (SNP) swept to victory in May and became the largest party in Scotland. One of its manifesto pledges had been to hold an inquiry into the contaminated blood scandal. Nicola Sturgeon, who was the Scottish Executive's health secretary at the time, restated her commitment to holding an inquiry in the early days of the administration. It was initially claimed that ministers would await the outcome of the Archer Inquiry in England before deciding on the scope and remit of the Scottish investigation. However, pressure mounted on Scottish ministers in February 2008, when a senior judge ruled that authorities had acted unlawfully by refusing an official investigation into the deaths of two patients who died after being infected with hepatitis C through blood transfusions. In an unprecedented move, Lord Mackay of Drumadoon quashed an early ruling not to hold fatal accident inquiries into the deaths of Eileen O'Hara and the Rev. David Black, who both died in 2003. O'Hara received blood transfusions in 1985 and 1991 and was later diagnosed with hepatitis C. Black was a haemophiliac who had received a liver transplant and received blood transfusions in the 1980s. He died of liver cancer due to hepatitis C. The ruling put an onus on the Scottish Executive to investigate all deaths caused by contaminated blood or blood products.

Two months later, Sturgeon renewed her government's commitment to hold a public inquiry. Lord Penrose, a senior judge and member of the Privy Council, was appointed to conduct the inquiry on 12 January 2009. The hearings would continue for the next six years.

A month later, the Archer Inquiry published its findings, which concluded that commercial interests had been given a higher priority than patient safety. While criticising the government's slow response, the inquiry apportioned no blame.

In spite of a series of strong recommendations to government to renegotiate a fair, direct and more substantial compensation package with survivors and their families, the Department of Health offered only sympathy and a promise to look at the findings. Archer said he had been surprised ministers and officials from the Department of Health were unwilling to take part in the inquiry, 'because there are things the government could have said in mitigation – things that weren't known about at that time'.[9]

When Dawn Primarolo, a health minister, responded to Archer's report in May, it was underwhelming. The only action taken was to double the average annual payment to those who received support from the Macfarlane Trust, the organisation set up to help patients who had been infected with HIV after being given contaminated blood products.

The government also offered a review of payments to those given hepatitis in another five years. This was the bare minimum that Lord Archer had recommended. Alan Johnson, who was then health secretary, has since said he believed the response was 'reasonable' because of the 'exceptionally difficult economic climate' caused by the impact of the global financial crisis and 'its profound fiscal and financial ramifications'.[10]

On the same day as Primarolo delivered her response to the report, it emerged that the government had also released hundreds of documents which had been withheld from the inquiry.

MPs who had been campaigning on behalf of their constituents were dismayed by the government's continued inertia surrounding a proper settlement for those affected, and compared the callous response to the experience of the victims of the contaminated blood scandal in the Republic of Ireland, who between 1997 and 2007 received an average of £150,000 each.

In a Westminster Hall debate in July 2009, Jenny Willott, the Liberal Democrat MP for Cardiff Central, said: 'The tragedy has affected a number of different countries around the world, yet the British government's behaviour is different from that of other governments . . . there is no difference between Irish and UK circumstances. Neither state has been found liable, but the Irish government have recognised their duty to support those whose health was ruined by treatment under the national health system.'[11]

But the UK Government remained steadfast in its refusal to discuss blanket compensation for struggling victims. It also refused to commit to a public inquiry with statutory powers, which could compel witnesses to give evidence.

In April 2010, the government came under renewed pressure to make higher compensation payments to the victims of the scandal. Andrew March, a classical music composer who was infected with HIV when he was nine and later developed hepatitis C, won a judicial review challenging the government's decision not to fully implement Archer's recommendations for a more substantial compensation package.

But the judge, Mr Justice Holman, warned campaigners against 'false optimism' over the outcome of the case, and said the size of the payouts remained a 'political' matter.[12]

Less than a month later, on 6 May 2010, a general election ushered in a new coalition government led by the Conservatives under David Cameron. The new prime minister's arrival in Downing Street was seen as a positive development by campaigners, who hoped it would signal a fresh approach, given his previous support for victims in his constituency.

In even better news, the Liberal Democrats under Nick Clegg, Cameron's new coalition partners, had committed to establishing a working group involving patient groups to determine 'appropriate levels of financial assistance' for those affected by the scandal in the party's 2010 manifesto.

Another positive development had also occurred shortly before the general election. Diana Johnson, Hull's first ever female Labour MP, was approached by one of her constituents for help with the campaign. Unbeknown to her at the time, it was a meeting that would help to define her political career.

Johnson was attending her last constituency surgery before the election at Bransholme Library in Hull when Glenn Wilkinson, a haemophiliac who had been infected with hepatitis C after receiving contaminated blood products, knocked on her door. Glenn had just returned from Lincoln, where he had been protesting in the constituency of the Labour health minister Gillian Merron.

'I remember that he was really cross and he explained his story to me,' Johnson told me. 'To be honest with you, I didn't know about the contaminated blood story at that point, so this was all . . . news to me.'

Her chances of winning her seat were on a knife edge, as her constituency was a target for the Liberal Democrats. Johnson promised Glenn that if she were re-elected, she would do whatever she could to help. She was returned to Parliament with a slim 641-vote majority. Remembering her promise to Glenn, Johnson decided to get involved with the All-Party Parliamentary Group on Haemophilia and Contaminated Blood, which she came to co-chair, first with the Conservative MP Jason McCartney, and later with the Conservative MP Peter Bottomley.

'The more I got involved with it, the more I realised what a scandal it was,' she reflected. 'When we began working with the APPG, it was mostly dominated by members of the House of Lords, and we decided we wanted to get a bit more of a campaign going. We started to look at various options, including [trying to] help with financial support and seeing what we could do to improve that.'

However, a message was quickly passed down to Johnson from government insiders, warning her that certain far-reaching measures would always be off-limits.

'I remember one of the things we were told was, "You're never going to get a public inquiry." It was basically accepted by those parliamentarians [on the APPG] seeking justice on behalf of their constituents that [it] just wasn't going to happen.'

This was bad news for the victims as a public inquiry was seen as the only way they could get justice – and answers.

Fortunately, however, Johnson was not the kind of woman who was going to take no for an answer.

•

Tony Farrugia remembers a nagging feeling of trepidation as he arrived at his stepmother's house in Ystradgynlais, an old mining town in the Swansea Valley, for a haunting family reunion.

It was 2010, the same year Cameron became prime minister and Prince William and Catherine Middleton got engaged.

Tony's life had been dominated by the contaminated blood scandal. He was just fourteen when his father, Barry, died of AIDS in 1986 after receiving diseased blood products. Over the next twenty years, two of his four uncles would also pass away after being treated with infected blood.

Barry's illness and subsequent death had ripped the family apart, ultimately leading to Tony and his twin brother, David, being separated and put into children's homes almost 100 miles away from each other.

By the time the reunion took place, Tony had not seen his oldest brother, Vincent, since their dad's death more than twenty years before, nor had he had contact with his stepbrother Paul for more than a decade. The high-stakes meeting in south Wales had been convened to try to convince their stepmother, Cheryl, to share an ex-gratia payment she was about to receive from the Skipton Fund, the organisation set up to make fixed payments to people infected with hepatitis C from contaminated blood products.

Ministers had recently agreed to remove the cut-off date

for claimants, meaning that Tony's family could make a posthumous claim on behalf of Barry.

'The meeting was about trying to build bridges,' Tony told me, more than a decade after the reunion. 'But it was clear that some of those bridges were being built on shaky ground, because not everyone was able to address the terrible events that had gone on in our family and what had caused it.'

The origins of the family's trauma began in 1971. Barry had emigrated to New Zealand with his wife, Yvonne, and young son, Vincent, to work on an oil platform.

Barry, who was a mild haemophiliac, had suffered a work injury, leading to a bleed. It is understood that he was refused treatment in New Zealand because there was not enough of the required blood products to treat the indigenous population. The couple returned home just weeks before the arrival of Tony and his twin brother, David. The marriage did not last, and Barry and Yvonne divorced in 1973.

Tony and his two brothers lived with their father in Dagenham, in east London.

However, Barry frequently had to travel for work. One of Tony's earliest memories is when he was three years old and he and his brothers were left at Redbridge Children's Home while his dad took a job in Port Talbot, south Wales.

During his time working in the industrial town, sitting between the foothills of the Brecon Beacons and the golden sands of Aberavon Beach, Barry suffered yet another work injury and was sent to University Hospital Wales in Cardiff for treatment.

It was here that he met Cheryl, who worked at the hospital as a nurse. The couple fell in love and married in 1976. Cheryl was twenty-one and Barry was twenty-six.

Although the family continued to live in London, they often took holidays to south Wales so Cheryl could visit her relatives. On one of the first of these holidays, in August 1977, an incident occurred that would shatter their lives forever.

It was a sunny afternoon on Aberavon Beach, and Barry had decided to take the boys out on a dinghy. Tony recalled the boat hit a wave and began to tip over. Panicking, Barry put his arm out to stop it capsizing, which led to the recurrence of a small forearm bleed that required treatment. Barry took himself off to University Hospital Wales, where he was treated by the notorious Professor Arthur Bloom, Britain's leading haematologist, who, as we have seen, performed secret clinical trials on his patients to service the desires of wealthy pharmaceutical companies.

Up until this moment, Barry had never been treated with anything other than cryoprecipitate at his local hospital, the Royal London. In Cardiff, however, Bloom started to administer cryoprecipitate to Barry, before claiming that his patient had developed an 'inhibitor', which stopped his body from accepting the treatment, and so he needed to be switched to deadly factor VIII.

According to typed notes in the medical records held by Dr Brian Colvin, the haemophilia centre director at the Royal London, Bloom called Barry's doctors in London to tell them the news. The note reads: 'Telephone call from Professor Bloom. This patient has now developed a . . . [cryoprecipitate] inhibitor and is in hospital in Cardiff being treated with high doses of factor VIII . . . We presently have him on very large doses of Hemofil in the region of 6,000 units a day.'[13]

The revelation that Barry was treated with Hemofil, a

blood product that had been embroiled in scandal after the 1975 exposé by *World in Action*, which linked it to cases of hepatitis, is disturbing.

However, what later emerges is even more shocking: Tony requested his father's medical records decades later, and there is no entry to show that Barry was ever given cryoprecipitate by Bloom.

Tony recalled: 'I approached Heath Park [in] around about 2012 for my father's medical notes. I had already received the London Whitechapel records. There seemed to be a document missing, so I approached Wales, at which point they told me that all my father's records were destroyed in 1989, eight years after his last treatment. But what they did send me was all his treatment cards of what he had actually received . . . All the treatment he ever received has all been noted down, but in 1977, where Professor Bloom has said, "We have given him cryoprecipitate and he has developed an inhibitor and we put him on factor VIII," the factor VIII is listed but the cryo is not there.'[14]

The claim that Barry had developed an 'inhibitor' to cryoprecipitate also astonished his regular doctor. Dr Colvin wrote to another clinician:

Professor Bloom's letter about Barry Farrugia is very disappointing news. We have really had no indication that he was developing an inhibitor, as in the past he has only had one or two treatments a year. I suppose we might have wondered when he presented on 1st August with a spontaneous bleed in the right forearm, but this seemed to improve with cryoprecipitate and we thought no more about it until Professor Bloom's telephone call.[15]

Tony now believes his father Barry was a PUP, one of the 'previously untreated patients' used as unwitting guinea pigs by Bloom and others for experimental medical research.

Whatever the truth of the matter, Barry's life quickly disintegrated. Within weeks of being treated by Bloom, he had developed hepatitis B. Tony recalled him looking jaundiced on several occasions after the first administration of factor VIII. His medical records confirm that the first positive antigen test came back on 2 September 1977.

Dr Colvin informed Bloom of the development in a letter dated 14 September. He wrote: 'As I mentioned in my last letter, he was formerly a mild haemophiliac, and we had no real warning of the development of the inhibitor. Even more surprising is the development of HBsAg positive hepatitis when he had only received tiny quantities of cryoprecipitate . . .'[16]

From then onwards, Barry was only ever treated with factor VIII.

This was not Barry's only brush with Bloom.

There is an even more sinister twist that only emerged years later, when Tony started investigating how his dad came to be infected with HIV. He uncovered documents relating to the AIDS litigation, which led to victims receiving an ex-gratia payment. These documents included a letter from June 1983 that claims Barry received blood from an infected batch while he was once again being treated by Bloom in 1980 (Barry was treated intermittently by Bloom between January and October 1980 when he fell down a drain leading to a bleed in his ankle during a visit to south Wales).

Further enquiries by Tony revealed that his father received blood from the same batch as Kevin Slater, the first haemophiliac in the UK to test HIV positive and die of AIDS. Bloom first recorded that Slater had 'probable AIDS' in March 1983, but two months later, as we saw in Chapter 4, he sent a note to all haemophiliac patients in the UK, distributed by the Haemophilia Society, in which he claimed he was unaware of any proven cases involving haemophiliacs in this country.

It is understood that by this stage, Bloom had gone back through his patients' notes and recorded that the same batch that had been used to treat Slater had also been used to treat others.

According to Tony's research, this included at least four other haemophiliacs, including his father. All but one are now dead.

It was not until 1984 that Barry started to suffer what would later be identified as AIDS-related symptoms. His medical notes reveal an agonising decline.

On 23 May 1984, there is a record of his attendance at hospital that notes: 'Intermittent nausea, especially when hungry. Feels bloated. Appetite reduced. Has lost half a stone in the last three months. Bowels normal. No jaundice. No change in stools or urine.'[17] The record also notes that he was feeling depressed and that it was unclear whether this was caused by the nausea or vice versa.

Two months later, Barry was no better, and his medical notes reported he was sleeping a lot and 'generally [felt] bilious without any vomiting'. The notes also show that he had undergone an abnormal ultrasound, which revealed he had an enlarged spleen. This was put down to 'continuing hepatitis'. There is also a question mark after the reference to his lymphocyte count, a white blood cell count that denotes the presence of a serious infection, which asks whether he is 'Pre-AIDS'. According to his notes, a HTLV-III test, an early HIV test, was carried out on 2 July 1984. The notes state that he was to be kept under review, and that John Craske, the leading virologist, should be notified. Inexplicably, during this period, Barry was still being given steroids for his 'active hepatitis',[18] which experts have since claimed would supress his immune system further, possibly advancing the onset of AIDS.[19]

On 9 October 1984, Barry's notes confirm that he had tested positive for HIV. The notes also claim that his status had been confirmed by samples from the AIDS Haemophil-iac Surveillance Group. However, Barry was not told of the diagnosis until February 1985 – in yet another shocking example of a patient being kept in the dark about the deadly disease ravaging their body. It is not clear whether Barry consented to the test or agreed to be included in the surveil-lance group, raising still more ethical questions.

Even before Barry's devastating diagnosis, his family life had begun to deteriorate and continued to decline almost as rapidly as his health.

Tony's relationship with his stepmother worsened as the pressure of his father's debilitating health took its toll on the family. The young teenager began running away, and on one occasion did not return home until 3a.m., by which time his father knew he had gone missing and had 'gone crazy'.

It was at this point that Barry asked Tony, who up until this moment had believed Cheryl was his birth mother, if he wanted to go and live with his real mum. In January 1985, Tony moved to Luton to live with Yvonne, but the reunion was brief; by June 1985, the relationship had broken down and he was living with a friend.

Tony was just thirteen. He recalled: 'During the summer

holidays, a car pulled up beside me and they said that they were social services. They took me to Houghton Lodge, where I stayed for about five weeks before they found me a placement in Brambles Children's Home, opposite my secondary school.'[20]

It wasn't until a week after Tony's fourteenth birthday, in November 1985 – a month after Rock Hudson had died from AIDS – that he learned his father had HIV when Barry and David, Tony's twin brother, visited him at the children's home. Tony said: 'I was on my own in a children's home at the time, and I had no support available to me . . . I think at that point, when he told me, I knew he was going to die.'[21]

Tony saw his father sporadically over the course of the next year. He spent Christmas with him in 1985 and then saw him again in April 1986, shortly before Barry was sectioned under the Mental Health Act.

By now, Barry's mental health was rapidly declining. He had developed Organic Brain Syndrome as the illness was attacking his brain, which led him to become 'aggressive towards everyone'.

'One weekend when dad was ill, his wife went away for the weekend,' Tony recalled. 'He served up my brothers a half-raw dinner, but my brothers just had to eat it. This wasn't who my dad was but it was the effect the illness was having on his mental health.'[22]

Tony visited his dad for the last time not long after he was admitted to hospital suffering from AIDS-related dementia, which at the time was put down to a 'nervous breakdown'. He remembers his dad was emaciated and not eating.

'He was awfully skinny, really, really skinny, and for a six-foot-two man, that was quite shocking to see,' recalled Tony. 'So, he didn't eat, but we . . . got ice cream and went back across to the hospital garden, and my dad asked me for a bit of ice cream. I handed it over, and the nurse stopped me and said, "You can't share that with him." He had . . . candida and he had loads of ulcers in his mouth, which could have been bleeding. So, I understand, but it is quite difficult at that age to be told you can't share an ice cream with your dad.'[23]

Barry briefly left hospital in August of that year to go on a holiday to Wales. Tony now believes this was to allow him to say goodbye to his extended family.

As the end neared in September 1986, Tony was summoned to the hospital to see his dad, who had been put into isolation. But on the afternoon of his expected visit, Tony was told by carers at the children's home that his father had died that morning. Barry was thirty-seven.

It wasn't until long after his death that it was discovered that Barry had also been infected with hepatitis C. Tony reflected: 'He had started to get ill in July 1984 and, in hindsight, that was when everything really fell apart at home. If I had known about my dad's infection and his health, I wouldn't have gone and stayed with my mum . . . My brother David had to stay there and live with it during this time, and it must have been terrible.'[24]

Thinking of Barry's funeral brings back still more haunting memories. There were rumours at the time that people who died of HIV could only be cremated due to the alleged risk of infection.

'I now often wonder what was actually in his coffin,' Tony told me.

With Barry's passing, the last remnants of the glue holding the broken family together were gone. Tony's brother David initially went to live with his uncle, but the day after the funeral he was put in a children's home in Dagenham East – almost 100 miles away from the children's home where his twin was living. The brothers did not see each other again until they turned eighteen.

Tony recalled: 'I was in a children's home and they were lovely . . . That's a real highlight of my childhood. You know, that was a godsend . . . It was a great place. They were very supportive, but . . . they weren't geared up for this . . . So as a child, yes, it is devastating. You have lost your dad. You don't understand. But, you know, you have to get on. And, as I say, at that point the whole family imploded.'[25]

Cheryl inherited Barry's estate and quickly sold the family home in Dagenham before returning to her native south Wales with her own son, Paul, who was only three when his dad died. Vincent, who was eighteen at the time of his dad's death, briefly went to live with Cheryl before deciding to go it alone.

However, the trauma did not end there.

Three weeks after his father's death, Tony learned that his Uncle Victor, a former merchant seaman who lived in East Ham, had also been infected with HIV. He was infected with contaminated blood products in the mid-1980s after undergoing routine dental treatment.

He died in 2002 at the age of sixty-three, and it was not until after his death that his family, including his son and daughter, discovered Victor had also been infected with hepatitis C.

A third brother, David, was the last brother to die when he suffered a brain haemorrhage, linked to the hepatitis C he had contracted after receiving contaminated blood products. He died in 2012 at the age of sixty-nine, leaving behind a daughter and grandson.

Their sister Angela told me of the horror she had experienced, watching her brothers die one by one. She spoke to me over the phone for more than an hour as she pieced together the story of her broken family. We had been put in touch by the Tainted Blood pressure group after I had put out a Facebook appeal for more families to come forward with their stories in a bid to ramp up the pressure on the government.

'My mother, Violet, died shortly after Victor was diagnosed after the rapid onset of cancer, and I am convinced she died of a broken heart. It was either that or she could not bear to see another child endure the same kind of slow and painful death.'[26]

Angela, who nursed Victor towards the end of his life, recalled the stigma he faced after being diagnosed with HIV.

'Victor would tell people that he had been diagnosed with HIV,' she said. 'He felt he had nothing to be ashamed of, since he had contracted the disease through no fault of his own. But his neighbours didn't see things in quite the same way, and his flat in East Ham was vandalised with words like "AIDS Scum" and crosses daubed on his door. The experience made him a virtual recluse, left waiting to die. In the end, even his carers didn't want to go into his flat and would put gloves on before they touched him.'[27]

Tony, who has become a seasoned activist, claims that discovering the truth about what happened to his father and uncles made him ill. However, he has found some comfort from within the Tainted Blood community and the knowledge that he is not alone in his suffering. Now, he is determined to help others through their grief.

The father of two, who lives in St Neots in Cambridgeshire, has been diagnosed with irritable bowel syndrome

(IBS), psoriasis and depression. He is angry at the lack of support given to the orphans of the victims. They have never been recognised, nor have they received any kind of compensation. They were forced, often at a young age, to fend for themselves. The only financial support he and his brothers have ever received came in the form of nominal payments from the Macfarlane Trust, and a cheque for £11,600 when Cheryl eventually agreed to share the Skipton Fund payout after the family reunion in 2010.

Tony's wife, Sarah, recently died of cancer. He can hardly believe the cards life has dealt him. 'I still cry every day,' he told me. 'My dad has eighteen grandchildren who he was never able to meet.'

The lack of official recognition of the scandal haunts him. 'I have never been able to even start the grieving process, as what really happened has never been publicly admitted,' he said. 'It is worse now for me than it was when I was a child, because I understand more now. At the moment, I am not sure if it has ruined my life, or defined it; only time will tell.'[28]

Diana Johnson and Glenn Wilkinson.

9

'TELL HER TO KEEP GOING'

2010–15

Glenn Wilkinson was tired. Tired of being fobbed off by the government. Tired of being portrayed as a conspiracy theorist. Tired of the never-ending lies.

Glenn, who has been on the frontline in the fight for justice for the victims of contaminated blood for years, decided the only way to get his campaign the attention it deserved was to take its demands all the way to the very top.

Having got nowhere after lobbying the Labour health minister Gillian Merron in Lincoln, the married father of two didn't think twice when he came up with the idea of taking the protest to the door of then-prime minister David Cameron.

With a group of activists, Glenn demonstrated outside Cameron's constituency office in Witney, Oxfordshire, in May 2014, demanding fairer compensation for those whose lives had been shattered by the diseases with which they'd been infected after receiving contaminated blood products. When Cameron refused to meet with the campaigners, Glenn and his fellow activists took their protest to the front door of his home, before being asked to leave by his security team.

When Cameron had first entered Downing Street, it was thought that he and his coalition partner Nick Clegg would be sympathetic to the cause. But just as Alan Milburn and so many others had done before him, once Cameron reached power, he appeared to lose interest. After four years of the Conservative–Liberal Democrat coalition, the campaign had barely moved forward.

The demonstration in 2014 was one of many attended by Glenn, who was getting increasingly frustrated that the campaigners' demands appeared to be falling on deaf ears.

He had been at it for some time.

A few months before we were first introduced by Diana Johnson, MP, in October 2010, he and his wife had been forced to remove their protest T-shirts before entering Parliament. They had been visiting the House of Commons to meet the Labour MP when a complaint about their clothing was made to the Serjeant at Arms, an ancient security role dating back almost 1,000 years to the time of the crusading king, Richard the Lionheart. These days, the Serjeant at Arms is responsible for maintaining order at the House of Commons and can often be seen carrying the mace during the Speaker's Procession.

Glenn and his wife tried to enter the Palace of Westminster wearing T-shirts bearing the slogan 'Silence is violence – 4,800 infected and counting'. Once the Serjeant at Arms had been informed of their attire, they were told they could not enter the historic building.

When I met Glenn in Portcullis House, the building that is home to the offices of MPs across the road from the House of Commons, he was bitterly disappointed. The government had rebuffed the campaign's latest demands for more generous financial assistance. Despite widespread support from a cross-party group of MPs, a motion calling on the government to apologise to the victims and implement the recommendations of the Archer report – including improved compensation payments to match those made in the Irish Republic – had just been voted down.

He told me: 'As approximately one hundred people from our infected and affected community looked down from the public gallery with the hope that after almost three decades of campaigning, their suffering would ease, their worst fears were realised when the government forced a three-line whip against the MPs. We now feel deceived, betrayed and incredibly angry.

'While in opposition, both David Cameron and Nick Clegg committed to finally resolve this issue – the Liberal Democrats even added this to their pre-election manifesto.

'As we all left the gallery, we felt incredibly dejected. However, we now know that by far the majority of MPs support our cause, and if it hadn't been for government intervention, we would have succeeded.'[1]

Glenn, just like Mike Dorricott, was a mild haemophiliac who had been infected with hepatitis C after undergoing a routine dental operation. The former engineer was nineteen when he went to Hull Royal Infirmary to have three teeth removed under general anaesthetic. While being treated, he was given factor VIII. At the time, Glenn had been unaware he would be receiving any kind of blood product during his treatment. His medical notes show that he was originally due to be treated with cryoprecipitate. But this was later scrubbed out and replaced with an entry confirming that he had received factor VIII.

When he was given a blood test in 1995, twelve years later, doctors revealed he had contracted hepatitis C through the contaminated factor VIII. When he was told the news, he was asked whether he was an alcoholic or a drug user, or if he had been sexually promiscuous. When he replied no, the doctor pointed to the entry in his medical notes that showed he had received factor VIII as the probable cause of his infection.

Glenn, like other mild haemophiliacs who were infected, believes he was treated as a PUP (previously untreated patient) and used as a guinea pig to test emerging new blood products. He claims that the factor VIII he received was 'wholly unnecessary', as his condition was mild and he was not being treated for a life-threatening bleed.

'My life changed irreversibly as a result of taking a risk which was not explained to me,' he told the inquiry. 'Part of my [decision] to become involved in campaigns over the years has been driven by my feeling that I was infected in circumstances where the blood products I received were, in fact, wholly unnecessary. I am not only one of the victims of this scandal, but am also one of those people who had no need to become a victim.'[2]

Glenn, whose hair is now greying, struggled on for years, his health failing, until he was finally forced to give up his job in 1999, leaving his family struggling on one income.

Many victims toiled for years in near-isolation, terrified of the stigma caused by their diseases and ashamed to speak out about their plight. The advent of the internet and mass communication was an important factor in the victims coming together and becoming more aware of the scale of the tragedy. Glenn was no different. After buying a computer and joining a number of Facebook groups, he realised that there were thousands of others just like him who were continuing to suffer.

Ever since then, his campaign for justice and calls for fair compensation arrangements have become almost a full-time job. Glenn's particular focus has been the discrimination he feels those infected with hepatitis C have suffered due to the greater financial support and assistance given to those infected with HIV.

'I have always taken the position that there was absolutely no justification for discriminating against HCV victims in comparison with HIV victims,' he said. 'I believe that medical science shows that [they] are both viruses that inflict lifelong devastating effects on those unfortunate enough to carry [them]. I simply do not believe there has ever been any proper justification for treating HCV victims as second class-victims in comparison to those unfortunate enough to have contracted HIV.'[3]

He has the evidence to back up his claims. Mortality data from the four UK infected blood support schemes, uncovered by Glenn under the Freedom of Information Act, reveals that between 2017 and 2021, those infected solely with hepatitis C are now dying at a faster rate than the co-infected or those suffering from HIV alone. This is in large part down to the effectiveness of HIV drugs, known as antiretroviral therapy, which works by reducing the amount of virus in the blood to undetectable levels, as well as the fact that many victims had been suffering from hepatitis C for a long time before it was detected, so they were delayed in taking steps to limit the damage to their liver.

Glenn felt so strongly about the issue that he helped set up his own pressure group, called the Contaminated Blood Campaign (CBC), to mount the case for support for all those affected, irrespective of whether they had a bleeding disorder or what they were infected with.

A decision by Andrew Lansley, the health secretary, in January 2011 did nothing to dispel Glenn's concerns. In response to calls for further support for hepatitis C sufferers, Lansley increased the Skipton Fund payments – but only for those suffering from second-stage hepatitis C, with liver complications such as cirrhosis or cancer.

Prior to his announcement, those affected were awarded £20,000 when they first developed chronic hepatitis C. A second-stage payment of £25,000 was then made when that person developed advanced liver disease, a complication of the condition. Lansley proposed increasing the second-stage payment to £50,000.

The announcement led Glenn to contact me again to highlight what he felt was a discriminatory decision against hepatitis C sufferers, who, unlike HIV victims, had to demonstrate the effects of the virus. When I spoke to him for an article for the *Hull Daily Mail*, he told me that he was concerned that proving his entitlement to the additional compensation could cost him his life, as he would need to undergo a dangerous liver biopsy.

'The derisory payments offered by government have failed to achieve settlement for the minority, never mind the majority,' he told me. 'I find it outrageous the government can find billions for the bankers, and they recently found £1.5 billion for those who invested with Equitable Life, but can, apparently, only find peanuts for those in our community whose lives have been left devastated by these infections given to us through no fault of our own, by the NHS, from the government's mismanagement of the blood supplies in the UK.'[4]

For the next few years, Glenn and I communicated regularly. He made several more appearances in the *Hull Daily Mail* before I moved to the *Sunday Express* in May 2014, where I took up the role as political editor. I was eager to harness the power of a national newspaper to the contaminated blood cause. One of the first stories I wrote for the paper was on Glenn's plight and the protest he led outside the prime minister's constituency office. As I was no longer constrained by the geography of working for a collection of regional newspapers, Glenn introduced me to other campaigners across the country, including Mike Dorricott, whose story we heard in Chapter 7.

But still the campaigners' demands fell on deaf ears. By now inertia had set in, as ministers awaited the findings of the Penrose Inquiry in Scotland. It seemed a convenient excuse for the government to sit on their hands and do nothing until they might be forced to respond. It was difficult not to suspect that Whitehall was desperately kicking the can down the road to play for time and save money as more and more victims who might qualify for compensation perished.

The victims and campaigners had high hopes for the Penrose Inquiry, which had taken six long years to conclude and cost the taxpayer £12 million. This optimism was short-lived.

When the Penrose report was published on 25 March, 2015, the Scottish judge tasked with leading the inquiry made only one clear recommendation. He said that everyone in Scotland who had received a blood transfusion before September 1991 should be offered a test for hepatitis C.

Angry victims branded the report a whitewash. Glenn was among those who had gone to the Museum of Scotland on Chambers Street to hear the report's findings. He was so disgusted that he was photographed setting fire to the report. He told me: 'We didn't expect the world from this inquiry, but we expected a lot more than this.'[5]

After the findings were published, Professor John Cash, the former president of the Royal College of Physicians of Edinburgh and the former director of the transfusion service, accused the inquiry of failing to get to the truth. In one of the last interviews he would ever give, Cash told me that the Inquiries Act 2005, which defines the parameters of public inquiries, enabled the executives responsible to avoid giving evidence.

'Did Lord Penrose get to speak to the people with the real answers? No, he didn't,' he told me. 'He tried but through no fault of his own, he couldn't get to the truth. He ran into serious problems because the Inquiries Act meant there was a whole area he could not address.'[6]

Cash had a long history with the contaminated blood scandal. As far back as 1976, he had warned in the *British Medical Journal* that bringing factor VIII blood-clotting products into Britain 'represents an unequivocal pathway by which the level of a potentially lethal virus into the whole community is being deliberately increased'.

Speaking about his earlier prophetic warning, Cash, who died in 2021, told me: 'One doesn't always want to be a prophet of doom, but I questioned whether we knew enough about what we were doing.'

However, he said the doctors always had the best interest of patients at heart, and although not a prescribing doctor, he recalled the dilemma they faced.

'I was involved with clinicians in the seventies who saw people in such pain that I can imagine them disregarding any worries they had,' he told me. 'The questions about this have to be addressed by those at the very top of government, ministers and civil servants. We were foot soldiers, given our instructions by officials in London, and it would be nice to know what was in their minds.'[7]

Although the campaigners were shocked by the findings of the Penrose Inquiry, there was even worse news to come. Hours before the report was due to be published, Glenn's fellow campaigner Mike Dorricott collapsed. He was taken to Royal Victoria Infirmary in Newcastle upon Tyne, where he was treated for a stomach and lung infection. He had also suffered organ failure, and loved ones at his bedside were told that he was unlikely to pull through.

Mike had hoped to die a 'happier man' in the knowledge that his family would be financially secure as a result of the Penrose report. Speaking to me as he lay gravely ill in hospital, his sister, Jane, told me: 'I am very close to my brother and upset at losing him to a disease that he shouldn't have been exposed to. He needs to be allowed to die in peace with the comfort of knowing he has fought for justice for himself and his family, and that they are financially supported because of him. He has been an amazing father and husband, and has always provided for his family. It would give him great comfort to know that he leaves them in a place where they can at least financially manage without him.'[8]

When Mike collapsed, he had not yet heard the recommendations made by Penrose. His wife, Ann, said she was at a loss as to what to tell him should he wake up.

'He was relying on Lord Penrose to reveal the truth so that there could be a proper compensation package put in place,' she told me. 'In his words, "Everything hangs on what Penrose recommends." By everything, he meant that he wanted to make sure that when he died, we would all be financially secure in the way we would have been, had his NHS treatment not resulted in infecting him with what he called "this nasty, nasty illness".

'We don't know whether he'll pull through. If he does, one of the first things he'll want to know is what is happened regarding the inquiry, and are we going to get proper compensation? What do we tell him? What would the prime minister or Jane Ellison [public health minister], or Lord Penrose himself tell him? Because we honestly don't have a clue what to say. I'm so disappointed with the Penrose Inquiry outcome. He has never complained about his situation. My husband has suffered enough battles with his health over the years. I really hoped for him that this was one he would win.'[9]

Mike's youngest daughter, Ellie, who was eighteen at the time, told me: 'I was really hoping the inquiry would give him a morale boost, but he would feel so frustrated by this outcome.'[10]

His eldest daughter, Sarah, who was twenty-four at the time, added: 'All this hard work that everyone has put into this – time and effort and money. There's nothing to show for it. My dad has put a lot into this himself. He has lobbied MPs, tirelessly campaigned, even met with ministers and put forward proposals. He will be so disappointed.'[11]

On the same day that Mike collapsed, Cameron apologised to victims of the contaminated blood scandal on behalf of the British government.

Speaking at Prime Minister's Questions in the Commons, Cameron said it was difficult to imagine the 'feeling of unfairness that people must feel at being infected with something like hepatitis C or HIV as a result of totally unrelated treatment within the NHS'.

He added: 'To each and every one of these people, I would like to say sorry on behalf of the government for something that should not have happened.'[12]

He also confirmed that the government would provide up to £25 million in 2015–16 to support any transitional arrangement to a better payment system.

The response to the additional funding was dismissed as a 'joke' and 'gesture' politics by campaigners, who believed it fell far short of what was needed to help the victims of this entirely avoidable scandal, who were still dying at the rate of one every four days.

Sadly, it was Mike who would become the scandal's latest victim. He spent the last days of his life at the Freeman Hospital drifting in and out of consciousness as his loved ones gathered beside him. Even as internal organs began to fail and it began to look increasingly likely that Mike's days could soon be numbered, Mike appealed to his sister, Jane, and wife, Ann, to remind me that his dying wish was for justice for him and his family.

'Tell her to keep going,' he implored them.

Mike was just forty-seven years old when the end finally came on 3 April 2015.

•

David Cameron's surprise general election victory – which came a little more than a month after Mike's untimely death – gave the campaign for justice renewed vigour. Cameron was returned to Downing Street on 7 May 2015, with a twelve-seat majority. His decision to appoint Alistair Burt, who had by now become an integral part of the campaign, as a health minister only added to the growing sense of optimism. Within days of arriving at the Department of Health, Burt held a number of meetings on the issue with Jeremy Hunt, the health secretary, and Jane Ellison, the health minister. According to Whitehall insiders, he made it clear he wasn't going to let the matter drop and was going to hold Cameron to his promise to adequately compensate the victims of the contaminated blood campaign.

Burt was already aware of some of the anomalies and problems with the existing support schemes, given his work with Diana Johnson on the APPG's inquiry into the issue earlier in the year. He had been tasked by Cameron to lead the discussion on compensation and how to overhaul the existing schemes to make them fairer.

By now, I had been introduced to several more campaigners, including the Farrugia family, who we met in Chapter 8. Their deeply shocking story appeared to resonate with Martin Townsend, the formidable editor of the *Sunday Express*. He had been moved by the story of young Tony, who had been left to fend for himself in a children's home after the untimely death of his father. With a history of campaigning, the paper had led a number of successful crusades on various issues, including the desire to achieve parity of esteem between physical and mental health.

Now Townsend had decided that he wanted to use the might of his paper to campaign on behalf of the victims of the contaminated blood scandal. Together, Townsend and I drew up a list of demands, including a 'full and fair' settlement for the victims of the tragedy and an inquiry into the Department of Health's role in the scandal.

The campaign was launched on 19 July 2015, with the stories of Nick Sainsbury, Ade Goodyear, Richard Warwick and Joe Peaty, who all told me how they had come to be infected with HIV while at school at Treloar's. They also revealed that only a handful of their school friends who had also been treated with factor VIII were still alive.

Peaty, who lives in Coventry and was at the school from 1979 to 1984, revealed that he was told of his HIV status while preparing to sit his A levels. He told me: 'I hadn't been having regular treatment until I arrived at the school, but they persuaded me to try a new treatment and got mine and my parents' consent for it. It meant I was given millions of units of factor VIII, sometimes up to a thousand units a day.

'They reassured us time and time again that it was safe. But it wasn't and there will always be a question mark in my head as to why these treatments were used when they had not been thoroughly tested and found to be safe.'[13]

Warwick, from Malton, North Yorkshire, who was at the school from 1976, was only told he had HIV in 1989 – an astonishing three years after he was first diagnosed. He told me: 'What is worse, I was told in front of my wife-to-be. We cried all the way home from the hospital.'[14]

This shocking story of lethal, institutionalised practices carried out on children by doctors at a respected school caused the contaminated blood campaign to snowball. The story was quickly retold by journalists at other media outlets, and used as the basis for a BBC *Panorama* documentary.

From that moment on, a steady flow of campaigners came forward to tell me of their own harrowing experiences after receiving encouragement from Sue Threakall and Andy Evans, who were then joint chairs of the pressure group Tainted Blood. Among them were Clair Walton, Chris Cornes, and even the Liberal Democrat peer Lynne Featherstone, whose nephew Nick had died after being infected with hepatitis C. The talented musician, who played with the Camden band The Dirty Feel, had died four years earlier at the age of thirty-five.

Baroness Featherstone told me: 'The government knew the treatments were contaminated. They were warned . . . But [they] carried on using contaminated blood products despite those warnings. Nick's mother, my sister, his father and his twin will never get over that loss.'[15]

The campaign started to have an effect. In August 2015, Tim Farron became the first party leader to give it his backing. Just a month after taking over as leader of the Liberal Democrats, Farron wrote an article for the *Sunday Express* saying he was 'delighted' to back the campaign and 'support the call for a long overdue settlement'.

'The prime minister in March finally apologised on behalf of the government. Now it is time those words were backed up by action. I am urging David Cameron to listen to victims and their families and ensure they finally get the full and fair compensation they so rightly deserve.'[16]

Progress was painfully slow. Positive announcements were often followed by little to no action. By Christmas 2015, it became apparent that not a penny of the £25 million promised by Cameron had actually reached the victims. At the time, it was estimated that at least nine people had died since the prime minister had made the pledge.

At the start of January 2016, a consultation on the reform of support arrangements for people affected by the scandal was finally launched after a lengthy delay. But with the forthcoming Brexit referendum dominating the headlines in first half of 2016, it felt like the issue was once again slipping off the government's agenda. When Cameron announced his resignation on the steps of Downing Street in the early hours of 24 June 2016, after the British public took the momentous decision to reject his entreaties and turn their back on the European Union, any victory in the campaign looked further away than ever.

However, to his credit, Cameron was determined not to leave office without delivering on his promise to help transition to a better compensation system for those affected. In one of his last acts as prime minister, during his final Prime Minister's Question Time, he announced that every victim of the contaminated blood scandal would receive a regular annual support payment. He also he announced that an extra £100 million would be allocated to help the victims, in addition to the £25 million he had promised in March 2015. The scheme offered payments to victims based on the number of viruses they had contracted and how seriously those viruses had affected their health. Sources close to the prime minister told me that the announcement had been motivated by the harrowing stories highlighted in our campaign.

Sadly, however, the new scheme appeared to create anomalies that left some claimants worse off. Those with hepatitis C were furious that they had again been awarded less than those with HIV, despite the fact that more people with the liver condition were now dying. Although widows were given a £10,000 one-off payment, many believed this to be a 'paltry sum' to compensate for the loss of a husband. The scheme also compared unfavourably to arrangements for contaminated blood victims in Scotland. This led campaigners to dismiss the new payment system as 'insulting and miserly'.[17]

Cameron also failed to commit to a public inquiry. He has since said he thought 'all efforts should be focused on getting the victims the help they deserved' rather than creating a lengthy inquiry that would have led to further delays in financial support being awarded.[18] Despite the pledge of more money, it was generally felt to have fallen far short of what was expected, and victims, their families, campaigners and MPs were left with a great sense of despondency. The campaign had thus far failed to deliver any of its key objectives. They had been campaigning for a full and final settlement, and believed the sums of money being offered by the government were piecemeal.

With a new prime minister, Theresa May, about to enter Downing Street, it felt like we were going back to square one.

●

In April 2016, shortly after an inquest ruled that the ninety-six victims who died in the Hillsborough football stadium disaster had been unlawfully killed, Diana Johnson asked Andy Burnham to address supportive MPs.

Burnham, the former health secretary and Labour MP for Leigh in Greater Manchester, had been instrumental in the creation of the Hillsborough Independent Panel. It had been set up shortly after the thirtieth anniversary of the tragedy after it emerged that police statements had been altered, leading to calls by Burnham for the disclosure of all documents relating to the disaster.

Johnson and her colleagues serving on the All-Party Parliamentary Group on Haemophilia and Contaminated Blood were feeling deflated, and were struggling to find a way forward to shake the government out of their current inertia over the issue of compensation and commitment to holding a public inquiry.

Johnson thought Burnham might be able to regalvanise the campaign by allowing the MPs to draw upon the lessons he had learned from his involvement unpicking the Hillsborough tragedy.

'I had always felt that the big problem around the parliamentary campaign on blood was that it was overly focused on finance,' Burnham told me in a coffee shop opposite the Home Office, several years after he had left Westminster to become the Mayor of Greater Manchester. 'From time to time, the government would throw a few scraps off the table to ease any pressure, but it rarely stopped to ask how we got to this position in the first place. With Hillsborough, I had managed to reopen it by putting a proposal to the Cabinet that at [the] very least, the families deserved answers, the full truth, no matter how difficult it might be. In answer to Diana's question, I suggested to the All-Party Group that they should do exactly the same. Go back to the beginning and demand the full truth.'

He added: 'With Hillsborough, the evidence I had that people had not been given the full truth was the emergence of police statements that had clearly been amended. I saw a direct parallel with the medical records of people who had been infected by contaminated blood or blood products. One of the things common to all MPs was they were in receipt of testimony from constituents reporting medical records being withheld, deleted, lost or even amended.'

Burnham believed the APPG could use a similar tactic to the one he'd used for the Hillsborough panel to force the government into action. He had first begun to see the parallels between the Hillsborough disaster and the contaminated blood tragedy back in January 2010, when he had first met with a group of campaigners from the Manor House Group.

The meeting had taken place at the insistence of his close friend Paul Goggins, the Labour MP for Wythenshawe and

Sale East. Goggins had implored Burnham, who was health secretary between June 2009 and May 2010: 'Just sit down, talk to them, hear it. Do what you did with the Hillsborough families.'

Burnham has since told me that officials at the Department of Health did 'everything they could' to try to get the meeting out of his diary. But in the end, he spent three hours with the families, listening to their plight. He said it was at that moment the 'scales fell from [his] eyes' and he started telling the Department of Health that there needed to be an independent disclosure panel on contaminated blood.

Among those who moved Burnham to act were Eleanor and Fred Bates. Fred, who was initially a mild haemophiliac, was infected with hepatitis A, B and C after receiving factor VIII in the late 1970s and early 1980s. He believes he was probably infected in 1984, when he was treated with factor VIII over a six-week period and remembers feeling 'very unwell'. His medical records show he first tested positive in November of that year, but he was not informed of his diagnosis until more than a decade later. Even then, he was told by a lawyer rather than his doctor.

The story planted a seed for Burnham that this behaviour amounted to a criminal offence, because withholding such information could have inadvertently led to a family member becoming infected, too. It was a theme he would return to in the coming years.

He said that after the conversation it struck him that there was 'something really, really wrong'. He recalled: 'I had this departmental line of no fault: no one did anything wrong, no fault. But then I had, sitting right in front of me, Eleanor Bates, who I was meeting for the first time, telling me that she went with Fred to see her lawyer in the mid-1990s because there was a litigation happening at that time . . . [and the lawyer] said: "And, of course, Fred is hepatitis B positive," and Eleanor said, "What?" That was the first time she had been told. And that, for me, was as revealing as the first time I knew there was an amended police statement around Hillsborough.'

Burnham also learned of the financial hardship suffered by the Bates family. He was told how they frequently had to 'beg' from the charities that were supposed to be supporting them.

He recalled: 'Again, I was in a position of asking, "Well, through no fault of your own, you and Fred are living this life, and you are having to kind of beg for basics."'

By the time he met the Bates family, Burnham had been health secretary for more than six months, and he admits to feeling a 'sense of guilt' that he had not been able to do more up to this point. 'But you are confronted with these firm lines and then . . . by the efforts of some very diligent MPs, you get to hear something very different, and that for me, was a massive moment . . . That was the day where I said, "OK, I'm doing something on this now." And that was the mood in which I went back down to London.'

Burnham, who faced strong resistance from within his department to his efforts to reopen the contaminated blood issue, believes he was 'misled' by officials who had provided 'inaccurate lines' to ministers regarding the scandal, 'primarily driven by a fear of financial exposure'.

He told me that had he known then what he knows now, he never would have sent a 2009 letter to an infected person saying: 'There is no evidence that individuals were knowingly infected with contaminated blood and blood products.'

He said: 'In my view, it was inaccurate. They were still putting that in letters that I was being asked to sign – things that were misleading – because it had been drilled into them in the seventies and eighties and was so baked in.'

Immediately prior to leaving office in May 2010, Burnham succeeded in announcing a review of the Skipton Fund payments. The government's response to the Archer report in 2009 had been to promise a review within five years. However, in one of his last acts as health secretary, Burnham overturned the decision and brought the review forward. But he claims even this decision was resisted by officials within his department, because at one point it was floated that the government should sell the Blood Products Laboratory to pay for the review – something he thinks was contrived to put him off the idea.

By the time Burnham spoke to the APPG, in the spring of 2016, he was preparing to leave Parliament. He was trying, before he went, to bring forward the Public Authority (Accountability) Bill, which became known as Hillsborough Law. The bill, which eventually ran out of time but has since been resurrected, proposed the introduction of a statutory duty of candour on public servants during all forms of public inquiry and criminal investigation. It also aimed to ensure proper participation of bereaved families at inquests, through publicly funded legal representation, and the provision of a public advocate to act for families of the deceased after major incidents.

'From all of the work I had done on justice campaigns, from Bloody Sunday [and] Hillsborough to contaminated blood, I was clear that the same pattern of events keeps repeating,' he told me. 'A major disaster or act of harm happened. The state would form a narrative to protect itself reputationally or financially. It would have access to all the levers of power to entrench that narrative at inquiries or inquests. And then families would be left fighting for years in the wilderness to try and unpick that narrative and get some form of redress. While we could individually help the Hillsborough families or those infected with [contaminated] blood, what was needed was a complete rebalancing of the system to prevent this pattern repeating and recurring long injustices that have scarred this country.'

He added: 'I believe there must have been people in the Department of Health, from the seventies onwards, who would have had serious concerns about some of the lines that were being put up to ministers. And if there was a statutory duty of candour, that would have allowed them to break the cycle of partial briefing [or] incorrect briefing without being in fear of losing their job for doing so, because there [would be] a law that would require them to come forward with information that they knew would have changed the complexion of the issue. It very much remains my view that that is essential.'

In hindsight, Burnham believes the Department of Health and bodies for which it is responsible have been 'grossly negligent of the safety of the haemophilia community in this country'. He told the inquiry there is 'even the possibility that the Crown Prosecution Service (CPS) should be asked to consider charges of corporate manslaughter'.[19]

Just days before Cameron's successor as prime minister, Theresa May, called a surprise snap general election on 18 April 2017, there was another dramatic twist in the campaign.

Burnham approached me with fresh evidence of what he described as a 'cover-up'.[20] The Labour MP and I had got to know each other well over the previous few years, and even more so since the advent of the *Sunday Express* crusade on contaminated blood, to which he had given his wholehearted support. He told me he had seen evidence of victims' medical records being altered, raising the prospect of a criminal investigation.

One of the cases that he had uncovered and subsequently raised in Parliament involved Ken Bullock, who died in 1998. Ken's widow said his diagnosis of hepatitis had been changed in 1983 to that of being a clinical alcoholic. According to Burnham, any mention of blood products in Bullock's medical records stopped 'very suddenly'. From then on, they refer only to 'alcoholic damage to the liver'.

It is possible that Bullock, a moderate drinker, was refused a liver transplant because of his falsified medical records saying he was an alcoholic.

'Falsification of a medical record is a criminal offence,' Burnham said. 'So, I don't know whether there was any instruction ever given to people working . . . in the NHS about withholding diagnosis or . . . withholding medical records, or amending medical records, or, in this case, falsifying medical records, but I do believe that those acts are criminal acts.'

Bullock's case is not unusual. There have been countless other examples of patients having their medical records withheld, or sometimes altered, with pertinent details blacked out. In some cases, this has made it impossible for those infected to apply for support from the Skipton Fund. However, Bullock's is one of the most egregious examples of medical records being changed in a way that suggest the motive was to cover up the cause of his infection.

Burnham was appalled by the revelation, and used

his last Commons speech as an MP, on 26 April 2017, to demand an inquiry into a 'criminal cover-up on an industrial scale' over the historic use of contaminated blood products in the NHS. Flanked by Diana Johnson, he said: 'Knowing what I know, and what I believe to be true, I wouldn't be able to live with myself if I left here without putting it on the official record.'

Burnham, whose speech was no less powerful despite the empty chamber he delivered it to, said campaigners had given him documents showing victims were used as 'guinea pigs' and subjected to 'slurs and smears' via falsified medical records. Others had had tests carried out without their knowledge or consent, with the results withheld 'for decades in some cases', even when they revealed positive results. It had also been suggested that the withholding of results led to infections being passed on to people living with the victims. The Labour MP cited three cases, including that of Bullock. He said the scandal had a 'very disturbing echo' of the Hillsborough stadium disaster. Victims of negligence by the state were 'suddenly the victims of smears perpetrated by those working on behalf of public bodies, particularly smears related to alcohol, to suggest the disease that afflicted Mr Bullock's liver was self-inflicted'.

The MP highlighted a 1975 letter from Stanford University's medical centre to a UK Government-owned blood products laboratory that warned of blood products coming on to the market 'from skid-row derelicts'. Another letter sent in 1982 from the Oxford Haemophilia Centre to all haemophilia centre directors in England raised concerns about the effectiveness of testing blood for 'infectivity' on chimpanzees.

Burnham said: 'In other words, let's find out if there's

"infectivity", in their words, in these products by using patients as guinea pigs.'

Burnham, who was able to use parliamentary privilege to make a number of detailed accusations, called for an independent panel or a public inquiry similar to the one launched into Hillsborough. He added: 'If the newly elected government after the general election fails to set up the process I've described, I will refer my dossier of cases to the police, and I will request a criminal investigation into these shameful acts of cover-up against innocent people.'[21]

Together he and I hatched a plan to go to the Metropolitan Police together and hand over a dossier of evidence before Parliament was due to rise for the summer recess at the end of July.[22]

We decided to act after the Conservative Party failed to address the issue in its 2017 election manifesto.

Burnham told me: 'It's disappointing that the Conservative Party have not pledged to hold an inquiry into the contaminated blood scandal. The case for holding one is overwhelming, and so how any political party can ignore it is really beyond me – but the fight goes on, and . . . I would encourage anybody who feels angry about what has happened [to] seek commitments directly from individual candidates.'

He added: 'I am now ready to take this evidence to the police. I am not going to go beyond when the House of Commons rises for the summer recess. I have made it very clear to the new government, whoever they are, that there is this opportunity to make amends and do things in a better way but let's be clear: this evidence is going to be investigated one way or another. I still think it is much more dignified and effective if we tie together the paperwork held by individuals and the paperwork held at national level, and I have learned that after Hillsborough that is the way to get to the truth more quickly – but if the incoming government don't do that, I will refer evidence to the police.'[23]

However, we never made our meeting with the police.

Before the deadline passed, the general election was held on 8 June 2017. The dramatic result, which saw May lose her majority, led to momentous developments that would change the course of the campaign forever.

•

A chance encounter a few weeks after the general election that left Theresa May clinging to power led to a break-through in the campaign.

May had failed in a spectacular gamble. She had sought to break the political deadlock over Brexit with a snap general election but, in the end, it led to her Conservative Party losing its Westminster majority.

May thought she could strengthen her position ahead of pivotal talks with the European Union after months of Brexit turmoil. But her audacious bid backfired, and she was left to rely on the support of Northern Ireland's Democratic Unionist Party (DUP) to prop up her minority government.

Towards the end of June, she struck a 'confidence and supply' deal with the DUP by promising at least an extra £1 billion in funding for the province that would enable her to stay in power.

Days after the agreement had been made, I bumped into Diana Johnson in Parliament. Our conversation quickly turned to the campaign and how we could leverage May's weakened position to bring about a change in government policy. The election had seen the Labour Party include a pledge in its manifesto to 'address historic public health injustices' by holding a public inquiry into the contaminated blood scandal. The Liberal Democrats had also repeated an earlier manifesto pledge to 'develop a just settlement for haemophiliacs who were given contaminated blood'. Crucially, I had also worked out that the DUP was supportive of a public inquiry. In a debate in the Commons the previous year, Jim Shannon, the party's health spokesman, had spoken up in support of the campaign for justice, saying: 'On such a sensitive matter, we need to be able to give our full empathy and sympathy to those affected. I really believe that the government needs to deliver.' It appeared that finally there was potentially a majority in Parliament in favour of holding a public inquiry. When I mentioned this to Johnson, she offered to test that assumption by asking all the main political parties to sign a letter to May calling for a Hillsborough-style inquiry.

By now, my home was *The Sunday Times*. In my second week as deputy political editor, the newspaper published the letter. It was signed by six party leaders: the DUP's Nigel Dodds; Ian Blackford, the leader of the SNP group in the Commons; Lib Dem leader Tim Farron; Plaid Cymru's Westminster leader Liz Saville Roberts; Green co-leader Caroline Lucas; and Labour leader Jeremy Corbyn.[24] The letter called for the establishment of an inquiry with the power to compel all those involved in the scandal to participate. It described the contaminated blood scandal as one of the 'worst peacetime disasters in our country's history', warning:

> We believe those affected have a right to know what went wrong; and why. Whenever public disasters of this kind take place, government has a fundamental

duty to support those affected in getting the answers they need; to disclose everything they know; and to ensure that officials are called to account for their actions. We regret that for many decades the victims of the contaminated blood scandal have been denied this right.

. . . Among many other considerations, it is alleged that victims' medical details were tampered with to hide the cause of their infections; that documents relating to the scandal were destroyed by Department of Health officials as part of a cover-up; and that patients were not told of the risks . . . once the dangers became known.

The editor of *The Sunday Times* wasn't quite as gung-ho about the campaign as Martin Townsend of the *Sunday Express*; the letter was featured in a short 350-word article on page four of my paper. Despite its lack of prominence, the piece was to have huge impact.

On the Monday, Diana Johnson used the letter to call for an urgent debate under Standing Order No. 24, where an MP can ask the Speaker of the House of Commons for a debate on a pressing issue. It is understood that behind the scenes, John Bercow, the former Speaker of the House of Commons, who had been a thorn in the government's side over the Brexit wars, had signalled to Johnson that if she applied for the debate, she was likely to be successful.

At teatime, Johnson made her impassioned appeal. She told MPs: 'The letter of 9 July raises the prospect that, if the matter of a public inquiry were put to a vote in the House, it would command the support of the majority of Members of Parliament. For all the reasons I have outlined, I believe that we now need an emergency debate. We need the government to do the right thing and secure justice for those affected in this scandal, including justice for the 2,400 people who have already died.'[25]

Bercow, who is known to have been privately supportive of the campaign, granted the debate, saying: 'I have listened carefully to the application from the Hon. Member, and I am satisfied that the matter raised by her is proper to be discussed under the terms of Standing Order No. 24.'

The debate was scheduled for the following day, putting the prime minister on a collision course with her backbenchers for the first time since the tumultuous election had left her eight seats short of a majority. More worryingly still, it would risk fracturing the fragile confidence-and-supply arrangement she had only recently agreed with the DUP.

Johnson recalled the tight spot that May was in. 'We had been granted a substantive motion, and if the opposition parties voted in a united fashion, we would have beaten the government . . . So, I think she was worried that [it] would be their first vote in Parliament as a new government, and she didn't have a majority, and she'd lose. It was clear pressure was building on May over the issue on multiple fronts.'

Pressure was also building in another arena. A few days earlier, an application had also been approved by the High Court for a group litigation order for more than 500 claimants – surviving victims of the contaminated blood scandal and the families of those deceased – to enable them to sue the government for compensation. At the time of writing this book, the group litigation order had been paused until three months after the publication of the final report by the Infected Blood Inquiry. The claimants were represented by the solicitor Des Collins, who was once dubbed Britain's Erin

Brockovich for settling the landmark eleven-year negligence claim against Corby Borough Council on behalf of children born with significant birth defects. Collins' claim alleged that the Department of Health failed in its duty to take reasonable care to prevent injury or loss to NHS patients when contaminated blood products were imported into the UK.

Diana Johnson told me: 'There was pressure on the . . . Department of Health about what was happening with these cases, and they might well lose them. But I certainly hold the view that without the pressure from all the different opposition parties in Parliament at that important point where the prime minister did not have a majority and she was desperately . . . wooing the DUP, and they'd signed this letter saying, "We think there's an injustice here and you need to do something about it," she wouldn't have found herself in such political hot water and looking for an easy way out.'

May's premiership was hanging by a thread, and there was already a question mark as to whether she would survive having almost led the party to electoral defeat. But she was also a woman of principle, who was well known in Westminster for her adherence to her moral compass, and she had already had her conscience pricked by the scandal.

After she became prime minister, May had set out her determination to deal with seven 'burning injustices'. It appeared that she had just added another one to her list. She was no stranger to shining a light on issues that were likely to deliver some uncomfortable truths. She had already played a pivotal role in the creation of independent inquiries into other, long-running scandals that the establishment had been keen to sweep under the carpet.

Only the week before Johnson demanded action in the Commons, May had pledged to examine the new evidence on contaminated blood that had been brought forward by Burnham. He was also still holding a sword of Damocles over the government with the threat to hand his dossier over to the police if a Hillsborough-style inquiry was not launched.

With hours to go before the debate was due to commence on Tuesday 11 July, May decided it was not worth expending the political capital on opposing a public inquiry when so many MPs, including those on her own side, were in favour of it.

I was standing in the atrium in Portcullis House when I received a phone call that I will never forget. It was the prime minister's special advisor Tim Smith. He rang me to deliver the momentous news about an hour before May was due on the floor of the House of Commons to respond to the debate.

'Well done,' he said. 'Just two weeks into your new job, and you have got your inquiry.'

I remember the call like it was yesterday. It was something that I, the MPs and the brave victims and their families had fought so long and hard for but feared might never happen. I was told that I could only tell close friends and family before the official announcement by May later that afternoon.

The first person I called was Diana Johnson, followed by Andy Burnham, then Sue Threakall, who was then co-chair of the pressure group Tainted Blood, and finally my mum. But this was not the end of the story. In many ways, it was just the next chapter, but it brought with it a small glimmer of hope that there might yet be a happy ending.

Colin Smith.

10

COLIN

2017–22

Even though it was almost thirty years since their beloved son 'little Colin' had died, the agony of his parents' loss was still etched on their faces as they gave evidence to the long-awaited Infected Blood Inquiry.

Seven-year-old Colin Smith weighed less than a four-month-old baby when he died on 13 January 1990. His tiny thirteen-pound body had been ravaged by AIDS, and towards the end he was so delicate he could only bear to be moved wrapped in a soft sheep fleece.

Colin was one of the youngest victims of the contaminated blood scandal, injected with HIV and hepatitis C when he had gone into hospital for a routine ear operation. He was just two years old when he was handed a death sentence.

His brave parents, Colin and Jan Smith, told the inquiry of their pain as they described taking their little boy home from hospital to spend one last Christmas with his family.

In heartbreaking testimony, Colin's mum described the anguish of 'having your child on your lap watching the rise and fall of his chest and waiting for it to stop'.[1] Colin's dad said he could never forgive himself for his little boy passing away before he did, buried underground in a 'grave on his own'.[2]

The evidence was so emotionally charged that at the end of their testimony, Jenni Richards, QC, counsel to the inquiry, wiped tears from her eyes. Sir Brian Langstaff, the inquiry's chairman, was also visibly moved.

The couple received a round of applause at the conclusion of their evidence, which laid bare the decades of deceit, denial and official neglect suffered by all contaminated blood victims. As the applause died down, Langstaff thanked them for their courage and reflected on the Smith family's suffering.

'What you might have expected with a seriously ill child was sympathy and help,' he said. 'What you described in brutal terms was that what you got was rejection, vilification and abuse . . . It takes a very special kind of resilience to be able now to talk to everyone about what happened to you and what happened to Colin, and to tell us in the most moving of ways how you have managed to keep Colin alive for you.'[3]

In a long list of impossible tragedies, Colin's story is always the one that touches everyone the most. It certainly touched me when I first wrote about the Smith family's devastating plight in the *Sunday Express* in July 2015.

The horror of Colin's short life, coupled with the courage and eloquence of his parents as they recalled what the family had suffered, was humbling.

Jessica Morden, the family's MP in Newport, said the case of Colin illustrated why the public inquiry could not 'come quickly enough'. A mother herself to an eight-year-old boy, she often imagined how she would feel if it was her own child who had suffered in this way. She believes the least the Smith family deserves is answers as to how and why their son died. In a speech in the House of Commons, she told MPs: 'Nothing can bring back Colin and others, but we can at least have a public inquiry that gets this right. We need to get it right this time, because Colin's family and others have been through so much over the years that we cannot let them down again.'[4]

Theresa May surprised many with the announcement that she was launching a UK-wide inquiry into the contaminated blood scandal – a decision her predecessors had dodged for the past thirty years. The day before she took the decision, Jeremy Hunt, the health secretary and Mike Dorricott's former constituency MP, informed the prime minister that he was 'minded' to hold an inquiry. According to documents released under freedom of information laws to the campaigner Carol Anne Grayson, his private secretary sent an email to the prime minister's office setting out his position. It stated: 'Following consultation with the Cabinet Office, SofS [Secretary of State] and the Department recommends a statutory inquiry to allow both documents and oral evidence to be considered, but that the inquiry should be based on the Hillsborough model.' An attached briefing note referred to the two previous inquiries held, the Archer Inquiry and the Penrose Inquiry in Scotland, but conceded that the 'victims remain of the view that there has been a cover-up and are not satisfied' by the previous inquiries.

The document added: 'Recent events including the announced inquiry into the Grenfell Tower fire and recent media articles on infected blood have increased the pressure to hold a "public inquiry".'[5]

Announcing the inquiry, May described the contaminated blood scandal as a 'tragedy which should simply never have happened'. Her statement continued:

Thousands of patients expected the world-class care our NHS is famous for, but they were failed. At least 2,400 people died and thousands more were exposed to hepatitis C and HIV, with life-changing consequences.

The victims and their families, who have suffered so much pain and hardship, deserve answers as to how this could possibly have happened.

While this government has invested record amounts to support the victims, they have been denied those answers for too long and I want to put that right. As prime minister, I am determined to stand up for victims and confront injustice and unfairness in our society at every turn.

We will work with the victims and their families to decide what form this inquiry should take so their voices are heard and they finally get the answers and justice they have spent decades waiting for.[6]

Although the carefully worded statement was short, it said everything the victims and their families had longed to hear. The only important questions that remained were how extensive the powers of the inquiry would be, and who would lead it.

In her response to the prime minister's statement, Diana Johnson made an impassioned appeal for a Hillsborough-style inquiry that could compel witnesses to give evidence and disclose documents. She told MPs: 'I do not need to remind the House of the damage that public disasters do to all those who are affected, as we know from the Hillsborough tragedy in 1989 and, more recently, the appalling fire at Grenfell Tower.

'Every public disaster of this kind is different: their causes differ; the victims suffer in different ways; and the measures necessary to support those affected, and their families, also differ. However, every victim has a fundamental right to one thing: answers. They deserve to be told what went wrong, why it went wrong, and who is responsible for what happened. The story of the injustice they have suffered needs to be set out and told to the wider public. Their voices need to be heard. Apologies, compensation and other forms of support are essential, but if their right to answers is not also satisfied, they will be denied true and meaningful justice.'

Johnson went on to praise those who had been involved in the campaign, including her constituent Glenn Wilkinson and the 111 MPs who had agreed to join the membership of the All-Party Parliamentary Group on Haemophilia and Contaminated Blood. She also paid tribute to the journalists, including myself, who had given a voice to the victims when no one else would listen.[7]

It was a moment of jubilation in a campaign where victories had been few and far between.

But we weren't complacent. History had taught us to be vigilant. Sure enough, it was not long before serious questions were raised about the independence of the inquiry. The government initially planned for the Department of Health to play a major role and refused to allow another department, such as the Cabinet Office or the Ministry of Justice, to take over. Campaigners believed the Department of Health was too embroiled in the scandal and its apparent cover-up to play any part.

With trust in the government among the campaigners in such short supply, May drafted in the Right Rev. James Jones, who had chaired the Hillsborough panel, to resolve the dispute.

After his meeting with campaigners, Jones said he completely agreed that the Department for Health 'cannot be responsible for investigating the Department of Health', adding: 'It would be an offence to natural justice.'[8]

Eventually, the government backed down and it was announced that the inquiry would fall under the jurisdiction of the Cabinet Office.

Given the row that had erupted over which department would lead the inquiry, the next hurdle facing the government was to find someone to chair it who would be acceptable to the campaigners. Among the names in the frame were Jones, Sir Robert Francis, who had led the inquiry into the Mid Staffordshire hospital scandal, and Sir Brian Langstaff, a retired High Court judge who had served as leading counsel to the inquiry into the Bristol Royal Infirmary that investigated the deaths of twenty-nine babies undergoing heart surgery.

It was at this point that Johnson was called into Downing Street to meet Damian Green, who was at the time May's deputy prime minister, and Sue Gray, the senior civil servant who went on to lead the investigation into Partygate. They wanted to seek her views on who would make an appropriate appointment.

'They were testing me to see what I thought might work,' Johnson told me.

When it was decided that Langstaff should take on the role, he came to Westminster for a private meeting with her in February 2018.

Johnson, who had previously shared the same chambers as Langstaff when she trained as a barrister, said: 'I remembered him being a very good barrister; he was very human, very bright and a really nice, decent man.'

Langstaff formally opened the three days of preliminary hearings on 24 September 2018, with a sombre warning that the true scale of the tragedy may yet be unknown.

'It is a truly sobering thought that if some claims are well-founded – and it will be for this inquiry to find out if they are – there may yet be many thousands more who do not feel well, but have not yet been told that the reason is that they suffer from hepatitis C,' he said. 'The consequences of what happened then may be continuing to cause death even now.'

Langstaff said that estimated figures for the total number of victims 'go far beyond 25,000', and there was a real chance that these 'may prove right'.[9]

A memorial event to mark the start of the hearings was held at Church House, the home of the headquarters of the Church of England, occupying the south end of Dean's Yard next to Westminster Abbey in London. Many of the campaigners featured in this book were present.

A choir sang as those affected by the scandal lined up to place glass phials carrying messages about those they had lost on medical-style laboratory racks in front of the stage.

The commemoration opened with a video sequence of pictures of the victims and their families, accompanied by Emeli Sandé's song 'Read All About It (Part III)', which contains the lines: 'You've spent a lifetime stuck in silence . . . So put it in all of the papers, I'm not afraid / They can read all about it, read all about it.'

A succession of unnamed victims then recounted in

short, prerecorded statements how they and their loved ones had contracted HIV, hepatitis C and other potentially fatal viruses from blood and plasma transfusions, mainly in the 1970s and 1980s.

One woman said: 'Every time I shut my eyes, I was looking at a coffin. I was sure I was going to die.'

Another victim said: 'It wrecked my marriage. It had a serious impact on my career.'

A man said: 'I was told I had two or three years to live: "Go away and make your will." Every day, I have to take a toxic combination of pills just to stay alive. I lost my job, I nearly lost my wife, and we have had to live on the breadline.'[10]

Closing the preliminary hearing, Langstaff said: 'These three days [of hearings] have made this scandal visible . . . This inquiry has shown a spirit of enthusiasm, cooperation and togetherness. Rest assured that tomorrow morning, I will be hard at work . . . and we shall stay hard at work until the job is done.'[11]

•

It was a day I believed would never come; a fantasy that only ever played out in my daydreams.

For almost two decades, I had been covering the contaminated blood scandal and working with the campaigners to expose the worst treatment disaster in NHS history.

For almost two decades, it felt like we had been howling into the wind while those affected, many of them already facing terminal illness, suffered the indignity of being forced into financial hardship, while all the time being ignored and stonewalled by the authorities who had caused their suffering in the first place.

But on a bright spring morning on 30 April 2019, our wish came true as the Infected Blood Inquiry opened its doors for the first time.

Finally, the stories of the campaigners, the brave men and women whose lives had been shattered by an entirely avoidable tragedy, would be heard. And finally, their insatiable quest for answers and justice would be realised.

Even as I awoke that morning and turned on the radio, it was clear the world had changed.

The contaminated blood scandal, a saga that had often been relegated to the backwaters of the news pages, despite being championed by a small handful of dogged MPs, lawyers and campaigning journalists, was leading the news bulletin on Radio 4's *Today* programme.

I had always planned to attend the first day of evidence at Fleetbank House, in central London. What I had not bargained for was how nervous I would feel. The campaign had already taken so many twists and turns along the way. There had been a few highs and many lows; hopes raised and hopes dashed.

We had campaigned for so long. Now the public inquiry was about to begin, and the stakes felt so high it was almost overwhelming.

If we didn't see justice this time, it felt unlikely that we ever would.

As I arrived at Fleetbank House, dozens of cameras were poised, ready to interview those who had gathered inside to deliver their testimonies. Almost every major news network was represented, as the story made it on to the primetime news slots for the first time. Finally, the world seemed ready to listen.

In an opening statement to the inquiry, Langstaff said

he had already read a large number of the witness state-ments from those infected or affected by the NHS blood, statements that he described as 'harrowing' and 'chillingly factual'. He added that making a statement for some people will be an 'act of bravery', with the possibility of stirring up 'distressing' memories.

Langstaff said the six principles of his inquiry were about 'putting people at its heart; being as quick as reasonable thoroughness permits; paying proper respect to a person's right to be heard; being as open and transparent as is legally possible to be; being independent of government; and [being] frightened of no one in the conclusions it draws'.[12]

They were words that the campaigners had waited dec-ades to hear.

Let down so many times by a recalcitrant state, trust in the establishment had, until then, been almost non-existent among the campaigners. But Langstaff immediately got off on the right foot. He has since come to be regarded with huge respect by virtually all those who have come before him.

The first witness to speak to the inquiry was given a standing ovation following his emotional evidence, during which he described being diagnosed with HIV and then losing his brother to AIDS.

Derek Martindale, who told the inquiry he was a severe haemophiliac, had been infected with HIV and hepatitis C through receiving blood products riddled with the diseases. He said he was twenty-three when he was diagnosed with HIV in 1985, and was given one year to live. Martindale said he had been told not to tell anyone, not even his family. He told the inquiry: 'When you're young, you are invincible; when you're twenty-three and generally fit, but then you are told you have twelve months to live – it's very hard to comprehend, so there was fear. There was no future, the likelihood of getting married or having children was very unlikely.'[13]

By the lunchbreak, the mood was sombre, but there was also a whiff of hope in the air. A hardcore group of campaigners, including Sue Threakall and Su Gorman, who were at the time running the Tainted Blood group, had travelled to London for the first week of hearings. Although I had spoken to them often during the course of the campaign, in most cases, it was the first time we had ever met in person. We hugged and chatted over plates of complimentary sandwiches and cups of tea. Tears were shed as we reflected on those members of the campaign group who had not lived long enough to see this day.

It did not feel like we were strangers. We had long since become a community, a family of sorts, united by one goal: to see justice finally delivered.

The inquiry has since taken evidence, either in the form of written statements or oral testimony – or both, in some cases – from at least 200 people involved in the scandal, including leading clinicians and scientists. It has held hearings in Belfast, Leeds, Cardiff, Edinburgh and London.

Among those to give evidence were the brave campaigners whose stories have been told in the pages of this book, including Nick Sainsbury, Ade Goodyear, Clair Walton, John Cornes, Mick Mason, Glenn Wilkinson and Colin and Jan Smith.

Other witnesses included civil servants, ministers and two former prime ministers. One gaping hole was evidence from the leading doctors of the time. They were the clinicians who decided to administer the dangerous blood products and conducted secret medical trials on innocent haemophiliacs. It seemed very odd to me that none of them were called to account for their actions, especially given some of the more questionable decisions they took: decisions that ultimately cost people their lives.

For some, it was already too late. Professor Arthur Bloom had died in 1992, aged sixty-two. But Bloom's ally, Dr Charles Rizza, the former director of the Oxford Haemophilia Centre, was allowed to submit a bland, two-page written statement and was not called to give evidence. He died in July 2022, at the age of ninety-three. Peter Jones, the former director of the Newcastle Haemophilia Centre, submitted more substantial written statements, but again was not called to give oral evidence. Jones at the time of writing is eighty-two. It is understood that he and Rizza were considered too old to be called on to give oral evidence, and that the events about which they may have been questioned happened so long ago they could not be relied upon as credible witnesses.

In his statement to the Infected Blood Inquiry, Jones defended his actions, claiming that he only used licensed products. He also repeatedly insisted that he only used commercial products because of the shortage of NHS blood products. In addition, he claimed that patients were given all the available information at the time and denied that those infected with HIV were told to keep it a secret. Jones also claimed that no research was carried out without ethical approval and insisted that he did tell patients who were being treated with factor concentrates that they were inevitably likely to be infected with non A non B hepatitis (now known as hepatitis C). And he claimed to have told those who were being treated with factor concentrates that a substantial proportion of them could go on to develop chronic liver disease.[14]

Beyond the doctors, much of the evidence was harrowing. All of it has been illuminating. Some of the most memorable evidence came from politicians, including the testimony of Jeremy Hunt, the former health secretary.

In an astonishingly frank cross-examination, he told the inquiry that institutions and the state can sometimes 'close ranks around a lie', and that it could be seen as a 'huge failing of democracy' that the victims had waited so long for justice.[15]

Hunt, like all the elected politicians involved in the scandal, said he had been misled by civil servants. He was asked by Jenni Richards, QC, counsel to the inquiry, whether a 2012 briefing for new ministers in the Department of Health – which he claimed 'almost certainly' was not shown to him at the time – stated that the contamination of Britain's blood supply had been an 'unavoidable problem'. Under a heading 'Key facts', the paper claimed that hepatitis C and HIV infection had been a problem in the 1970s and 1980s, 'before it was possible to screen donors and make products safer'.

Hunt, who was health secretary for six years until July 2018, replied: 'That briefing is wrong, and it shouldn't say that. At the very least, ministers should be aware as politicians that this is contentious and disputed by families – but I'm afraid it tries to suggest the issue is closed when it is not.'

Hunt described a situation in the civil service and government where 'people collectively try and remember things as they would like them to have been, rather than as they actually were.' He said the language used in documents suggested an 'institutional closing of ranks' that tried to protect people perceived to be 'doing the right thing'.[16]

Hunt also paid tribute to campaigners and families of those infected, including his constituent Mike Dorricott, whose story was shared in Chapter 7.

'In some ways, you could look at this as a huge failing of our democracy, that it's taken so long to resolve this issue,' Hunt said. 'In another way, the families and campaigners, including Mike, were entirely responsible for justice being done in the end, by the way they campaigned, by the way they put pressure on all of us in Parliament and created that moment in which the public inquiry should happen.'[17]

While Hunt's evidence was welcomed by campaigners, not every politician has received a warm reception – most notably Ken Clarke, the former health minister during the advent of the AIDS crisis. The Tory grandee was heavily criticised for displaying 'contempt' in his evidence after he showed a reluctance to answer questions.

Clarke, who was a Conservative health minister from 1982 to 1985, and health secretary from 1988 to 1990, appeared to become irritated with the level of detail he was asked to recall when he was being examined by the lead counsel. At one point, he asked: 'Why do we have to go through such meticulous detail through who said what and when, when did he change his mind?' He added that it was 'interesting' but 'pretty pointless'.

Further protestations from Clarke even led Langstaff to slap him down. The retired judge told Clarke that it was for the chair of the inquiry to 'ultimately determine' what questions were relevant. Langstaff said: 'If I think the questions are unhelpful, then I will indicate that. But at the moment, it would be helpful to me, I think, and we may get on a little bit more quickly, if we just deal with the questions as they come and leave the motive or the purpose of asking the questions to counsel.'[18]

Earlier, Clarke had said he was not responsible for blood products during the early days of the infected blood scandal, despite being a health minister at the time. He said he was dealing with policies such as closing 'old Victorian asylums' or getting rid of 'old geriatric hospitals'. However, he did admit that he believed there was a 'strong possibility' blood had been infected with AIDS, despite famously telling the public at the time that there was 'no conclusive proof'. Clarke was asked whether he was being 'straightforward and candid with the public' as he was 'not acknowledging the likely causal connection between AIDS and blood products'.

Clarke responded: 'The line did not say "blood products don't cause AIDS". That would be quite wrong and inaccurate and untrue. In my opinion, if you give the ordinary meaning of the words "there's no conclusive proof", and if you look at the sentence as rounded, it's quite clear we're saying there's a strong possibility at least that it causes AIDS, but there is at the moment no conclusive proof.

'I used it, but it's not my medical opinion. I'm using the English language. That is clearly what the department was saying. I'm convinced that was the collective view of the scientific experts in the department and those they consulted outside.'

When asked by lead counsel if he was not being less than 'candid' with the public, he said: 'Most definitely not. It's an absurd tabloid newspaper spin you're putting on it.'[19]

Dr Diana Walford, who served as the principal medical officer from 1979 to 1983 before holding other senior roles in the DHSS, said that doctors at the time 'really didn't want to accept there was a safety issue' with the blood products used to treat their patients.

She told the inquiry: 'They didn't want to accept that there was a genuine issue here – a safety issue. They felt that we were going to, in some way, circumscribe their ability to prescribe and that was never the intention. It was a sort of travesty of what we were trying to do.'

Dr Walford was shown a letter in which she was described as saying 'the value of factor concentrates to severe haemophiliacs far outweigh the possible, and as yet unproven hazards of transmission of [AIDS]'.

She said she would defend that position then, adding: 'I still think now – of course I now know about AIDS and its terrible consequences – but I still believe that, at that time, the hazards were unproven of transmission, and basically what one knew was that the severe haemophiliacs desperately needed factor VIII or factor IX.'[20]

John Major, the former prime minister, also incurred the wrath of campaigners after he said those affected had 'incredibly bad luck'. He suggested that no amount of money could have offered true compensation for what happened, which triggered gasps from those victims present at the inquiry, who felt Major clearly had no idea of the impoverished circumstances forced upon those lucky enough to survive.[21]

Another former prime minister, David Cameron, also gave a written statement to the inquiry explaining how he had personally intervened to increase a financial package of support for the victims from £25 million to £125 million. He also set out why he blocked a public inquiry, insisting that he believed his efforts were better focused on providing additional monetary support.[22]

Perhaps surprisingly, Theresa May, the prime minister who finally gave the victims a public inquiry, was not called to give evidence. However, she agreed to speak to me.

•

There was no lightbulb moment for Theresa May when she decided to announce the inquiry. Instead, the former prime minister claims it was a 'gradual realisation' of the significance of what had happened in the late 1970s and 1980s. 'In Parliament, MPs will be standing up raising issues of concern with you and you hear so many different things,' she told me. 'You can't alight on everything. But sometimes if something's repeated and repeated, and then you start to see the . . . evidence and then it . . . dawns on you exactly what lies behind this.'

May had not had any victims in her constituency and was unfamiliar with the details of the scandal when she entered Downing Street. However, the more she learned about the issues as they rose up the political agenda, the more she started to smell a rat. As home secretary and prime minister, May had set up inquiries into child abuse, the Grenfell Tower fire, and the conduct of undercover police. She also established an independent review into the unsolved murder in 1987 of Daniel Morgan, a private detective who was killed amid claims of police corruption. The common theme that ran through all these inquiries like letters through a stick of rock was that they involved an arm of the recalcitrant state. Speaking in her spacious corner office in Portcullis House, May told me that it was her experience of some of these cases that led her to ask more questions about the scandal.

'It was, in a sense, another example of a bit of the public sector that just shut its doors when there was a problem . . .

and . . . refused to accept that anything had gone wrong, in the hope that it would go away. It was also clear that no one was really thinking about the impact on the people who has been affected by it.'

Speaking about her involvement with the Hillsborough panel, the child abuse inquiry and the Morgan review, May added: 'There were a number of things where I just came up against the system saying "no". And it's difficult to explain, but sometimes it's just a gut feeling that there's just something there that genuinely does need to be properly investigated.

'The problem is with the public sector. I think the Department of Health has been particularly guilty of this over time, because we saw it with vaginal mesh implants, pregnancy test Primodos and epilepsy drug sodium valproate cases . . . there is this sense of it wanting to defend itself . . . rather than thinking about the people that it's supposed to be serving. And it seemed to me that this was yet another example of that.'

May's initial dealings with the Department of Health on the issue proved frustrating. In the end, she concluded it was being 'deliberately difficult'.

She told me: 'As I was interacting with the department, I got to the point where I thought, well, hang on a minute. No. There is something here and they're just being awkward, and they're doing the general thing of defending the institution. And you see it time and time again. You saw it at Hillsborough, you saw it in all the cases of child sexual abuse, you know, in . . . children's homes, the local authority involvement, church involvement . . . et cetera. People had a greater interest in defending the institution than they did in actually getting to the bottom of the truth of what had happened. And so it was just like gradual realisation that here was another case . . . of the intransigence of the department.'

She added: 'I guess I just had that perhaps not consciously, but subconsciously – that sort of sense that there were issues on which the public sector needed to be held to account.'

May said that civil servants can often tell ministers what they think they want to hear. She said: 'I said it when I became chairman of education at Merton Council, and I said it to the permanent secretary when I went into the Home Office – don't try to bring me the evidence for the answer you think I want to have. What you owe me is your best possible fact-proofing of facts. Your best advice. And I'll listen to those facts and advice on the back of that. I then take the political decision. So, it's up to me whether I listen to that. I might challenge it and ask for more, or whatever. But don't try to second-guess what you think I want as the answer.'

May said some of the resistance she met from the department was around concerns about costs, and fears that any moves towards compensating the victims would open the floodgates to other causes.

'Sometimes there's a concern that if they accept . . . that mistakes were made and that this is going to lead to compensation . . . it will open up other cases and therefore there are going to be huge economic costs down the line,' she said.

May claims she had been thinking about launching a public inquiry for some time before she announced it. She does not believe it came about because pressure was exerted on her by the DUP, or by the threat of litigation led by Des Collins, the maverick senior partner at Collins Solicitors, who represents more than 1,500 families infected and affected by the contaminated blood scandal. May is renowned for having a strong moral compass; however, I find it unlikely that the timing of the announcement was a complete coincidence. It is possible that the political pressure exerted upon her pushed open a door that was already ajar.

However, she told me emphatically: 'I think as PM, I was clear that it needed to be done. It shouldn't have taken so long . . . I don't want to take credit for it, because so many people have been involved over the years. It was down to those who campaigned over the years and . . . kept the issue at the forefront of people's minds. Journalists like yourself, and MPs like Diana Johnson and Alistair Burt . . .'

May recalled the meetings she had with Johnson and Cabinet Office officials about the arrangements for the inquiry and who would lead it. She said: 'What was imperative was that the people affected actually were willing to accept the inquiry, and the way that it was set up. That's why those meetings, I think, were so important. Because [these are] the people . . . for whom this is being done, to try to provide them with that closure, that . . . greater sense of justice, and . . . if they walk away from it, then obviously it's sort of dead in the water. So, building that relationship was [very] important.'

The former prime minister is hopeful that the families affected will get the recognition they deserve from the inquiry. Speaking just weeks before the final submissions were made to the inquiry, she said: 'There is a sense that often, for a lot of people, it is the recognition of what has happened that is important. It's about being able to raise their voice and somebody listening to it, and not just dismissing it . . . But then somebody acknowledging the mistakes. So . . . something that actually sort of says: you weren't a group of people that were shouting about something that was nothing. You're a group of people who've been horrendously affected by this. And sadly, there are not so many of you today, because of the impact. So, for me, first of all, it's about recognising the severity of the issue. And then looking at the mistakes that government made, and how those mistakes came about. And although it's all a while back now, I'm sure there will be important lessons to be learned.'

May believes that one change that could be made to help families like those embroiled in the contaminated blood scandal is the creation of a public advocate. She is working with Labour MP Maria Eagle, the former justice minister, on the initiative.

She said: 'It would mean that if something happens, like Hillsborough, like Grenfell, potentially like discovering something on contaminated blood, that there is somebody there who victims and survivors and families will be able to go to, if they wish to, to help them get through the system. To help them get to the truth. And I think that is . . . important.' She also believes such a system would help expedite the process, meaning that families will not be left in limbo for decades, as they have in the contaminated blood scandal, for justice to be delivered. 'It shouldn't take that long,' she told me. 'And that's partly the idea with the independent public advocate . . . that they would be able to help families, if they wanted to have that help. Help them . . . get through the system and get to the truth . . . at a much earlier stage. So, they weren't having to fight for years and years and decades and decades.'

Despite suggestions from Andy Burnham that there may be a case for charges of corporate manslaughter in relation to individuals involved in the contaminated blood scandal, May is more sceptical. Expressing a view that may disappoint some campaigners who are desperate to see those responsible punished, the former prime minister said: 'I think if you look at Hillsborough, obviously Dave Duckenfield, who was the superintendent in charge, [and] made the decision in terms of opening the gates, is the one who was particularly in people's line of sight. But there have been court cases against him and he's not been found guilty. And the only . . . charges that have led to a prosecution were on health and safety. And so, even at Hillsborough, where, if you like, there were individuals who could be identified, it hasn't been possible.'

I asked if she thought it was unlikely that any individual would face prosecution in relation to the contaminated blood scandal. May responded: 'If I'm honest, yes. I think it is unlikely blame will be apportioned.'

•

Even as the inquiry was underway, one minister was working hard behind the scenes to shift the dial on Whitehall's attitude towards compensation.

Penny Mordaunt, who was paymaster general between 2020 and 2021, was determined to ensure that no time would be lost in compensating the victims once Langstaff published the findings of his inquiry. Mordaunt, a little-known hero of the campaign, was responsible for persuading officials that a compensation package for victims did not have to be put in the 'too-difficult-to-do box'.

It was March 2021 when I discovered that she was drawing up plans to set up an independent review to examine proposals for a compensation scheme. It was, for me, a breakthrough moment, because the very existence of such plans was the first ever admission of culpability by the government. Unlike the earlier support given to victims in the form of ex-gratia payments, the proposals under consideration were for compensation.

The news, which I reported in *The Sunday Times* on 21 March 2021, was welcomed by Clive Smith, chairman of the Haemophilia Society. He told me: 'Setting up a compensation framework is the closest any UK Government has ever come to admitting liability for the contaminated blood scandal, and the significance of this moment for our community cannot be overstated.'[23]

The following week, Mordaunt announced that she had commissioned a review by Sir Robert Francis, KC, on a compensation framework. By May 2022, it appeared more good news was on the way. I had seen a Cabinet Office document circulated to ministers that suggested the government was preparing to accept there was a 'strong moral case' for compensation. Francis published the findings of his review in June of the same year. In the report, he suggested thousands of people should receive minimum payments of £100,000 each.

In his study, Francis said there is a compelling case for awarding interim payments as soon as possible, explaining: 'Many wish to be able to settle their affairs before they die. Challenging though it is to do this before the scheme has been set up and is fully operational, and before the conclusions of the [public] inquiry are available, I suggest that such a payment should be made now, reflecting the minimum any infected person could be expected to receive under the scheme. I have suggested this is unlikely to be less than £100,000 in any case.'

His report also recommended that victims should be compensated, among other things, for physical and social injury, stigma and social isolation, the cost of care and the loss of income. Crucially, it also recommended that partners, children, siblings and parents of infected people who suffered mental or physical consequences should be admitted to the compensation scheme.[24]

However, within weeks of his review being published, the government was plunged into turmoil with the resignation of Boris Johnson, who was forced to stand down following a series of sleaze scandals. With victims facing a potential summer of government inertia as Tory contenders jockeyed to replace Johnson, Langstaff took the unusual step of making a personal intervention. He recommended that victims of the contaminated blood scandal, or their bereaved partners, should receive at least £100,000 in compensation each 'without delay', saying: 'I am obliged to recognise that the practical way to make payments swiftly is to do so through the current infected blood support schemes. This is why I have decided to recommend that interim payments of no less than £100,000 are made to all infected people, and to all the bereaved partners currently registered with the schemes, and those who register between now and the inception of any future scheme.'[25]

Andy Burnham was also concerned at potential delays, and called on the outgoing prime minister Johnson to approve the payments immediately. 'Please, Prime Minister, do this today. Say you'll do it today; no one will disagree, every single Member of Parliament will support it, people have waited far, far too long.'[26]

On the same morning as he made his appeal, Burnham called me and asked me to ask the two Tory leadership candidates, Liz Truss and Rishi Sunak, to publicly back the calls for interim payments. Both agreed.

Sunak told *The Sunday Times*: 'The contaminated blood scandal is a tragic injustice and we must now match words with action, just as we did with those affected by the thalidomide scandal. Survivors and their families need to have certainty now, so I'd ensure the interim compensation payments recommended by Sir Brian Langstaff are made without delay.'

Truss said: 'They have waited long enough to get the compensation they need and deserve, so as prime minister, I will ensure interim payments are made as soon as possible.'[27]

With the pressure building on the government to act, I privately contacted Stephen Barclay, the health secretary, to urge him to intervene. He agreed to speak to the Cabinet Office and said he would 'push the issue'. We messaged several times over the course of the next few weeks, and in early August, Number 10 finally gave me the nod that Johnson was prepared to sign off on the money. A source told me: 'The prime minister strongly believes that all those who suffered so terribly as a result of this injustice should receive compensation as quickly as possible.'

The government made the announcement on 17 August 2021, and it was welcomed by campaigners, including Su Gorman of the campaign group Tainted Blood. Her husband, Steve Dymond, died at sixty-two of organ failure after being infected with hepatitis C via factor VIII blood products administered in 1976 – something he did not discover until twenty-one years later. Gorman described the payouts as a 'landmark', but told me it was shameful that it had taken more than forty years to deliver justice.

For some, the announcement came only just in time.

Barrie Dennis, who lived with his family in Stratford-upon-Avon in Warwickshire, was infected with hepatitis C after receiving contaminated blood products. He had Christmas disease, a form of haemophilia caused by deficiency of the blood-clotting factor IX rather than the more commonly deficient factor VIII.

Despite having an 'amazing sense of humour', his laughter had stopped in the last few months of his life, replaced by a gnawing anxiety that he would not live long enough to see the conclusion of the public inquiry into the tragedy that has blighted his life.

His wife, Debra, said: 'Barrie hasn't been himself for the past few months . . . He's more worried now than he's ever been. He's told me he won't make the end of the inquiry. He says he knows his own body and doesn't think he has long left.'

She told me that receiving compensation while Barrie was still alive would make all the difference to her family.

'It would just mean that we wouldn't have to worry,' she said. 'I wouldn't have to work so much, and we could spend what time we have left together. More importantly, it would give him peace of mind that he had left me with some kind of financial security.'

Barrie died on 21 August 2022 – just four days after he became eligible for the £100,000 interim payment. Debra told me she believes he died peacefully, knowing she was going to be looked after.

However, the announcement did not please everyone, and led to divisions within the campaign, with some believing that the group who benefited was too narrow and that the payment should also have gone to other groups, including orphans and parents who had lost children. There were also concerns that the interim payments would delay compensation for the other groups, including orphans and widows.

The government promised to publish a response to Sir Robert Francis's nineteen recommendations, but has so far failed to do so, causing yet further anguish to the victims.

Acknowledging the difficulty successive governments have faced in their efforts to grapple with the issue, Steve Barclay, the current health secretary, compared the contaminated blood scandal to a 'derelict building'.

In an interview for this book in the winter of 2022, ahead of the conclusion of the inquiry, he said: 'The derelict building syndrome is where you get used to a building being derelict and it's never quite the right time to fix it. There are other priorities that accumulate. And before you know it, it's been derelict for twenty years.'

Barclay was determined not to ignore the issue when it landed on his plate when he first took over as health secretary in July 2022 – a strange twilight zone for the UK Government after Boris Johnson had announced his resignation and was serving as caretaker prime minister while his successor was chosen. Speaking in a meeting room in the Department of Health, he told me: 'One of the things I was worried about in the summer was there was quite a strong narrative saying the government had gone to sleep. Linked to that, Whitehall was very vigorously enforcing the Cabinet decision that the prime minister shouldn't have any new policies. So, the agreement had been that nothing major would be entered into by the PM.

'I felt that was being, to some extent, gold-plated, almost to the point that the PM shouldn't be making any policy decisions. Which wasn't realistic, given that he was still going to be in [place] for a further two months. So, this was the context . . . when I got in touch with Boris [Johnson] . . . to say, look – if you're being told you can't make new policy decisions, well, actually, contaminated blood isn't new. You're within scope to be able to act.'

Barclay claims his concern was that if the announcement was not signed off before Johnson left Downing Street, the payments would be delayed. 'The attraction was that it was unfinished business . . . And having been his chief of staff, obviously, I think he knew that I was coming at it constructively: "There is a pressing issue in terms of people dying each week. And this is a process you've set up. Therefore, can we get it over the line?" And they accepted that argument. In terms of what comes next, they will have to look at it in the round . . . I think what the journey to date shows is there is a genuine issue that needs to be addressed.'

Moving forwards, Barclay wants to help draw a line under the scandal. 'I think it should be the job of the Secretary of State to try and put it to bed.' He also wants to see the introduction of much greater transparency to counter claims of cover-up and ensure 'the bad stuff' comes out. He believes the lack of transparency is often where things have gone wrong, and that issues are not identified quickly enough, which has 'led to a big scandal'. Barclay also wants to see more focus on personalised care and screening to spot the next AIDS-like epidemic before it hits. He recently visited Kings Hospital, where they screen patients' blood for HIV and hepatitis B and C when they are admitted. He believes this is something that can ultimately be rolled out nationwide with a national screening centre, like the one used during Covid at Rosalind Franklin Laboratory in Leamington Spa, Warwickshire.

The health secretary is also in favour of erecting a memorial to those victims who died as a result of the scandal. He told me: 'Where there's been huge personal tragedy, then I think the country's got a long history of recognising that. So, I think as part of the grieving process, having memorials is part of our DNA, really. It's part of the mourning process, isn't it? I think it needs to be done very sensitively and in a way there's probably people better placed than me to do that, because when you're dealing with human loss, it mustn't be a party political football.'

•

Little Colin Smith was just seven years old when he finally took his last breath and succumbed to the disease that had taken over his achingly fragile body. His death was both a tragedy and a blessed relief for his family, who had watched him transform from a bouncing baby boy into an emaciated skeleton, often too weak to even lift his own head and limbs.

Colin was the baby of the family, a beautiful blond cherub, the youngest of four sons. Unusually, given that the condition runs in the family, he was the only one of the Smith boys to be diagnosed as a haemophiliac.

The bleeding disorder was first discovered when he was four months old. Colin's aunt found a bruise on his knee as she changed his nappy, and correctly diagnosed the condition. He was a severe haemophiliac, and his parents were convinced to transfer his care from the Royal Gwent Hospital, close to their home in Newport, to Heath Hospital in Cardiff, under the care of Professor Arthur Bloom. It was a decision the family would later come to bitterly regret.

Bloom has since fallen into disgrace. University Hospital

of Wales in Cardiff, as it has since become known, removed a bust of the haemophilia expert shortly after Colin's parents gave evidence to the inquiry in July 2019.

His name has repeatedly cropped up during the Infected Blood Inquiry. Relatives of those infected have accused Bloom of keeping secret the risks of treating his patients with imported blood products. He also conducted trials of dangerous blood products on previously untreated patients (PUPs) without their consent.

In their evidence to the inquiry, Colin's parents shared their son's medical notes, which confirm that he was used as a guinea pig. They reveal that when he first came into Bloom's care as a baby, he had never received any kind of treatment for his condition. Indeed, the words 'not treated' were underlined in his clinical notes dated 21 July 1983. His nursing notes show that the very next day he was given his first dose of factor VIII.

A letter from Bloom to Colin's GP, dated 3 August 1983, recorded his treatment. It stated:

> I saw Colin in the clinic again this week. I understand that he turned up in the paediatric ward about a week ago having fallen down and hit the back of his head.
>
> He received an intravenous injection of one bottle of 250 units of factor VIII concentrate and made an uneventful recovery without any evidence of intercranial bleeding.
>
> The concentrate which we used was prepared from British blood from the Lister Institute. However, all these materials carry the risk of hepatitis, particularly non-A non-B [the name for hepatitis C at the time], but this is something that haemophiliacs have to accept.[28]

However, Colin's parents were never told that there was a risk of hepatitis C transmission. What is even more outrageous is that one month prior to Colin being injected with factor VIII, Bloom and other haemophilia centre directors in the UK had agreed that children should only be treated with cryoprecipitate because of the risk of AIDS.* The decision was made in response to reports that the first haemophiliac in the UK had been infected with HIV. In a letter dated 24 June 1983, Bloom and Charles Rizza, of the Oxford Haemophilia Centre, refer to a meeting that took place on 13 May 1983. They state: 'For treatment of children and mildly affected patients or patients unexposed to imported concentrates, many directors already reserve supplies of NHS concentrates (cryoprecipitate or freeze-dried) and it would be circumspect to continue this policy.'[29]

If this was Bloom's official position, what on earth had he been doing with Colin?

The Smiths were also left in the dark over the risks posed by HIV. They were never informed about the difference between the different types of products.

'It was never spoken about,' Jan told the inquiry. 'We just believed the doctor. You know, they were treating Colin, and it sounds terrible, but he was like a god to us, Prof Bloom, because he was looking after my son. So why would

---

* When asked for comment on Bloom giving Colin Smith factor VIII, even when there had been a directive not to give children factor VIII after the advent of AIDS, a spokesperson for Cardiff and Vale University Health Board said: 'In the interest of confidentiality, the Health Board is unable to comment on the care of individual patient cases and the treatment they received. However, as an organisation, we are committed to an open and transparent approach, and we have fully co-operated with the Inquiry at all stages, including those related to the patient case referenced; details of which are yet to be released by the Inquiry.'

I ask any questions about [it]? We thought he was getting the best treatment possible.'[30]

Colin believes his son was a PUP. 'There is no doubt they treated and tested him for the purposes of research as they could have seen him as an easy target,' he claimed. 'He was just unlucky enough to be diagnosed with haemophilia at the same time as these trials were starting.'[31]

Jan is also convinced her son was a guinea pig. The first time we spoke, when the family threw their support behind the *Sunday Express* campaign, she told me: 'The devastating thing is that he didn't even need factor VIII. It was also a product that was never supposed to have been given to children under a certain age, so he should never have been given it in the first place.'[32]

According to his parents, Colin also regularly had his blood tested without their consent. They even found a letter to a pharmaceutical company saying the hospital was no longer able to send any more samples of his blood after they withdrew him from treatment close to the end of his life. 'We were just told they were checking his blood count,' his father said.[33]

Colin's parents were told the devastating news that he had been infected with HIV in 1984 when he was just two years old and being treated in hospital for a chest infection. When the couple were approached by Bloom in the corridor outside their son's ward, they had no forewarning that their lives were about to change forever, as they had not even been informed that Colin was being tested.

Jan recalled: 'Bloom came down to see him and then called us out and then just told us that he's HIV [positive], in the corridor, with children running around and other parents . . . but we still didn't comprehend what that meant to us, because it had never been discussed. Nobody had told us what HIV was.'[34]

Many of their questions remained unanswered, and nobody informed them of the risk to their three older sons, Darren, Patrick and Daniel. The couple only began to realise how serious the condition was when Colin had a serious nosebleed while sharing a bed with Daniel.

Jan told me: 'We called the hospital. They asked whether any of the blood had got on to Daniel, and told us that we must burn the mattress – so they knew the risks, but nobody ever told us.'

It wasn't until the advent of Norman Fowler's 'Don't Die of Ignorance' public health campaign in 1986 that the severity of Colin's illness began to sink in. It was also at this time, when the family was most in need of support, that their community turned their back on them as the panic around the 'gay plague' reached fever pitch.

'Those adverts were devastating. They destroyed a lot of people,' recalled Jan. 'We started getting "AIDS dead" written on the house – not little letters, six-foot letters on the side of the house, crosses on the door, the car vandalised, people going across the street from us, you know, threatening to take their children out of school if Colin went there. It was devastating.'[35]

Colin's dad said he made the mistake of telling a family friend about their son's condition, and before long, everybody knew. He remembered getting up one morning in the dark to paint the front door after someone daubed it with the words "AIDS dead".

'The boys come out and asked what I was doing, so I just said, "Your Mum didn't like the colour," and they accepted that,' he recalled. 'Then "AIDS dead" [was] scratched on the car. Constant phone calls day and night – he [Colin] should be put down, put on an island, shouldn't be allowed to sleep with his brothers. It just went on and on.'[36]

Smith, who had previously served in the armed forces, even lost his job because his boss was scared of losing customers if they found out about Colin's illness. He was told by the Job Centre that he was unemployable, and told to sign on until the week after Colin died, when he was advised to get a job. However, throughout most of the abuse, which eventually led to the family moving home, little Colin was oblivious to the turmoil.

His dad recalled: 'Colin was Colin; he just went round the house destroying stuff . . .'[37]

Colin was eventually put on AZT, the revolutionary AIDS treatment, which Bloom told his family could save his life. The drug would prove controversial in its early years of use, as it was often given in copious quantities, leading to further health problems.

It was at this stage his health began to deteriorate. Jan reflected: 'I can remember going to a meeting and somebody just pointed a finger at me and said, "Get him off it, you're killing him," and I think they were right.'

By now, Colin was starting to lose weight and have complications with his chest. He was also spending more and more time in hospital. His parents only learned after his death that during this period he had been treated for pneumonia twice and once for suspected meningitis.

'We took him to the hospital . . . and I said to Prof [Bloom] that . . . he was complaining of chest pains, and he just looked at me, smiled and said, "He's got a good imagination, that kid." That's what he told me, and he had pneumonia twice, but we were never, ever told that. We only saw that when it was in his records.'[38]

Despite growing increasingly frail, Colin still had a zest for life. His dad remembered: 'He loved driving, so we'd sit in the car park and drive him round on my lap. He'd do the steering; I'd do the pedals. We got stopped one night by the police going to the hospital, and they gave us an escort and my car blew up on the way home because they went faster than I did. But he just loved . . . life.'[39]

By now, it was clear that Colin knew he was dying, but his parents claim he never complained or asked what was going to happen to him. Instead, he would express himself through his drawings, which were often of crosses and headstones. His brother Daniel, who stayed with him at the hospital during the last months of his life, remembered getting into an argument with Colin, as the end drew nearer.

'I said to him, "I will break your Lego," and he said, "Do not do that, you will miss me when I'm gone."' He added: 'My grandmother passed away six months before Colin. He [Colin] mentioned that he was not scared of death. He said he knew he was going to see her, and she passed away to be there for him and did not want to suffer any more pain.'[40]

His parents only knew that their son was dying when Professor Bloom objected to them taking Colin home from hospital a week before Christmas in 1989, telling them that he 'had to die in hospital because there were no undertakers that would take an AIDS patient'.

The family ignored the advice and on the morning of 19 December they unhooked Colin's drips and carried him out of the hospital.

Colin's death certificate recorded the cause of death as a) PCP pneumonia and b) AIDS due to contaminated factor VIII infusion and c) haemophilia. He was one of around 380 children with haemophilia and other blood disorders to die of AIDS. Shockingly, this means that almost one in every three people infected with HIV through contaminated NHS blood products in the 1970s and 1980s was a child.

After his death, the family even had to battle to get the burial they wanted for their son. 'We wanted somewhere to go to remember him,' Jan told me. 'The hospital was adamant he must be cremated, but we stood our ground and finally found a sympathetic vicar to perform the service.'[41]

The cemetery close to their home in Newport is where Colin now rests.

The couple admit that in the aftermath of Colin's death, their lives fell apart, and it nearly ended their marriage.

'When Colin died, we couldn't talk about it,' recalled Jan. 'If I went into the room, [my husband] would walk out, or vice versa. There was just this silence. The kids were walking on eggshells and it was horrendous, and it all came to a head . . . the first Christmas that we didn't have Colin . . . I can remember arguing, and I picked up a bottle of drink – I don't drink, I'm literally teetotal – and was going out of the house. I was going to get in the car, drink it and just crash into a wall . . . and my other kids were screaming, "Mummy, mummy, don't go, don't go, please," and that brought me back. It brought us back . . . because we realised then those kids needed us.'[42]

Colin's father admitted he felt suicidal and would frequently visit his son's grave at the cemetery, where he would 'rant and rave'. He reflected: 'I've seen a lot of death in my life, when I was in the forces, in the Troubles – violent and

other. With training, you can handle that. There's no training for what was about to be dropped on us, with what
happened to Colin. There's no way that a child should have
to die the way he did.' He added: 'I could cope with death,
but not with the death of my son. I still have trouble today
[with] the fact that he's in a grave on his own, and the guilt
will never go away.'[43]

His brother's death also had a profound effect on Daniel.
He kept Colin's things as a shrine to him and slept in his
clothes so he could smell him. When he got married, one of
Colin's trinkets was sewn into his wife's wedding dress, and
he had one of Colin's toy cars in his pocket.

The family still visit Colin's grave every week, and each
Christmas they take him a card or present. Although he has
been gone now for more than thirty years, he lives on in
their hearts.

'We talk about him every day,' said Jan. 'The grandkids,
they know who Colin is. They never met him, but they just
talk about him. It's just natural.'[44]

CONCLUSION

The last time I spoke to Nick Sainsbury he was weary. It was as if he knew the end was not far away. The previous few years of his life had been particularly challenging. The former Treloar's pupil had developed a love of travel from a young age and used the meagre amount of money he had saved to explore the world with friends. It gave him a sense of escapism after the trauma of being diagnosed with HIV and hepatitis C and being forced to live with the grim spectre of death never far away. Tragically, his last trip abroad would prove to be disastrous, and this had a deleterious effect on his already fragile mental and physical health.

In March 2020 – as the world was waking up to the threat of coronavirus – Nick and a friend arrived in Cape Verde, a volcanic island off the western coast of Africa, for a ten-day holiday. The pair had been looking forward to enjoying some sun, good food and relaxation.

On 16 March, Nick's friend developed symptoms of, and tested positive for, Covid. While he was taken to hospital, Nick was quarantined in his hotel room for five days, during which time he also developed symptoms of coronavirus. Not long afterwards, Nick tested positive. He was taken to hospital, where there was no Wi-Fi communication and the conditions left a lot to be desired, with cockroaches and power cuts. Nick's friend deteriorated and he had to be put on a ventilator. Efforts to save his life proved futile and he eventually died.

Nick was not told of his friend's death until the following morning. Astonishingly, such was the panic around Covid, the authorities in Cape Verde had already buried him. With the island in lockdown, and no commercial flights entering or leaving, Nick remained in isolation at the hospital until arrangements could be made to repatriate him back to the UK. The air ambulance bringing Nick home landed at Doncaster Airport on 27 March – just four days after Boris Johnson introduced the first national lockdown. The former civil servant, who was still in shock and grieving for his dead friend, went back to his home in Hull alone. Due to his underlying health conditions, he would spend much of the next year shielding from the deadly virus.

When I spoke to Nick about the ordeal, he admitted that he had been left heartbroken by his friend's death and lonelier than he had ever been. The emotional trauma seemed to have a physical impact on his severely weakened body. In the winter of 2021, Nick developed pneumonia and a heart infection, spending seven weeks in hospital. In January 2023, he was diagnosed with cancer in his right knee and had to undergo an operation to have the tumour removed. Speaking to me in April 2023, Nick described life as an endurance test. With his health in free fall, he feared he would not live long enough to see the end of the public inquiry. Sadly, he was proved correct. He died weeks later.

Though the Infected Blood Inquiry hearings ended in February 2023, the clock has not stopped ticking. Those who have been infected with deadly diseases are all anxiously awaiting the findings of the public inquiry, which are expected to be published in the autumn of 2023. But not all will live long enough to see justice served. Nick will not be the last to die before Sir Brian Langstaff, the judge leading the inquiry, delivers his report. As previously stated, it is estimated that one victim of the scandal dies every four days.

Langstaff seems acutely aware of the time pressure. In April 2023, he took the unusual step of urging the government to award interim compensation payments of £100,000 to parents and children who suffered bereavements as a result of the contaminated blood scandal. This was in addition to the interim payments awarded in October 2022 to infected individuals and their bereaved partners, which had been prompted by another intervention from Langstaff. In his second interim report, the judge called on the payments to be extended to 'recognise deaths to date unrecognised'. Langstaff said the victims and their families were living on 'borrowed time' as he demanded 'appropriate redress to all those who have been wronged,' adding: 'Time without redress is harm.'[1]

Giving a firm indication of his final conclusions, Langstaff said in his report: 'It is now accepted that wrongs have been done. The Government was absolutely right to accept this. My conclusion is that wrongs were done on individual, collective and systemic levels. Not only do the infections themselves and their consequences merit compensation, but so do the wrongs done by the way in which authority responded to what had happened.'[2] In a sign that the judge had grasped the wide-ranging features of the tragedy, Langstaff said that, in his opinion, compensation should cover all classes of victims, both direct and indirect. The judge said this should be extended to people whose careers suffered as a result of the care they had to provide to loved ones who were infected with deadly diseases.

While no one has definitive insight into the judge's thinking, campaigners believe Langstaff decided to publish his second interim report after growing deeply frustrated with the government yet again choosing to kick the can down the road. As we have seen, the government reneged on a commitment to publish a response to compensation proposals ahead of the conclusion of the inquiry. Sir Robert Francis, KC, delivered his report on compensation on 14 March 2022, but the government did not publish it until 7 June 2022. Campaigners were told that the reason for the delay was that the government would be publishing its response simultaneously. However, this never happened. At the time of writing Langstaff was preparing to exert yet further pressure on the government to release details of the compensation arrangements as it was announced that the Infected Blood Inquiry would be reconvening its public hearings in July 2023. It is understood that the purpose of the new hearings is to force ministers, including Cabinet Office minister Jeremy Quin, to explain the delay when some victims have such limited time left.

•

While compensation and the acceptance of liability is vital for the campaigners, it has never been their only priority. They also wanted an answer to the crucial question: How on earth could this tragedy have happened in the first place? There is no straightforward answer. But in the next few pages I will try to outline some of the factors that I believe are relevant to how the tragedy unfolded.

CONCLUSION

Self-sufficiency

It is my view that achieving self-sufficiency in blood products would have given Britain the best chance of stopping or limiting the impact of the impending disaster. It is worth considering that in Finland, where the decision was taken not to use factor concentrates until they had been heat-treated, only two haemophiliacs became infected with HIV. The case of Finland also shows that using disease-riddled factor VIII products was not essential, as many experts have claimed. It was a clinical choice not to continue using cryo-precipitate. And a catastrophic one at that.[3]

Had self-sufficiency been achieved, it is likely that the spread of AIDS through blood products could have been reduced. As Lord Fowler, the former health secretary, said in his evidence to the Infected Blood Inquiry: 'If David Owen's advice had been taken and we'd gone for self-sufficiency as a nation, then much of the ensuing tragedy, probably not all of it, but much of it, could have been avoided.'[4] Lord Morris, the president of the Haemophilia Society, said much the same when he addressed Parliament in March 2002. 'Self-sufficiency was not achieved as planned but this was not reported to Parliament, although failure to achieve it meant continued reliance on less safe imports,' he said. 'One is entitled to ask how many people with haemophilia could have been saved from life-threatening viral infection had the policy announced in Parliament been duly implemented?'[5]

Ken Clarke's false claim when health minister in November 1983 that there was 'no conclusive proof that AIDS was transmitted by blood products' was also extremely unhelpful and inevitably cost lives. With no information to the contrary, people continued to expose themselves to dangerous blood products while erroneously assuming them to be safe.

Underclass

For decades, the haemophilia community enjoyed a unique relationship with the medical establishment. It is my belief that those with chronic bleeds were treated as an underclass, or second-class citizens. Following centuries of haemophiliacs dying at such young ages, there was a sense of fatalism amongst clinicians about their life expectancy and potential quality of life. It was still believed among some within the UK medical community that haemophilia itself – and the risk of a fatal head bleed – was more dangerous than the risk of being infected with a deadly virus through contaminated blood products. This is a theory that some experts maintain to this day given that, before advances in treatment, the life expectancy of haemophiliacs was not much more than forty. As we saw in Chapter 4, Ade Goodyear's father, Bernard, was advised by one clinician in charge of his son's care that in his 'professional opinion, it would be best just to let the children with haemophilia go as it was a terrible condition to live with'.

In his evidence to the Infected Blood Inquiry, Lord Glenarthur, who was a junior health minister between 1983 and 1985, during the peak of the AIDS crisis, revealed how he felt he had no choice but to allow the continued import of American factor VIII because he feared haemophiliacs would die. He said: 'There seemed no practical alternative, other than to suddenly imperil the lives of haemophiliac patients.' In his oral evidence, he expanded: 'I understood that . . . bleeding intracranially and joints, the damage, and that sort of thing were the issues that arose. Untreated haemophiliacs . . . were in peril of dying . . . if things went badly wrong and that was what I was advised.'[6]

The inquiry also heard repeated evidence from the infected and affected of patients and their families being treated by clinicians in an unacceptably paternalistic manner, even by the standards of the 1970s and 1980s. Given the frequency of their visits to hospital, they often considered haematologists to be an extension of the family and their advice went almost completely unchallenged. Those who gave evidence, without exception, said that they would have preferred to have lived with their underlying condition, whether untreated or treated with safer products, such as cryoprecipitate, rather than run the risk of contracting deadly diseases through factor concentrates. Sue Threakall, who lost her husband, Bob, in 1991 after he contracted HIV, told the Infected Blood Inquiry: 'I am completely convinced that from the outset haemophiliacs were viewed as expendable. Not by all the doctors and certainly not by most of the nurses. But the UK Haemophilia Centre Directors' Organisation (UKHCDO), the unknown (as yet) civil servants, the pharmaceutical companies, and members of the British government (some still serving) truly have blood on their hands.' She added: 'Haemophiliacs in the early days were a compliant, finite, trusting group that was well used to hospitals, blood tests and so on. They readily co-operated with their doctors, believing them to be acting in their best interests. I make no apology for saying that the majority of our community are not like that now.'[7]

Guinea pigs

One of the most shocking revelations in the contaminated blood scandal is the extent to which those suffering from bleeding disorders became unwitting guinea pigs. Evidence presented to the Infected Blood Inquiry exposed a worryingly cosy relationship between haematologists and some of the pharmaceutical companies that were peddling factor VIII. This appears not too dissimilar to concerns raised about the strong links between the pharmaceutical companies and doctors in the recent lawsuits in the United States involving the Sackler family and the overprescription of addictive opioids, including OxyContin.

Treloar's school appears to have been the epicentre of a secret medical testing regime with little to no informed consent. The first suggestion that Treloar's would be used for medical trials emerged in correspondence in September 1967. The school warden said in a letter: 'There are nearly 40 haemophiliacs in the college, and we have long felt that they provide an opportunity for research, which should not be missed . . . The project has the enthusiastic support of the Haemophilia Society and will be carried out with the closest possible co-operation of the Oxford Haemophilia Centre, Medical Research Council Laboratory . . .'[8]

According to evidence presented to the Infected Blood Inquiry, the first of a series of hepatitis studies of haemophiliac boys took place between 1970 and 1973.[9] It is understood that these trials happened despite previously being rejected by other haemophilia centres on ethical grounds. The Infected Blood Inquiry identified countless examples of interactions between Treloar's and their pupils' home haemophilia centres about the trials but no records of any information being relayed to the children or their parents about it. Instead, the inquiry has seen evidence of a 'generic' consent form produced by Dr Aronstam, the director of the Haemophilia Centre at Treloar's, which does not identify any specific product, any risks, or any rights of the patient. There was little or no evidence suggesting the pupils, or their families, ever had any idea that they were the subjects of experiments. Such behaviour raises worrying ethical questions and flies in the face of the established practice of informed consent. Doctors are required to give patients all the information about their treatment, including the benefits and risks, whether there are alternatives and the consequences if the treatment does not go ahead.

Although I have chosen to focus on Treloar's, denying patients informed consent was a pattern of behaviour repeated by clinicians across the country. In Chapter 5, we saw that Clair Walton and Sue Threakall were advised to pursue their dream of having a baby – despite the risk of them being infected with AIDS by their partners. In other chapters, I have revealed how patients had their HIV and hepatitis C diagnoses withheld from them by doctors – in some instances for years. Campaigners have also complained about medical records being inexplicably altered or destroyed, leading many to conclude it was part of a cover-up by the medical establishment.

It is unclear what prompted this cavalier attitude towards medical ethics. Some campaigners have speculated that it was because the lives of haemophiliacs taking part in the trials were considered of less value than the general population because of their shortened life expectancy. Others think the answer is considerably more sinister. They believe the haemophilia community provided pharmaceutical companies with a lucrative supply of human guinea pigs to test their new products on. In return, they think, the doctors were rewarded handsomely with generous research grants, freebies, and possibly even hospitality and honorariums, though there is no evidence of this. Increasingly, campaigners believe the doctors involved not only broke the Hippocratic oath, but also the Nuremberg Code, which governs the research ethics for human experimentation.

Collins Solicitors, who are acting on behalf of more than 1,500 core and non-core participants in the inquiry, claim that many of those they are representing were shocked to hear that pharmaceutical companies were 'providing grants to the [Treloar's] college to fund research, with the acknowledgements in a written report including Armour Pharmaceutical for funding it'. They were also alarmed to learn that the company was 'involved in setting out the protocols for research being conducted' at the school in what amounts to a clear conflict of interest. The law firm also used their closing submission to point to minutes of a Cutter Laboratories board meeting in December 1980, which was 'looking at providing some form of official financial support for a research fellowship to Dr Aronstam'.[10] It is not known whether such a grant was ever made. Reflecting on his experience at Treloar's, Ade told the Infected Blood Inquiry: 'I believe that Treloar's was a "gift" of an establishment for pharmaceutical companies to try out their products whilst knowing little boys and young adults were being maimed and harmed en masse. The pharmaceutical companies left gifts, which the staff would give to us as incentives to take treatments and likewise when we behaved. It was positive reinforcement. We were even offered branded gifts such as chronograph watches, pyramid clocks, stationery kits (Bayer Filofax and pens), back packs and so on all branded with certain pharmaceutical company logos, mainly American. Looking back now, it was like being groomed by the "peddlers of death".'[11]

Human agency

One of the most startling statistics presented to the Infected Blood Inquiry was that almost one out of every three people infected with HIV through contaminated NHS blood products in the 1970s and 80s was a child. About 380 children with haemophilia and other blood disorders are now thought to have contracted the virus. This leads to the question: was this a strange accident or was there some kind of agency involved which meant that children were more likely to be exposed to hazardous blood products? Sadly, it appears that the latter is true. Many of the victims, or their families, who gave evidence to the public inquiry believe that they or their loved ones were involved in secret trials to find out the extent to which the infectivity of the various factor concentrates had been reduced. In January 1982, Professor Arthur Bloom wrote a letter that appeared to confirm that haemophiliacs were being experimented on. He wrote: 'This study shows that it is possible to demonstrate infectivity effectively using quite small numbers of PUPs [previously untreated patients].'[12]

Little Colin Smith's parents believe their son was used as a PUP, despite, as we have seen, Bloom and other haemophilia centre directors agreeing that children should only be treated with cryoprecipitate due to the risk of AIDS.

It emerged in evidence to the Infected Blood Inquiry that the policy was not universally applied. And it was not just Bloom who chose to ignore his own advice.

Alder Hey Hospital, in Liverpool, had the worst HIV infectivity rates for children in the country. At the height of the AIDS crisis in the mid-1980s, ninety per cent of its young haemophiliac patients were infected with HIV. The mother of two boys, who were treated at Alder Hey and died of HIV, told the Infected Blood Inquiry: 'At Alder Hey it was like a conveyor belt of children dying. We would constantly get phone calls from other parents and families telling us that another child had died.'[13] By contrast, only a few miles across the Pennines at Sheffield Children's Hospital, the picture could not have looked more different, and patients experienced one of the lowest infectivity rates in the country. This has in part been credited to the work of Professor Francis Eric Preston, whose particular awareness of the risks of hepatitis led him to a focus on the use of cryoprecipitate for children, not exclusively, but at least as a main form of treatment, in marked contrast to the position in Liverpool, where cryoprecipitate appears to have played little or no part in treatment.

The tale of two cities and the maverick behaviour by Bloom suggests that even where there were policies in place to mitigate the risks of factor concentrates, they were not uniformly observed. This means that active human agency or error played at least some part in the life-or-death decisions being made by doctors. To make matters worse, the inquiry was presented with considerable evidence that the vast majority of factor VIII was given to patients for non-life-threatening situations.

Reflecting on the disproportionate number of children

infected with HIV in the wake of the scandal, Haemophilia Society chief executive Kate Burt said: 'We know that some very young children with bleeding disorders were given high-risk factor-concentrate treatment from mid-1983 onwards, which went against guidance at the time. As a result, some parents have had to live with the unbearable question of whether their child's death or infection could have been prevented.'[14]

•

Sir John Major, the former prime minister, drew gasps from families watching him give evidence to the public inquiry when he described the contaminated blood scandal as 'incredibly bad luck'.[15] In reality, this was an entirely avoidable tragedy, as can be seen by the experiences of other countries, such as Finland. It arose from a combination of disparate factors which, once they began to collide, created the perfect storm. This included the thirst for profit coupled with unsafe practices adopted by pharmaceutical companies; a blasé approach to the emerging evidence of a catastrophe, both in the UK and across the Atlantic; and insufficient foresight and planning by government to achieve self-sufficiency. This was in addition to a general societal view of haemophiliacs as a 'doomed' group of individuals, whose lives were valued less than others who could expect to lead a longer life.

Decisions to experiment on the haemophilia community were particularly egregious given the vast majority of patients who were infected with deadly diseases through contaminated blood products were mild haemophiliacs, or those who were not suffering from life-threatening conditions. Despite safeguarding procedures being introduced to mitigate the risks of the imported factor VIII, the new rules were often ignored. For years, the scandal was kept under wraps as victims grappled to come to terms with their destroyed lives. It wasn't until the advent of social media that many of them realised that they were not alone and a number of new campaign groups were born, including Tainted Blood and Factor 8. But for years they were fobbed off by the government, who, as Jeremy Hunt, a former health secretary, said in his evidence to the inquiry, 'closed ranks around a lie'.[16]

In a desperate bid to avoid admitting liability for the scandal, which had claimed thousands of lives, the government 'took on the attitude of a defendant asserting that it had done nothing wrong'.[17] This meant that even when campaigners took the government to court, including the notorious HIV litigation in 1991, when victims were forced to sign away all future legal claims without knowing they had been given a second deadly condition, they were only awarded ex-gratia payments rather than compensation. As former prime minister Theresa May told me in an interview for this book shortly before the end of the inquiry, it marked another instance of the public sector shutting its doors and refusing to accept that there is an issue, as well as demonstrating a lack of thought with regards to the impact on those affected.

The impact of this tragedy cannot be underestimated. Many of those affected have suffered the terrible physical and psychological effect and symptoms of infection with HIV or hepatitis C. They have lived with the fear of infecting their partners, spouses, family or friends. In some cases, it has led to the breakdown of relationships and stopped people from marrying or having children. Victims have often faced stigma and the loss of careers. They have lost earnings and, in many instances, have been denied the opportunity of financial security due to an inability to obtain life insurance or mortgage protection policies. Many have suffered multiple bereavements and now struggle with survivor's guilt. For parents who have lost children, they have had to endure the incredible emotional trauma that comes with such tragedy. For children who have lost parents, they have had to cope with their own grief while often dealing with the permanent collapse of a stable family life. Many orphans have ended up in care or, worse still, homeless.

But even as their suffering is plain to see, they continue to wait for government to finally do the right thing. While a backbench MP, Jeremy Hunt admitted that the victims had already waited too long for justice. He told the Infected Blood Inquiry: 'I think it is absolutely true: that it took too long for the state to resolve this issue and I don't think any of us who were in government can escape our share of the responsibility that it took too long over successive governments to resolve it . . . I think the totality of this was a failure by the British state.'[18]

Whatever justice may be achieved, it will come too late for John Cornes, one of the last remaining brothers of a doomed Birmingham family. He passed away in May 2023. The funeral was held in the same cemetery where his four brothers Alan, Garry, Roy and Gordon have all been laid to rest. John, who was infected with hepatitis C, died in May after developing inoperable brain tumours. The last exchange I had with him was not long before his death in a final interview for this book. He told me that the last three years of his life had been 'hell'. 'My liver has been playing up, I have been hospitalised and had a stent fitted,' he said.

'It ended up with me having to give up work, which was not an easy decision. Before I was a workaholic and felt alive. Now I feel nothing.'

When I first got involved in this campaign more than twenty years ago, it was almost impossible to comprehend how these individuals could have been left to suffer for so long. Once I had been welcomed into their world, I felt it was my duty to help them. As I rose to more senior jobs in journalism, I kept trying to use my position to highlight the victims' plight. I disagreed with the state quantifying their lives in terms of pounds and pence, inconvenient numbers on a spread sheet that would never add up. When Theresa May finally recognised their suffering and granted a public inquiry, it was the proudest moment of my career. But even now – after all these years of campaigning – many people still have not heard about the tragedy. My motivation for writing this book was to ensure that the valiant campaign led by the victims of the worst treatment disaster in NHS history is never forgotten. They are warriors who have all overcome their own personal tragedies and somehow still found the strength to continue their fight for justice. I am humbled to have played even a small part in that battle.

References

Introduction

1 This introduction is based on a story I wrote for *The Sunday Times* on the eve of the Infected Blood Inquiry opening. Wheeler, Caroline. 'Contaminated blood inquiry: The decades-long fight for justice', *The Sunday Times*, 23 September 2018

2 'PRSE0004591 – Transcript – *World in Action:* "Blood Money"; 01 Dec 1985', *Infected Blood Inquiry*, https://www.infectedbloodinquiry.org.uk/evidence/prse0004591-transcript-world-action-blood-money-01-dec-1975

3 'Transcript – London – Wednesday 23 September 2020 (Knowledge of Risk – Inquiry Presentation)', *Infected Blood Inquiry*, https://www.infectedbloodinquiry.org.uk/sites/default/files/documents/Transcript%20-%20London%20-%20Wednesday%202023%20September%20%28Knowledge%20of%20Risk%20-%20Inquiry%20Presentation%29%20.pdf, p. 52

4 'Contaminated Blood Scandal in France', *Wikipedia*, https://en.wikipedia.org/wiki/Contaminated_blood_scandal_in_France

5 Contaminated Blood Scandal in Japan', *Wikipedia*, https://en.wikipedia.org/wiki/Contaminated_blood_scandal_in_Japan

6 'Presentation Note on the Role of the Chief Medical Officer', *Infected Blood Inquiry*, https://www.infectedbloodinquiry.org.uk/sites/default/files/documents/Presentation%20Note%20on%20the%20Role%20of%20the%20Chief%20Medical%20Officer_1.pdf, p. 67

7 'Second Written Statement of Kenneth Clarke', *Infected Blood Inquiry*, https://www.infectedbloodinquiry.org.uk/sites/default/

REFERENCES

files/documents/WITN0758012%20-%20Second%20written%20
statement%20of%20Lord%20Kenneth%20Clarke%3B%20
12%20Jul%202021.pdf, pp. 77–8

8 Ellison, Jane, UIN 211081 (written question), HC Deb, 27 October
   2014, https://www.theyworkforyou.com/wrans/?id=2014-10-
   20.211081.h&s=hepatitis+%2B+waiver+%2B+HIV+%2B+1991
   #g211081.r0

9 Factor 8 Scandal, 'Factor 8 supplies chronology of Haemophiliac
   Hepatitis C cover-up', 22 October 2018, https://www.
   factor8scandal.uk/campaign-history/2018/10/22/factor-8-supplies-
   chronology-of-haemophiliac-hepatitis-c-cover-up

10 Borland, Sophie, 'New tainted blood scandal: Patients infected
   with HIV were each paid around £24,000 to sign away their rights
   to sue – before being told they'd also contracted hepatitis C',
   Daily Mail, 21 October 2018, https://www.dailymail.co.uk/news/
   article-6300933/Patients-infected-HIV-paid-24-000-sign-away-
   rights-sue.html

11 Wheeler, Caroline, 'I'm not taking any more risks', *Sunday
   Mercury*, 25 February 2001

12 Wheeler, Caroline, 'Dying father's plea over infected blood', *Sunday
   Express*, 8 June 2014

13 Wheeler, Caroline, 'EXCLUSIVE: I saw all three of my brothers die
   after they were given contaminated blood', *Daily Express*, 4 July
   2015

14 Wheeler, Caroline, 'Tears for tainted blood boy will never ever dry',
   Sunday Express, 26 July 2014, https://www.express.co.uk/finance/
   crusader/593816/Tears-tainted-blood-boy-will-never-ever-dry

15 Wheeler, Caroline, 'Chris Cornes, orphan in contaminated bloody
   scandal, still fighting for justice 20 years on', *The Sunday Times*,
   4 April 2021, https://www.thetimes.co.uk/article/chris-cornes-
   orphan-in-contaminated-blood-scandal-still-fighting-for-justice-20-
   years-on-j58wsjl7n

16 'Theresa May urged to hold inquiry into contaminated blood', *The
   Times*, 10 July 2017

1: Blood Money

1 Godfrey, Miles, 'Dame Anita's husband speaks of grief', *Brighton
   Argus*, 22 October 2007

2 Wheeler, Caroline, 'Daughter says transfusion "roulette" killed
   Anita Roddick', *The Sunday Times*, 16 July 2017

3 Forster, Katherine, 'I fight on for my mum, Anita Roddick,
   whirlwind of the Body Shop', *The Times*, 23 September 2018

REFERENCES

4 George, Rose, *Nine Pints: A Journey Through the Miraculous World of Blood*, Granta, 2019

5 Sugg, Richard, *Mummies, Cannibals and Vampires: The History of Corpse Medicine from the Middle Ages to the Falun Gong*, 2020

6 Groopman, Jerome, 'The History of Blood', *New Yorker*, 7 January 2019

7 Ibid

8 Wallace, Rob, 'Medical Innovations: Charles Drew and Blood Banking', National WWII Museum, 4 May 2020, https://www. nationalww2museum.org/war/articles/medical-innovations-blood-banking

9 American Red Cross, 'World War II and the American Red Cross', https://www.redcross.org/content/dam/redcross/National/history-wwii.pdf

10 Byrne, Eugene, 'D-Day 75 years on – How Bristol was the blood donation epicentre for the war effort', *Bristol Post*, 6 June 2019

11 Titmuss, Richard, *The Gift Relationship: From Human Blood to Social Policy*, Policy Press, 2019

12 Parker, Suzi, 'Blood money', *Salon*, 24 December 1998, https:// www.salon.com/1998/12/24/cov_23news/

13 Duda, Kelly (dir.), *Factor 8: The Arkansas Prison Blood Scandal* documentary film, 2005

14 Ibid

15 Ibid

16 Ibid

17 GM Watch, 'Bayer and the holocaust', 27 January 2012, https:// www.gmwatch.org/en/news/archive/2012/13646-bayer-and-the-holocaust

18 Ibid

19 Havery, Gavin, 'He died after NHS blood transfusion gave him HIV and Hepatitis C, now there are calls for a Hillsborough-style inquiry', *Northern Echo*, 10 May 2017

20 'Transcript – London – Wednesday 16 March 2022 (Presentation by Counsel about self-sufficiency cont.), Infected Blood Inquiry, https:// www.infectedbloodinquiry.org.uk/sites/default/files/documents/ Transcript%20-%20London%20-%20Wednesday%2016%20 March%202022%20%28Presentation%20by%20Counsel%20 to%20the%20Inquiry%20about%20self-sufficiency%20and%20 domestic%20production%20of%20blood%20products%20in%20 England%20and%20Wales%20continued%29.pdf

21 'Chapter 10: Trends in demand for and use of blood products and in production and supply of NHS products', *Penrose Inquiry*, https://www.penroseinquiry.org.uk/preliminary-report/chapter-10/ index.html

22 World Health Organization, 'Utilization and supply of human

blood and blood products (WHA28.72), 28 May 1975, https://www.who.int/publications-detail-redirect/WHA28.72

23 'PRSE0004591 – Transcript – World in Action: "Blood Money"; 01 Dec 1985', *Infected Blood Inquiry*, https://www.infectedbloodinquiry.org.uk/evidence/prse0004591-transcript-world-action-blood-money-01-dec-1975

24 Ibid
25 Ibid
26 Ibid
27 Ibid
28 Ibid

29 'Final Report', *Penrose Inquiry*, https://www.penroseinquiry.org.uk/finalreport/pdf/PEN0131400.PDF, p. 10

30 'LDOW0000039 – Transcript – *World in Action* "Blood Money Part 2" – undated', *Infected Blood Inquiry*, https://www.infectedbloodinquiry.org.uk/sites/default/files/Lord%20Owen%20publication_1/Lord%20Owen%20publication/LDOW0000039%20-%20Transcript%20for%20%27World%20in%20Action%20Blood%20Money%20Part%202%27%20-%20undated.pdf

31 Ibid
32 Ibid

2: School of Death

1 'Transcript – London – Tuesday 22 June 2021 (Nicholas Sainsbury, John Peach & Gary Bennett)', *Infected Blood Inquiry*, https://www.infectedbloodinquiry.org.uk/sites/default/files/documents/Transcript%20-%20London%20-%20Tuesday%2022%20June%202021%20%28Nicholas%20Sainsbury%2C%20John%20Peach%20%26%20Gary%20Bennett%29.pdf

2 Ibid

3 'Our history', Treloar's, https://www.treloar.org.uk/about-us/our-history/

4 'Transcript – London – Tuesday 22 June 2021 (Nicholas Sainsbury, John Peach & Gary Bennett)', *Infected Blood Inquiry*

5 Ibid
6 Ibid
7 Ibid

8 'SUBS0000053 – Written Submissions on behalf of the Treloar Trust – 16 Dec 2022', *Infected Blood Inquiry*, https://www.infectedbloodinquiry.org.uk/sites/default/files/Final%20Written%20Submissions%20for%20Publication%20copy/Final%20Written%20Submissions%20for%20Publication%20copy/

SUBS0000053%20-%20Written%20submissions%20on%20
behalf%20of%20the%20Treloar%20Trust%20-%2016%20
Dec%202022.pdf

9 'Transcript – London – Tuesday 22 June 2021 (Nicholas Sainsbury, John Peach & Gary Bennett)', *Infected Blood Inquiry*

10 Ibid

11 Ibid

12 Ibid

13 'Transcript – London – Monday 21 June 2021 (Presentation by Counsel to the Inquiry about Treloar's, Gary Webster & Mr BA)', *Infected Blood Inquiry*, https://www.infectedbloodinquiry.org.uk/ sites/default/files/documents/Transcript%20-%20London%20-%20 Monday%2021%20June%202021%20%28Presentation%20 by%20Counsel%20to%20the%20Inquiry%20about%20 Treloar%27s%2C%20Gary%20Webster%20%26%20Mr%20 BA%29.pdf

14 'Transcript – London – Tuesday 22 June 2021 (Nicholas Sainsbury, John Peach & Gary Bennett)', *Infected Blood Inquiry*

15 Wheeler, Caroline, 'Justice fight for pupils of Treloar College who were killed by tainted blood', *Sunday Express*, 19 July 2015, https://www.express.co.uk/news/uk/592179/blood-hiv-treloar- college-scam-nhs-medicine-positive-hiv

16 'LIT0010245', *Penrose Inquiry*, https://www.penroseinquiry.org. uk/finalreport/pdf/LIT0010245.PDF

17 Wheeler, Caroline, 'Six-year inquiry "failed to find full awful truth about scandal of tainted blood"', *Sunday Express*, 6 September 2015

18 'Written statement of the Rt Hon Lord David Owen', 5 February 2020, https://www.lorddavidowen.co.uk/wp-content/ uploads/2020/10/Lord-Owen-Written-statement-o.pdf

19 'Chapter 4 – Self-Sufficiency', *Archer Inquiry*, https://archercbbp. wordpress.com/report/chapter-4-self-sufficiency/

20 Tainted Blood, 'The Tainted Blood Timeline – what really happened', https://www.taintedblood.info/timeline/

21 BBC News, 'Scotland "could have helped hundreds avoid HIV"', 3 January 2020, https://www.bbc.co.uk/news/uk- scotland-50976611

22 'Chapter 4 – Self-Sufficiency', *Archer Inquiry*

23 Ibid

24 'Tainted Blood – Accusations Document', *Archer Inquiry*, https:// archercbbp.files.wordpress.com/2017/03/taintedbloodaccuse.pdf

25 'Transcript – London – Monday 21 June 2021 (Presentation by Counsel to the Inquiry about Treloar's, Gary Webster & Mr BA)', *Infected Blood Inquiry*

26 'HHFT0000916_003 – Letter from J Craske to Dr A Aronstam,

Treloar Haemophilia Centre, re: use of factor VIII during study of hepatitis in patients treated with designated batches of NHS Factor; 10 May 1979', *Infected Blood Inquiry*, https://www. infectedbloodinquiry.org.uk/sites/default/files/documents/ HHFT0000916_003%20-%20Letter%20from%20J%20 Craske%20to%20Dr%20A%20Aronstam%2C%20Treloar%20 Haemophilia%20Centre%20re%20use%20of%20factor%20 VIII%20during%20study%20of%20hepatitis%20in%20 patients%20treated%20with%20designated%20batches%20 of%20NHS%20Factor%20-%2010%20May%201979.pdf

27 'HHFT0000916_002 – Letter from A. Aronstam to Dr J. Craske re: use of Factor VIII and trial material on mild haemophiliacs; 14 May 1979', *Infected Bloody Inquiry*, https://www.infectedbloodinquiry. org.uk/sites/default/files/documents/HHFT0000916_002%20-%20 Letter%20from%20A%20Aronstam%20to%20Dr%20J%20 Craske%20re%20use%20of%20Factor%20VIII%20and%20 trial%20material%20on%20mild%20haemophiliacs%20-%20 14%20May%201979.pdf

28 'Transcript – London – Monday 21 June 2021 (Presentation by Counsel to the Inquiry about Treloar's, Gary Webster & Mr BA)', *Infected Blood Inquiry*

29 Ibid

30 Siddique, Haroon, 'Infected blood scandal: Ex-pupil tells inquiry he did not know he was in a trial', *Guardian*, 21 June 2021

31 'WITN1723001 – Written statement of Gary James Webster', *Infected Blood Inquiry*, https://www.infectedbloodinquiry.org. uk/sites/default/files/documents/WITN1723001%20Written%20 Statement%20of%20Gary%20Webster.pdf

32 'Transcript – London – Monday 21 June 2021 (Presentation by Counsel to the Inquiry about Treloar's, Gary Webster & Mr BA)', *Infected Blood Inquiry*

33 *World in Action*, 'Blood Business', 22 December 1980, https://www. youtube.com/watch?v=5duZkdEN-N8

34 Tainted Blood, 'The Tainted Blood Timeline – what *really* happened', https://www.taintedblood.info/timeline/

35 Burgess, Kaya, 'Tainted blood scandal: officials knews of hepatitis risk of US blood in 1980', *The Times*, 22 September 2020, https:// www.thetimes.co.uk/article/tainted-blood-scandal-officials-knew-of-hepatitis-risk-from-us-blood-in-1980-cftfslldf

36 Tainted Blood, 'The Tainted Blood Timeline – what *really* happened'

37 Wheeler, Caroline, 'Sick children infected with HIV and used as guinea pigs as NHS said chimps "too expensive"', *Sunday Express*, 23 August 2015

38 'Document displayed for Milners Solicitors (Day 2, PM),

25 September 2018', *Infected Blood Inquiry*, https://www. infectedbloodinquiry.org.uk/sites/default/files/Document%20 displayed%20for%20Milners%20Solicitors%20(Day%20 2%2C%20PM)%2C%2025%20September%202018.pdf

3: The Plague

1 'Transcript – London – Wednesday 05 June 2019 (Adrian Goodyear)', *Infected Blood Inquiry*, https://www. infectedbloodinquiry.org.uk/sites/default/files/documents/ Transcript%20Adrian%20Goodyear%20%5BW1243%5D%20 -%2005%20June%202019.pdf
2 Ibid
3 School of Global Health, University of Copenhagen, 'After hard working days she rested by the beautiful River Ebola', 22 July 2020, https://globalhealth.ku.dk/news/2020/after-hard-working-days-she-rested-by-the-beautiful-river-ebola/
4 University of Oxford, 'HIV pandemic's origins located', 3 October 2014, https://www.ox.ac.uk/news/2014-10-03-hiv-pandemics-origins-located#:~:text=The%20team's%20analysis%20 suggests%20that%2C%20between%20the%201920s%20and%20 1950s,and%20spread%20across%20the%20globe.
5 School of Global Health, University of Copenhagen, 'After hard working days she rested by the beautiful River Ebola', 22 July 2020
6 I. C. Bygbjerg, 'AIDS in a Danish Surgeon (Zaire, 1976)', letter to the editor, Lancet, 23 April 1983
7 Johnson, Brian D., 'How a typo created a scapegoat for the AIDS epidemic', *Maclean's*, 17 April 2019, https://macleans.ca/culture/ movies/how-a-typo-created-a-scapegoat-for-the-aids-epidemic/
8 https://www.marxists.org/history/haiti/1972/dollars-blood.htm
9 'Robert Rayford', *Wikipedia*, https://en.wikipedia.org/wiki/Robert_ Rayford
10 Moran, Mike, 'Forgotten History: The Sad and Mysterious Tale of America's First AIDS Victim', *Medium*, 8 April 2019, https:// medium.com/@michaelmoran/the-sad-and-mysterious-case-of-the-first-known-american-aids-victim-6dfe2975b1f6
11 Specter, Michael, 'Larry Kramer, public nuisance', *New Yorker*, 5 May 2002, https://www.newyorker.com/magazine/2002/05/13/ public-nuisance
12 Ibid
13 'Ryan White, *Wikipedia*, https://en.wikipedia.org/wiki/Ryan_White
14 Lopez, German, 'The Reagan administration's unbelievable response to the HIV/AIDS epidemic', *Vox*, 1 December 2016, https://www.vox.com/2015/12/1/9828348/ronald-reagan-hiv-aids

REFERENCES

4: Guinea Pigs

1 'WITN1243001 Written Statement of Adrian Goodyear
20 February 2019', *Infected Blood Inquiry*, https://www.
infectedbloodinquiry.org.uk/sites/default/files/documents/
WITN1243001%20Written%20Statement%20of%20Adrian%20
Goodyear%2020%20February%202019.pdf
2 Ibid
3 Ibid
4 'Transcript – London – Wednesday 05 June 2019 (Adrian
Goodyear)', *Infected Blood Inquiry*, https://www.
infectedbloodinquiry.org.uk/sites/default/files/documents/
Transcript%20Adrian%20Goodyear%20%5BW1243%5D%20
-%2005%20June%202019.pdf
5 Ibid
6 'Presentation note on the work and evidence of Dr Richard
Lane – 17 Mar 2022', *Infected Blood Inquiry*, https://www.
infectedbloodinquiry.org.uk/sites/default/files/documents/
INQY0000331%20-%20Presentation%20note%20on%20
the%20work%20and%20evidence%20of%20Dr%20Richard%20
Lane%2017%20March%202022.pdf, p. 46
7 'Transcript – London – 30 September 2020 – Professor Bloom and
Cardiff Haemophilia Centre – Inquiry Presentation Continued'
Infected Blood Inquiry, https://www.infectedbloodinquiry.org.uk/
sites/default/files/documents/Transcript%20-%20London%20-%20
30%20September%202020%20-%20Professor%20Bloom%20
and%20Cardiff%20Haemophilia%20Centre%20-%20Inquiry%20
Presentation%20continued.pdf, p. 34
8 'Transcript – London – Tuesday 2 February 2021 (Presentation
on First Cardiff AIDS Patient and Presentation on Newcastle
Haemophilia Centre)', *Infected Blood Inquiry*, https://www.
infectedbloodinquiry.org.uk/sites/default/files/documents/
Transcript%20-%20London%20-%20Tuesday%202%20
February%202021%20%28Presentation%20on%20First%20
Cardiff%20AIDS%20Patient%20and%20Presentation%20on%2-
0Newcastle%20Haemophilia%20Centre%29.pdf
9 Letter from Arthur Bloom to the Haemophilia Society, 4 May
1983, https://www.taintedblood.info/tb/tlfiles/Professor%20A%20
Bloom%204%20May%201983.pdf
10 INQY0000323 – 'Presentation Note on the Oxford Haemophilia
Centre – 30 Sep 2020', *Infected Blood Inquiry*, https://www.
infectedbloodinquiry.org.uk/sites/default/files/documents/
INQY0000323%20-%20Presentation%20Note%20on%20
the%20Oxford%20Haemophilia%20Centre.pdf, p. 15
11 Ibid, p. 16

REFERENCES

12 'Transcript – London – Thursday 11 February 2021 (David Watters)', *Infected Blood Inquiry*, https://www. infectedbloodinquiry.org.uk/sites/default/files/documents/ Transcript%20-%20London%20-%20Thursday%2011%20 February%202021%20%28David%20Watters%29.pdf

13 'WITN4120001 – Written statement of Susan Douglas; 28 October 2021', *Infected Blood Inquiry*, https://www.infectedbloodinquiry. org.uk/sites/default/files/documents/WITN4120001-%20 Written%20Statement%20of%20Susan%20Douglas%20%3B%20 28%20October%202021.pdf

14 Siddique, Haroon, 'Infected blood scandal: government knew of contaminated plasma "long before it admitted it"', *Guardian*, 7 June 2021

15 *BMJ*, Spencer Galbraith obituary, https://www.bmj.com/content/ suppl/2009/05/07/bmj.b1827.DC1/galbraith0409long.pdf

16 'PEN0150054', *Penrose Inquiry*, https://www.penroseinquiry.org. uk/finalreport/pdf/PEN0150054.PDF, p. 6

17 Hall, Sarah, 'Government knew of HIV risk from imported blood', *Guardian*, 25 May 2007

18 Ibid

19 Tainted Blood, 'The Tainted Blood Timeline – what *really* happened', https://www.taintedblood.info/timeline/

20 Ibid – see 1983

21 Tainted Blood, Letter re: heat-treating factor VIII, https://www. taintedblood.info/tb/tlfiles/NBTS%20Heat%20Treated%20 Factor%20VIII%20RHA%20Finances%2029%20June%201983. pdf

22 Tainted Blood, 'The Tainted Blood Timeline – what *really* happened'

23 Hall, Sarah, 'Government knew of HIV risk from imported blood', *Guardian*, 25 May 2007

24 Tainted Blood, 'The Tainted Blood Timeline – what *really* happened'

25 Ibid

26 'WITN5282001 – Written statement of Lord Simon Glenarthur; 9 Jul 2021', *Infected Blood Inquiry*, https://www. infectedbloodinquiry.org.uk/sites/default/files/documents/ WITN5282001%20-%20Written%20statement%20of%20 Lord%20Simon%20Glenarthur%3B%2009%20Jul%202021.pdf

27 Burgess, Kaya, 'Tainted blood scandal: officials knew of hepatitis risk of US blood in 1980', *The Times*, 22 September 2020, https:// www.thetimes.co.uk/article/tainted-blood-scandal-officials-knew- ofhepatitis-risk-from-us-blood-in-1980-cftfslldf

28 'WITN0758001 – Written statement of Lord Kenneth Clarke; 01 Jul 2021', *Infected Blood Inquiry*, https://www.

infectedbloodinquiry.org.uk/sites/default/files/documents/
WITN0758001%20-%20Written%20statement%20of%20
Lord%20Kenneth%20Clarke%3B%2001%20Jul%202021.pdf

29 'Transcript – London – Wednesday 28 July 2021 (Lord
Kenneth Clarke continued', *Infected Blood Inquiry*, https://
www.infectedbloodinquiry.org.uk/sites/default/files/documents/
Transcript%20-%20London%20-%20Wednesday%2028%20
July%202021%20%28Lord%20Kenneth%20Clarke%20
continued%29.pdf

30 'WITN4461001 – Written statement of Dr Diana Walford; 05 Jul
2021', *Infected Blood Inquiry*, https://www.infectedbloodinquiry.
org.uk/sites/default/files/documents/WITN4461001%20
-%20Written%20statement%20of%20Dr%20Diana%20
Walford%3B%2005%20Jul%202021.pdf

31 'Transcript – London – Tuesday 20 July 2021 (Dr Diana
Walfrod Continued', *Infected Blood Inquiry*, https://www.
infectedbloodinquiry.org.uk/sites/default/files/documents/
Transcript%20-%20London%20-%20Tuesday%2020%20
July%202021%20%28Dr%20Diana%20Walford%20
Continued%29.pdf

32 'Transcript – London – Tuesday 27 July 2021 (Lord Kenneth
Clarke), *Infected Blood Inquiry*, https://www.infectedbloodinquiry.
org.uk/sites/default/files/documents/Transcript%20-%20
London%20-%20Tuesday%2027%20July%202021%20
%28Lord%20Kenneth%20Clarke%29.pdf

33 'Transcript – London – 30 September 2020 – Professor Bloom and
Cardiff Haemophilia Centre – Inquiry Presentation Continued',
Infected Blood Inquiry

34 'INQY0000323 – Presentation Note on the Oxford Haemophilia
Centre – 30 Sep 2020', *Infected Blood Inquiry*, p. 17

35 'HCDO0000394_117 – Minutes of a Haemophilia Reference
Centre Directors Meeting re: blood donor testing and screening
for HTLV III antibodies; 10th December 1984', *Infected Blood
Inquiry*, https://www.infectedbloodinquiry.org.uk/sites/default/files/
WinterPN/WinterPN/HCDO0000394_117%20-%20Minutes%20
of%20a%20Haemophilia%20Reference%20Centre%20
Directors%20Meeting%20re%20blood%20donor%20testing%20
and%20screening%20for%20HTLV%20III%20antibodies%20
-%2010th%20December%201984.pdf

36 Boseley, Sarah, 'Officials worried about saving money amid infected
blood scandal', *Guardian*, 23 March 2010

37 'Transcript – London – Wednesday 05 June 2019 (Adrian
Goodyear, Susan Gorman, Irene Ruth Spellman)', *Infected Blood
Inquiry*, https://www.infectedbloodinquiry.org.uk/sites/default/files/
documents/Transcript%20-%20London%20-%20Wednesday%20

05%20June%202019%20%28Adrian%20Goodyear%2C%20
Susan%20Gorman%2C%20Irene%20Ruth%20Spellman%29_0.
pdf

38 Ibid

39 Ibid

40 Ibid

41 'Transcript – London – Thursday 24 June – Alex Macpherson &
Presentation by Counsel to the Inquiry about Treloar's (continued)',
Infected Blood Inquiry, https://www.infectedbloodinquiry.org.
uk/sites/default/files/documents/Transcript%20-%20London%20
-%20Thursday%2024%20June%202021%20%28Alec%20
Macpherson%20%26%20Presentation%20by%20Counsel%20
to%20the%20Inquiry%20about%20Treloar%27s%20-%20
continued%29.pdf

42 Wheeler, Caroline, 'We told them the truth: the boys were infected,
some would die early', *The Times*, 13 June 2021

43 'Transcript – London – Thursday 24 June – Alex Macpherson &
Presentation by Counsel to the Inquiry about Treloar's (continued)',
Infected Blood Inquiry

44 'Transcript – London – Wednesday 05 June 2019 (Adrian
Goodyear)', *Infected Blood Inquiry*

45 'WITN1243001 Written Statement of Adrian Goodyear
20 February 2019', *Infected Blood Inquiry*

46 Ibid

47 Ibid

48 Ibid

5: Until Death Do Us Part

1 'Transcript – London – Thursday 02 May 2019 (Clair Walton,
Mrs A, Lesley Brownless)', *Infected Blood Inquiry*, https://
www.infectedbloodinquiry.org.uk/sites/default/files/documents/
Transcript%20-%20London%20-%20Thursday%2002%20
May%202019%20%28Clair%20Walton%2C%20Mrs%20
A%2C%20Lesley%20Brownless%29.pdf

2 Ibid

3 Ibid

4 Ibid

5 Ibid

6 Ibid

7 Ibid

8 Ibid

9 Ibid

10 Ibid

REFERENCES

11 Ibid

12 'Transcript – London – Tuesday 8 October 2019 (Opening Remarks, Colin Turton, Denise Turton, Sue Threakall, Barry Fitzgerald and Ronan Fitzgerald)', *Infected Blood Inquiry*, https://www.infectedbloodinquiry.org.uk/sites/default/files/documents/Transcript%20London%20Tuesday%208%20October%202019%20%28Colin%20Turton%2C%20Denise%20Turton%2C%20Sue%20Threakall%2C%20Barry%20Fitzgerald%20and%20Ronan%20Fitzgerald%29.pdf

13 'WITN1564001 – Written statement of Susan Threakall', *Infected Blood Inquiry*, https://www.infectedbloodinquiry.org.uk/sites/default/files/documents/WITN1564001%20Written%20Statement%20of%20Susan%20Threakall.pdf

14 'Transcript – London – Tuesday 8 October 2019 (Opening Remarks, Colin Turton, Denise Turton, Sue Threakall, Barry Fitzgerald and Ronan Fitzgerald)', *Infected Blood Inquiry*

15 Ibid

16 Ibid

17 Ibid

18 Ibid

19 Wheeler, Caroline, 'Tainted blood: "Bob died a death you would not wish on a rabid dog"', *Sunday Express*, 20 September 2015

20 'Transcript – London – Tuesday 8 October 2019 (Opening Remarks, Colin Turton, Denise Turton, Sue Threakall, Barry Fitzgerald and Ronan Fitzgerald)', *Infected Blood Inquiry*

21 Wheeler, Caroline, 'Tainted blood: "Bob died a death you would not wish on a rabid dog"', *Sunday Express*, 20 September 2015

22 Ibid

23 'Transcript – London – Tuesday 8 October 2019 (Opening Remarks, Colin Turton, Denise Turton, Sue Threakall, Barry Fitzgerald and Ronan Fitzgerald)', *Infected Blood Inquiry*

24 Caroline, 'Tainted blood: "Bob died a death you would not wish on a rabid dog"', *Sunday Express*, 20 September 2015

25 'Transcript – London – Wednesday 22 September 2021 (Lord Norman Fowler)', *Infected Blood Inquiry*, https://www.infectedbloodinquiry.org.uk/sites/default/files/documents/Transcript%20-%20London%20-%20Wednesday%2022%20September%202021%20%28Lord%20Norman%20Fowler%29.pdf

26 Tainted Blood, 'The Tainted Blood Timeline – what *really* happened', https://www.taintedblood.info/timeline/ – see 1985

27 'WITN0771001 – Written statement of Lord Norman Fowler 17 Jul 2021', *Infected Blood Inquiry*, https://www.infectedbloodinquiry.org.uk/sites/default/files/documents/WITN0771001%20-%20

Written%20statement%20of%20Lord%20Norman%20
Fowler_17%20Jul%202021.pdf, p. 10

28 'Transcript – London – Tuesday 21 September 2021 (Lord Norman
Fowler)', *Infected Blood Inquiry*, https://www.infectedbloodinquiry.
org.uk/sites/default/files/documents/Transcript%20-%20
London%20-%20Tuesday%2021%20September%202021%20
%28Lord%20Norman%20Fowler%29.pdf, pp. 62–3

29 'Transcript – London – Wednesday 22 September 2021 (Lord
Norman Fowler)', *Infected Blood Inquiry*

30 'WITN0771001 – Written statement of Lord Norman Fowler
17 Jul 2021', *Infected Blood Inquiry*, p. 197

31 'Transcript – London – Wednesday 22 September 2021 (Lord
Norman Fowler)', *Infected Blood Inquiry*, pp. 118–9

32 'WITN5287001 – Written Statement of Edwina Currie Jones;
09 August 2022', *Infected Blood Inquiry*, https://www.
infectedbloodinquiry.org.uk/sites/default/files/documents/
WITN5287001-%20Written%20Statement%20of%20Edwina%20
Currie%20Jones%3B%2009%20August%202022.pdf, p. 49

33 Dr Tony Aronstam – HIV Haemophilia & Compensation',
BBC TV South, November 1987, https://www.youtube.com/
watch?app=desktop&v=1q6Y4PeNWeQ

34 The All-Party Parliamentary Group (APPG) on Haemophilia and
Contaminated Blood, *Inquiry into the current support for those
affected by the contaminated blood scandal in the UK*, January
2015, https://haemophilia.org.uk/wp-content/uploads/2017/02/
appg_hcb_fr.pdf.pdf

35 'Transcript – London – Thursday 02 May 2019 (Clair Walton, Mrs
A, Lesley Brownless)', *Infected Blood Inquiry*

36 Ibid

37 Ibid

38 Ibid

39 Ibid

40 Ibid

41 Ibid

42 Ibid

43 Ibid

44 'Transcript – London – Tuesday 8 October 2019 (Opening
Remarks, Colin Turton, Denise Turton, Sue Threakall, Barry
Fitzgerald and Ronan Fitzgerald)', *Infected Blood Inquiry*

45 Ibid

46 Ibid

47 Ibid

48 Ibid

REFERENCES

6: Seven Brothers

1 Driscoll, Margarette, 'Focus – Sex, Lies and Propaganda – Birmingham AIDS scare', *The Sunday Times*, 28 June 1992
2 Ibid
3 Gardner, David, and Golden, James, 'AIDS SCARE: WHO IS TELLING THE TRUTH? Conflict of evidence as man is named', *Daily Mail*, 24 June 1992
4 Ibid
5 Barlass, Tim, and Shaw, David, 'Baby victim caught up in the AIDS affair; Sufferers won't be prosecuted', *Evening Standard*, 26 June 1992
6 Arlidge, John, 'Five contact lifeline over HIV lover', *Independent*, 25 June 1992
7 Driscoll, Margarette, 'Focus – Sex, Lies and Propaganda – Birmingham AIDS scare', *The Sunday Times*, 28 June 1992
8 Ibid
9 Arlidge, John, and Celia Hall, 'Health Secretary Bottomley rejects legal moves to combat AIDS', *Independent*, 27 June 1992
10 Wheeler, Caroline, 'NHS contaminated blood scandal: tragic story of seven brothers', *The Sunday Times*, 5 May 2019
11 Ibid
12 'Transcript – Leeds – Tuesday 11 June 2019 – (John Cornes, Jo-Ann Cohrs, Graham Binks)', *Infected Blood Inquiry*, https://www.infectedbloodinquiry.org.uk/sites/default/files/documents/Transcript%20-%20Leeds%20-%20Tuesday%2011%20June%202019%20-%20%28John%20Cornes%2C%20Jo-Ann%20Cohrs%2C%20Graham%20Binks%29.pdf
13 Ibid
14 Pavison, John, and Driscoll, Margarette, 'Blood money: the battle for justice', *The Sunday Times*, 1 October 1989
15 'WITN7068001 Written Statement of David Mellor 25 Apr 2022', *Infected Blood Inquiry*, https://www.infectedbloodinquiry.org.uk/sites/default/files/documents/WITN7068001%20Written%20Statement%20of%20David%20Mellor%2025%20Apr%202022.pdf, p. 36
16 Driscoll, Margaret, 'HIV and hepatitis: How *The Sunday Times* exposed the NHS blood transfusion scandal'. *The Sunday Times*, 16 July 2017
17 Ibid
18 'WITN7068001 Written Statement of David Mellor 25 Apr 2022', Infected Blood Inquiry, p. 78
19 'Presentation Note on the Role of the Chief Medical Officer', *Infected Blood Inquiry*, https://www.infectedbloodinquiry.org.uk/sites/default/files/documents/Presentation%20Note%20on%20

the%20Role%20of%20the%20Chief%20Medical%20Officer_1.
pdf, p. 67

20 Wheeler, Caroline, 'Ken Clarke rejected infected blood scandal
   advice', *The Sunday Times*, 25 July 2021

21 Ibid

22 'DHSC0046964_024 – Letter from Harry Ognall – 26 Jun 1990',
   Infected Blood Inquiry, https://www.infectedbloodinquiry.org.uk/
   sites/default/files/20230-06-08%20Part%2012_4/20230-06-08%20
   Part%2012/DHSC0046964_024%20-%20Letter%20from%20
   Harry%20Ognall%20-%2026%20Jun%201990.pdf

23 Ellison, Jane, UIN 211081 (written question), HC Deb, 27 October
   2014, https://www.theyworkforyou.com/wrans/?id=2014-10-
   20.211081.h&s=hepatitis+%2B+waiver+%2B+HIV+%2B+1991
   #g211081.r0

24 Factor 8 Scandal, 'Factor 8 supplies chronology of Haemophiliac
   Hepatitis C cover-up', 22 October 2018, https://www.
   factor8scandal.uk/campaign-history/2018/10/22/factor-8-
   supplieschronology-of-haemophiliac-hepatitis-c-cover-up

25 Borland, Sophie, 'New tainted blood scandal: Patients infected
   with HIV were each paid around £24,000 to sign away their rights
   to sue – before being told they'd also contracted hepatitis C',
   Daily Mail, 21 October 2018, https://www.dailymail.co.uk/news/
   article-6300933/Patients-infected-HIV-paid-24-000-sign-away-
   rights-sue.html

26 'WITN5288001 – Written Statement of William Waldegrave',
   Infected Blood Inquiry, https://www.infectedbloodinquiry.org.uk/
   sites/default/files/documents/WITN5288001%20-%20Written%20
   Statement%20of%20William%20Waldegrave.pdf, p. 71

27 'Transcript – London – Monday 27 June 2022 (Sir John Major)',
   Infected Blood Inquiry, https://www.infectedbloodinquiry.org.uk/
   sites/default/files/documents/Transcript%20-%20London%20-%20
   Monday%2027%20June%202022%20%28Sir%20John%20
   Major%29.pdf

28 Borland, Sophie, 'New tainted blood scandal: Patients infected with
   HIV were each paid around £24,000 to sign away their rights to
   sue – before being told they'd also contracted hepatitis C', *Daily
   Mail*, 21 October 2018

29 'Transcript – Leeds – Tuesday 11 June 2019 – (John Cornes, Jo-Ann
   Cohrs, Graham Binks)', *Infected Blood Inquiry*

30 Wheeler, Caroline, 'Chris Cornes, orphan in contaminated blood
   scandal, still fighting for justice 20 years on', *The Sunday Times*,
   4 April 2021 https://www.thetimes.co.uk/article/chris-cornes-
   orphan-in-contaminated-blood-scandal-still-fighting-for-justice-20-
   years-on-j58wsjl7n

REFERENCES

31 'Transcript – Leeds – Tuesday 11 June 2019 – (John Cornes, Jo-Ann Cohrs, Graham Binks)', *Infected Blood Inquiry*

32 Wheeler, Caroline, 'NHS contaminated blood scandal: tragic story of seven brothers', *The Sunday Times*, 5 May 2019

33 'Transcript – Leeds – Tuesday 11 June 2019 – (John Cornes, Jo-Ann Cohrs, Graham Binks)', *Infected Blood Inquiry*

34 Ibid

35 Wheeler, Caroline, 'NHS contaminated blood scandal: tragic story of seven brothers', *The Sunday Times*, 5 May 2019

36 Ibid

37 Ibid

38 'Transcript – Leeds – Tuesday 11 June 2019 – (John Cornes, Jo-Ann Cohrs, Graham Binks)', *Infected Blood Inquiry*, p. 44

39 Wheeler, Caroline, 'NHS contaminated blood scandal: tragic story of seven brothers', *The Sunday Times*, 5 May 2019

40 Ibid

7: Shredded

1 'Transcripts – Leeds – Friday 21 June 2019 (Jennifer Dorricott, Eleanor Dorricott, Sarah Dorricott, Ann Dorricott, Peter Burney)', *Infected Blood Inquiry*, https://www.infectedbloodinquiry.org. uk/sites/default/files/documents/Transcripts%20-%20Leeds%20 -%20Friday%2021%20June%202019%20%28Jennifer%20 Dorricott%2C%20Eleanor%20Dorricott%2C%20Sarah%20 Dorricott%2C%20Ann%20Dorricott%2C%20Peter%20 Burney%29.pdf

2 Ibid

3 Ibid

4 'WITN1198001 – Written statement of Jennifer Dorricott', *Infected Blood Inquiry*, https://www.infectedbloodinquiry.org.uk/sites/ default/files/documents/WITN1198001%20-%20Written%20 Statement%20of%20Jennifer%20Dorricot.pdf

5 'WITN3448001 – Response of David Birkenhead (on behalf of Huddersfield and Calderdale NHS Foundation Trust) to the Written Statement of Ann Dorricott, *Infected Blood Inquiry*, https:// www.infectedbloodinquiry.org.uk/sites/default/files/documents/ WITN3448001%20-%20Response%20of%20David%20 Birkenhead%20%28on%20behalf%20of%20Calderdale%20 and%20Huddersfield%20NHS%20Foundation%20Trust%29%20 to%20the%20Written%20Statement%20of%20Ann%20 Dorricott.pdf

6 Wheeler, Caroline, 'Dying father's plea over infected blood', *Sunday Express*, 8 June 2014

7 Ibid

8 Ibid

9 Ibid

10 Ibid

11 'Transcripts – Leeds – Friday 21 June 2019 (Jennifer Dorricott, Eleanor Dorricott, Sarah Dorricott, Ann Dorricott, Peter Burney)', *Infected Blood Inquiry*

12 Ibid

13 Wheeler, Caroline, 'Dying father's plea over infected blood', *Sunday Express*, 8 June 2014

14 'Transcripts – Leeds – Friday 21 June 2019 (Jennifer Dorricott, Eleanor Dorricott, Sarah Dorricott, Ann Dorricott, Peter Burney)', *Infected Blood Inquiry*

15 'Transcript – London – Thursday 14 July 2022 Alan Milburn', *Infected Blood Inquiry*, https://www.infectedbloodinquiry.org.uk/sites/default/files/documents/Transcript%20-%20London%20-%20Thursday%2014%20July%202022%20Alan%20Milburn.pdf, p. 55

16 Ibid, pp. 66–7, 72

17 Ibid, p. 82

18 'Transcript – London – 28 July 2022 – Malcolm Chisholm', *Infected Blood Inquiry*, https://www.infectedbloodinquiry.org.uk/sites/default/files/documents/Transcript%20-%20London%2028%20July%202022%20-%20Malcolm%20Chisholm.pdf

19 Ibid

20 'Transcript – London – Thursday 21 July (Lord John Reid and Hazel Blears)', *Infected Blood Inquiry*, https://www.infectedbloodinquiry.org.uk/sites/default/files/documents/Transcript%20-%20London%20-%20Thursday%2021%20July%202022%20%28Lord%20John%20Reid%20and%20Hazel%20Blears%29.pdf

21 'WITN5426001 Written Statement of Anita James 18 May 2022', *Infected Blood Inquiry*, https://www.infectedbloodinquiry.org.uk/sites/default/files/documents/WITN5426001%20Written%20statement%20of%20Anita%20James%2018%20May%202022.pdf

22 Ibid

23 'WITN7169001 – Written Statement of Dr Patricia Troop; 12 September 2022', *Infected Blood Inquiry*, https://www.infectedbloodinquiry.org.uk/sites/default/files/documents/WITN7169001%20-%20Written%20Statement%20of%20Dr%20Patricia%20Troop%3B%2012%20September%202022.pdf, p. 14

24 'WITN4912001 – Written Statement of Zubeda Seedat; 23 Aug 2022', *Infected Blood Inquiry*, https://www.infectedbloodinquiry.org.uk/sites/default/files/documents/WITN4912001%20-%20

Written%20Statement%20of%20Zubeda%20Seedat%3B%20
23%20Aug%202022.pdf, p. 34

25 'WITN4505389 – Third Written Statement of Charles Lister
OBE, 19 May 2022', *Infected Blood Inquiry*, https://www.
infectedbloodinquiry.org.uk/sites/default/files/documents/
WITN4505389%20Third%20Written%20Statement%20of%20
Charles%20Lister%20OBE%2019%20May%202022.pdf

26 Ibid

27 'WITN4912001 – Written Statement of Zubeda Seedat; 23 Aug
2022', *Infected Blood Inquiry*, p. 20

28 'ARCH0002968 – Written statement of the Rt Hon Lord Jenkin
of Roding for the Archer Inquiry – 20 Apr 2007', *Infected Blood
Inquiry*, https://www.infectedbloodinquiry.org.uk/sites/default/files/
OE%20Pub%20Part%201%20copy_0/OE%20Pub%20Part%20
1%20copy/ARCH0002968%20-%20Written%20statement%20
of%20the%20Rt%20Hon%20Lord%20Jenkin%20of%20
Roding%20for%20the%20Archer%20Inquiry%20-%2020%20
Apr%202007.pdf, pp. 2, 3

29 'LDOW0000345 – Transcript of part of Lord David Owen's
evidence to the Archer Inquiry – undated', *Infected Blood Inquiry*,
https://www.infectedbloodinquiry.org.uk/sites/default/files/
Lord%20Owen%20publication_1/Lord%20Owen%20publication/
LDOW0000345%20-%20Transcript%20of%20part%20of%20
Lord%20David%20Owen%27s%20evidence%20to%20the%20
Archer%20Inquiry%20-%20undated.pdf

30 Sheard, Sally, 'Doctors in Whitehall: medical advisers at the 60th
anniversary of the NHS', University of Liverpool Repository,
https://livrepository.liverpool.ac.uk/1185/

8: A Chance Encounter

1 Wheeler, Caroline, 'I'm not taking any more risks', *Sunday
Mercury*, 25 February 2001

2 Ibid

3 Brook, Sally, 'Real Lives: I found my dream man . . . then
discovered he was HIV positive', *Daily Mirror*, 26 March

4 Ibid

5 Ibid

6 Ibid

7 Mick and Caroline Mason's story was recounted to the author in a
telephone interview, combined with their statements to the Infected
Blood Inquiry, which are not online but wwere shared by the
couple

REFERENCES

8 'Probe into deaths of patients exposed to HIV', *Daily Mail*, 1 April 2007, https://www.dailymail.co.uk/health/article-444990/Probe-deaths-patients-exposed-HIV.html

9 Boseley, Sarah, and Alex Topping, '"A horrific human tragedy": report criticises response to blood scandal', *Guardian*, 24 February 2009, https://www.theguardian.com/society/2009/feb/24/haemophilia-contamination-report

10 'WITN7197001 – Witness Statement of Alan Johnson; 30 August 2022, *Infected Blood Inquiry*, https://www.infectedbloodinquiry.org.uk/sites/default/files/documents/WITN7197001%20-%20Witness%20Statement%20of%20Alan%20Johnson%3B%2030%20August%202022_0.pdf, p. 19

11 *Hansard*, HC Deb, col. 127WH–132WH, 1 July 2009, https://publications.parliament.uk/pa/cm200809/cmhansrd/cm090701/halltext/90701h0010.htm

12 'Composer wins compensation review over contaminated blood', *Daily Telegraph*, 15 April 2010, https://www.telegraph.co.uk/news/health/news/7597423/Composer-wins-compensation-review-over-contaminated-blood.html

13 'Transcript – London – Friday 18 October 2019 (Anthony Farrugia, David Farrugia, Juliet Batten, Rosamund Cooper, Mrs AO, Mrs AP)', *Infected Blood Inquiry*, https://www.infectedbloodinquiry.org.uk/sites/default/files/documents/Transcript%20-%20London%20-%20Friday%2018%20October%202019%20%28Anthony%20Farrugia%2C%20David%20Farrugia%2C%20Juliet%20Batten%2C%20Rosamund%20Cooper%2C%20Mrs%20AO%2C%20Mrs%20AP%29.pdf

14 Ibid

15 Ibid

16 Ibid

17 Ibid

18 Ibid

19 Ibid, p. 19

20 'WITN1218001 – Written Statement of Anthony Farrugia', *Infected Blood Inquiry*, https://www.infectedbloodinquiry.org.uk/sites/default/files/documents/WITN1218001%20-%20Written%20Statement%20of%20Anthony%20Farrugia.pdf

21 Ibid

22 Ibid

23 'Transcript – London – Friday 18 October 2019 (Anthony Farrugia, David Farrugia, Juliet Batten, Rosamund Cooper, Mrs AO, Mrs AP)', *Infected Blood Inquiry*

24 'WITN1218001 – Written Statement of Anthony Farrugia', *Infected Blood Inquiry*

25 'Transcript – London – Friday 18 October 2019 (Anthony Farrugia, David Farrugia, Juliet Batten, Rosamund Cooper, Mrs AO, Mrs AP)', *Infected Blood Inquiry*
26 Wheeler, Caroline, 'EXCLUSIVE: I saw all three of my brothers die after they were given contaminated blood', *Sunday Express*, 4 July 2015
27 Ibid
28 'WITN1218001 – Written Statement of Anthony Farrugia', *Infected Blood Inquiry*

9: 'Tell her to keep going'

1 Wheeler, Caroline, 'Blood payouts rejected; HULL: Increased compensation for victims has been ruled out', *Hull Daily Mail*, 20 October 2010
2 'WITN2050001 – First Written Statement of Glenn Wilkinson – 14 Aug 2020', *Infected Blood Inquiry*, https://www.infectedbloodinquiry.org.uk/sites/default/files/2021-12-16%20WS/2021-12-16%20WS/WITN2050001%20-%20First%20Written%20Statement%20of%20Glenn%20Wilkinson%20-%2014%20Aug%202020.pdf
3 Ibid
4 Wheeler, Caroline, 'Risking his life in bid for payments justice; A Government review into payments for the victims of the contaminated blood scandal has forced a Hull dad to consider undergoing potentially life-threatening surgery', *Hull Daily Mail*, 5 February 2011
5 Herbert, Dean, '"Whitewash" fury of blood scandal victims: £12m six-year inquiry only makes ONE suggestion', *Daily Express*, 26 March 2015
6 Wheeler, Caroline, 'Six-year inquiry "failed to find full awful truth about scandal of tainted blood"', *Sunday Express*, 6 September 2015
7 Ibid
8 Wheeler, Caroline, 'EXCLUSIVE: Infected by NHS blood, Mike's last wish is justice for his family', *Sunday Express*, 29 March 2015
9 Ibid
10 Ibid
11 Ibid
12 BBC News, 'Penrose inquiry: David Cameron apologises over infected blood', 25 March 2015, https://www.bbc.co.uk/news/uk-scotland-32041715
13 Wheeler, Caroline, 'Justice fight for pupils of Treloar College who were killed by tainted blood', *Sunday Express*, 19 July 2015,

REFERENCES

https://www.express.co.uk/news/uk/592179/blood-hiv-treloar-college-scam-nhs-medicine-positive-hiv

14 Ibid

15 Wheeler, Caroline, 'Lib Dem peer: I'll fight for nephew killed by the bad blood scandal', *Sunday Express*, 18 April 2016

16 Farron, Tim, 'Lib Dems backing Express crusade', *Sunday Express*, 2 August 2015

17 Gilbert, Dominic, 'David Cameron reveals £125m of contaminated blood victim payments as one of last acts as Prime Minister, which campaigners brand "an insult"', *Eastern Daily Press*, 13 July, 2016, https://www.edp24.co.uk/news/health/20867346.david-cameron-reveals-125m-contaminated-blood-victim-payments-one-last-acts-prime-minister-campaigners-brand-insult/

18 'WITN3903001 – Witness Statement of David Cameron', *Infected Blood Inquiry*, https://www.infectedbloodinquiry.org.uk/sites/default/files/documents/WITN3903001.pdf

19 'Transcript – London – Friday 15 July 2022 (Andy Burnham)', *Infected Blood Inquiry*, https://www.infectedbloodinquiry.org.uk/sites/default/files/documents/Transcript%20%E2%80%93%20London%20%E2%80%93%20Friday%2015%20July%20%28Andy%20Burnham%29.pdf

20 Wheeler, Caroline, 'Fresh "cover-up" evidence found in contaminated blood scandal', *Sunday Express*, 28 May 2017

21 Burnham, Andy, HC Deb 25 April 2017, https://www.theyworkforyou.com/debates/?id=2017-04-25b.1070.2&s=speaker%3A10766#g1072.1

22 Wheeler, Caroline, 'Mayor of Manchester: I'll call in police if I have to over blood contamination scandal', *Sunday Express*, 21 May 2017

23 Ibid

24 'Theresa May urged to hold inquiry into contaminated blood', *The Times*, 10 July 2017

25 Johnson, Diana, HC Deb, 10 July 2017, https://www.theyworkforyou.com/debates/?id=2017-07-10a.62.0&s=Diana+Johnson+%2B+emergency+debate+%2B+justice+%2B+died#g62.2

10: Colin

1 'Transcript – Cardiff – Wednesday 24 July 2019 (Colin Smith, Janet Smith, Elaine Huxley, Mr AE, Judith Thomas)', *Infected Blood Inquiry*, https://www.infectedbloodinquiry.org.uk/sites/default/files/documents/Transcript%20-%20Cardiff%20-%20Wednesday%2024%20July%202019%20%28Colin%20Smith%2C%20Janet%20

REFERENCES

Smith%2C%20Elaine%20Huxley%2C%20Mr%20AE%2C%20
Judith%20Thomas%29_0.pdf

2 Ibid

3 Ibid

4 Morden, Jessica, HC Deb, 11 July 2017, https://www.
theyworkforyou.com/debates/?id=2017-07-11g.174.0&s=%22Noth
ing+can+bring+back+Colin+and+others+but+we+can+at+least+hav
e+a+public+inquiry%22#g207.0

5 Volpe, Sam, 'Government changed its mind on Infected Blood
Inquiry "because of pressure from campaigners"', *Chronicle Live*,
30 March 2022, https://www.chroniclelive.co.uk/news/north-east-
news/infected-blood-inquiry-documents-revealed-23536730

6 Sky News, 'PM orders inquiry into 'appalling' contaminated blood
scandal', 11 July 2017, https://news.sky.com/story/pm-orders-
inquiry-into-contaminated-blood-scandal-10944595

7 Johnson, Diana, HC deb, 11 July 2017, https://www.
theyworkforyou.com/debates/?id=2017-07-11g.174.0&

8 Harpin, Lee, 'EXCLUSIVE: Head of contaminated blood inquiry
backs calls for probe to be independent from government', *Daily
Mirror*, 2 August 2017, https://www.mirror.co.uk/news/politics/
head-contaminated-blood-inquiry-backs-10919322

9 ITV News, 'Thousands could be infected by contaminated blood
scandal, inquiry hears', 24 September 2018, https://www.itv.com/
news/2018-09-24/thousands-could-be-infected-by-contaminated-
blood-scandal-inquiry-hears

10 Bowcott, Oliver, 'Infected blood victims "may still not know they
have hepatitis C"', *Guardian*, 24 September 2018, https://www.
theguardian.com/society/2018/sep/24/infected-nhs-blood-inquiry-
opens-with-tribute-to-victims

11 Bowcott, Oliver, and Rebekah Evans, 'Infected blood scandal:
government expresses "sorrow and regret"', *Guardian*,
26 September 2018, https://www.theguardian.com/uk-news/2018/
sep/26/key-documents-being-withheld-infected-blood-inquiry-told

12 'Transcript – Opening statements – 30 April 2019', *Infected Blood
Inquiry*, https://www.infectedbloodinquiry.org.uk/sites/default/files/
documents/Transcript%20-%20Opening%20statements%20-%20
30%20April%202019.pdf

13 'Transcript - London - Tuesday 30 April 2019 (Derek Martindale,
Carole Hill, Perry Evans), *Infected Blood Inquiry*, https://
www.infectedbloodinquiry.org.uk/sites/default/files/documents/
Transcript%20London%20Tuesday%2030%20April%20
2019%20%28Derek%20Martindale%2C%20Carole%20
Hill%2C%20Perry%20Evans%29.pdf

14 WITN0841005 - Written statement of Dr Peter Jones; 17 Sep

2020', *Infected Blood Inquiry*, https://www.infectedbloodinquiry.
org.uk/sites/default/files/Part%201_4/Part%201/
WITN0841005%20-%20Written%20statement%20of%20Dr%20
Peter%20Jones%3B%2017%20Sep%202020.pdf

15 'Transcript – London – Wednesday 27 July 2022 (Jeremy Hunt)',
Infected Blood Inquiry, https://www.infectedbloodinquiry.org.
uk/sites/default/files/documents/Transcript%20-%20London%20
-%20Wednesday%2027%20July%202022%20%28Jeremy%20
Hunt%29%20.pdf, p. 46

16 'Transcript – London – Wednesday 27 July 2022 (Jeremy Hunt)',
Infected Blood Inquiry, https://www.infectedbloodinquiry.org.
uk/sites/default/files/documents/Transcript%20-%20London%20
-%20Wednesday%2027%20July%202022%20%28Jeremy%20
Hunt%29%20.pdf

17 Ibid

18 'Transcript – London – Tuesday 27 July 2021 (Lord Kenneth
Clarke)', *Infected Blood Inquiry*, https://www.infectedbloodinquiry.
org.uk/sites/default/files/documents/Transcript%20-%20
London%20-%20Tuesday%2027%20July%202021%20
%28Lord%20Kenneth%20Clarke%29.pdf

19 'Transcript – London – Wednesday 28 July 2021 (Lord Kenneth
Clarke continued)', *Infected Blood Inquiry*, https://www.
infectedbloodinquiry.org.uk/sites/default/files/documents/
Transcript%20-%20London%20-%20Wednesday%2028%20
July%202021%20%28Lord%20Kenneth%20Clarke%20
continued%29.pdf

20 'Transcript – London – Tuesday 20 July 2021 (Dr Diana
Walford Continued)', *Infected Blood Inquiry*, https://www.
infectedbloodinquiry.org.uk/sites/default/files/documents/
Transcript%20-%20London%20-%20Tuesday%2020%20
July%202021%20%28Dr%20Diana%20Walford%20
Continued%29.pdf

21 'Transcript – London – Monday 27 June 2022 (Sir John Major)',
Infected Blood Inquiry, https://www.infectedbloodinquiry.org.uk/
sites/default/files/documents/Transcript%20-%20London%20-%20
Monday%2027%20June%202022%20%28Sir%20John%20
Major%29.pdf

22 WITN3903007 – Second Written Statement of David Cameron;
13 December 2021', *Infected Blood Inquiry*, https://www.
infectedbloodinquiry.org.uk/sites/default/files/documents/
WITN3903007-Second%20Written%20Statement%20of%20
David%20Cameron%3B%2013%20December%202021.pdf

23 Wheeler, Caroline, 'Compensation at last for lives ruined by NHS
contaminated blood scandal', *The Sunday Times*, 21 March 2021,

REFERENCES

https://www.thetimes.co.uk/article/compensation-at-last-for-lives-ruined-by-nhs-contaminated-blood-scandal-27gb6fjmx

24 Francis, Sir Robert, QC, 'Compensation and Redress for the Victims of Infected Blood', https://www.infectedbloodinquiry.org.uk/sites/default/files/2022-06/Compensation_and_Redress_for_the_Victims_of_Infected_Blood_-_Recommendations_for_a_Framework_-_Sir_Robert_Francis__Final_.pdf

25 Thomas, Tobi, 'Infected blood inquiry: victims should receive £100,000 each 'without delay', *Guardian*, 29 July 2022, https://www.theguardian.com/uk-news/2022/jul/29/infected-blood-inquiry-victims-should-receive-100000-each-without-delay

26 yahoo! finance, 'Three ex-health secretaries urge immediate payouts for infected blood victims', 30 July 2022, https://uk.finance.yahoo.com/news/three-ex-health-secretaries-urge-091033173.html?guce_referrer=aHR0cHM6Ly93d3cuZ29vZ2xlLmNvLnVrLw&guce_referrer_sig=AQAAALRBaaQ3mXo0Ra2js0QtCnSFqcxJHsmg7GXpJZmIMqpofiEz11G3t-dOaE5mvl75OCsudiJ2QUA_7A2o3vVMSMES7W0YbUDMJdHfVO0jeernE_6nzobsj3Qs_u4GaiBOopLRqDKCPJC5GcJy3aQUY_WxOAnNtuajixu_Zr2jZ6YJ&guccounter=2

27 Wheeler, Caroline, 'Urgent blood payouts backed', *The Sunday Times*, 31 July 2022

28 'Transcript – Cardiff – Wednesday 24 July 2019 (Colin Smith, Janet Smith, Elaine Huxley, Mr AE, Judith Thomas)', *Infected Blood Inquiry*

29 Tainted Blood, 'The Tainted Blood Timeline – what *really* happened', https://www.taintedblood.info/timeline/

30 'Transcript – Cardiff – Wednesday 24 July 2019 (Colin Smith, Janet Smith, Elaine Huxley, Mr AE, Judith Thomas)', *Infected Blood Inquiry*

31 Ibid

32 Wheeler, Caroline, 'Tears for tainted blood boy will never ever dry', *Sunday Express*, 26 July 2014, https://www.express.co.uk/finance/crusader/593816/Tears-tainted-blood-boy-will-never-ever-dry

33 'Transcript – Cardiff – Wednesday 24 July 2019 (Colin Smith, Janet Smith, Elaine Huxley, Mr AE, Judith Thomas)', *Infected Blood Inquiry*

34 Ibid
35 Ibid
36 Ibid
37 Ibid
38 Ibid
39 Ibid
40 Ibid

REFERENCES

41 Wheeler, Caroline, 'Tears for tainted blood boy will never ever dry', *Sunday Express*, 26 July 2014
42 'Transcript – Cardiff – Wednesday 24 July 2019 (Colin Smith, Janet Smith, Elaine Huxley, Mr AE, Judith Thomas)', *Infected Blood Inquiry*
43 Ibid
44 Ibid

Conclusion

1 'Second Interim Report', *Infected Blood Inquiry*, file:///D:/Blood/Infected%20Blood%20Inquiry%20Second%20Interim%20Report.pdf
2 Ibid
3 'SUBS0000063 – Submission of Collins – 16:12:22'. *Infected Blood Inquiry*, https://www.infectedbloodinquiry.org.uk/sites/default/files/documents/SUBS0000063%20-%20Submission%20of%20Collins%20-%2016%3A12%3A22.pdf
4 'Transcript – London – Tuesday 21 September 2021 (Lord Norman Fowler)', *Infected Blood Inquiry*, https://www.infectedbloodinquiry.org.uk/sites/default/files/documents/Transcript%20-%20London%20-%20Tuesday%2021%20September%202021%20%28Lord%20Norman%20Fowler%29.pdf
5 *Hansard*, HL Deb, col. 766, 12 March 2002, https://https://publications.parliament.uk/pa/ld200102/ldhansrd/vo020312/text/20312-25.htm
6 'Transcript – London – Thursday 22 July 2021 (Lord Simon Glenarthur), *Infected Blood Inquiry*, https://www.infectedbloodinquiry.org.uk/sites/default/files/documents/Transcript%20-%20London%20-%20Thursday%2022%20July%202021%20%28Lord%20Simon%20Glenarthur%29.pdf
7 'Transcript London Tuesday 8 October 2019 (Colin Turton, Denise Turton, Sue Threakall, Barry Fitzgerald and Ronan Fitzgerald)', *Infected Blood Inquiry*, https://www.infectedbloodinquiry.org.uk/sites/default/files/documents/Transcript%20-%20London%20-%20Tuesday%208%20October%202019%20%28Opening%20Remarks%2C%20Colin%20Turton%2C%20Denise%20Turton%2C%20Sue%20Threakall%2C%20Barry%20Fitzgerald%20and%20Ronan%20Fitzgerald%29.pdf, p. 96
8 'SUBS0000063 – Submission of Collins – 16:12:22'. *Infected Blood Inquiry*
9 Ibid
10 Ibid

REFERENCES

11 'WITN1243001 Written Statement of Adrian Goodyear 20 February 2019', *Infected Blood Inquiry*, https://www.infectedbloodinquiry.org.uk/sites/default/files/documents/WITN1243001%20Written%20Statement%20of%20Adrian%20Goodyear%2020%20February%202019.pdf

12 'Document displayed for Milners Solicitors (Day 2, PM), 25 September 2018', *Infected Blood Inquiry*, https://www.infectedbloodinquiry.org.uk/sites/default/files/Document%20displayed%20for%20Milners%20Solicitors%20(Day%202%2C%20PM)%2C%2025%20September%202018.pdf

13 'WITN1267001 – Written Statement of Susan Hallwood – 03:01:2020', *Infected Blood Inquiry*, https://www.infectedbloodinquiry.org.uk/sites/default/files/documents/WITN1267001%20-%20Written%20Statement%20of%20Susan%20Hallwood%20-%2003%3A01%3A2020.pdf

14 BBC News, '1 in 3 infected with HIV in blood scandal was a child', 9 November 2022', https://www.bbc.co.uk/news/health-63569463

15 'Transcript – London – Monday 27 June 2022 (Sir John Major)', *Infected Blood Inquiry*, https://www.infectedbloodinquiry.org.uk/sites/default/files/documents/Transcript%20-%20London%20-%20Monday%2027%20June%202022%20%28Sir%20John%20Major%29.pdf

16 'Transcript – London – Wednesday 27 July 2022 (Jeremy Hunt)', *Infected Blood Inquiry*, https://www.infectedbloodinquiry.org.uk/sites/default/files/documents/Transcript%20-%20London%20-%20Wednesday%2027%20July%202022%20%28Jeremy%20Hunt%29%20.pdf, p. 46

17 'SUBS0000063 – Submission of Collins – 16:12:22'. *Infected Blood Inquiry*, https://www.infectedbloodinquiry.org.uk/sites/default/files/documents/SUBS0000063%20-%20Submission%20of%20Collins%20-%2016%3A12%3A22.pdf

18 'Transcript – London – Wednesday 27 July 2022 (Jeremy Hunt)', *Infected Blood Inquiry*, https://www.infectedbloodinquiry.org.uk/sites/default/files/documents/Transcript%20-%20London%20-%20Wednesday%2027%20July%202022%20%28Jeremy%20Hunt%29%20.pdf, p. 164

Acknowledgements

Death in the Blood would not have been possible without my agent and now editor, Martin Redfern. I had thought about writing a book on the contaminated blood scandal for years but would never have succeeded had it not been for his gentle encouragement and support.

The driving force behind writing this book was to ensure that the brave campaign led by the victims of the contaminated blood scandal is never forgotten. I am constantly surprised by how many people still don't know about the disaster. With the Infected Blood Inquiry expected to deliver its findings shortly, there is never going to be a better time to publish a book about the long, hard-fought battle for truth and justice, and the heroic role played by a group of campaigners in for what for decades felt like the impossible. Many of them have taken on the battle while suffering from debilitating illnesses after receiving blood products riddled with deadly diseases but they have still somehow found the strength to take on the fight.

Sadly, some of them have not made it to the end of the journey. During the course of writing this book, Nick Sainsbury, who was infected with HIV, and John Cornes, who was infected with hepatitis C, passed away. I will forever be grateful to them for trusting me with their stories.

ACKNOWLEDGEMENTS

Mike Dorricott died from liver cancer linked to hepatitis C in 1995. I am enormously indebted to him and his family for their support and help in writing this book, especially his wife, Ann, and daughters, Sarah and Eleanor. I hope this book will now ensure the voices of those who are no longer here will continue to be heard long after death and that they will become an important footnote in history.

This book and, more importantly, this campaign would not have succeeded had it not been for Sue Threakall, Andrew Evans, Andrew March and Su Gorman. They have all held prominent roles in the Tainted Blood group and all played an instrumental role in supporting me when we launched the crusade in the *Sunday Express*. There were often late-night and early-morning phone calls, and Sue even stepped in at one point to tell her own story when one of the weekly articles I was writing collapsed. Similarly, Glenn Wilkinson, from the Contaminated Blood Campaign, and Jason Evans, the founder of Factor 8, have both played a pivotal role.

With thanks also to Mick and Caroline Mason, with whom my interest in the campaign first began. Thank you for educating me and not freaking out when I called you out of the blue almost twenty years after I had first spoken to Mick and was writing a piece for *The Sunday Times* about the start of the public inquiry.

The first time I heard Ade Goodyear's story it nearly broke my heart. Yet, even after everything he has endured, Ade is like a ray of sunshine, always happy to meet up and chat whenever I was stuck or needed inspiration. I am also enormously grateful to Gary Webster, who also shared details about this traumatic school years at Treloar's.

My heart goes out to Tony Farrugia, who had already been through so much when life gave him lemons again with the death of his beloved wife, Sarah. I can't thank him enough for all the help he gave me writing this book, even when he was juggling two traumatised children along with his own grief. I am sure he will eventually get the lemonade he deserves.

There can be no braver campaigners than Janet and Colin Smith. My admiration for them and their entire family knows no bounds. The pain and trauma they have suffered since the loss of little Colin is incomprehensible and yet they have always conducted themselves with great warmth and dignity.

Diana Johnson has worked tirelessly on the contaminated blood campaign. She listened to the concerns of her constituent Glenn Wilkinson and decided to take on the establishment. She was rightly honoured for her role in exposing the scandal and deserves huge credit for forcing the government to launch the public inquiry. I am proud of the double act we have forged to affect change.

Andy Burnham, the Mayor of Greater Manchester, also deserves huge credit for his role in exposing the scandal. Although he had been a health secretary, once the scales fell from his eyes, Andy has done everything he can, including using his last speech in Parliament, to raise the profile of the campaign.

Theresa May, the former prime minister, also deserves plaudits for agreeing to the public inquiry, a decision which governments of all colours had ducked for decades. I am very grateful to her for agreeing to be interviewed for this book.

Thanks also go to Lord David Owen, for inviting me to his home and allowing me to pick his considerable brains about his planned drive towards self-sufficiency and his concerted efforts to keep this scandal in the spotlight.

I am also grateful to Steve Barclay, the health secretary, for speaking to me for this book and for his efforts in ensuring the interim payments were made to victims last autumn.

ACKNOWLEDGEMENTS

I have been incredibly fortunate to have been supported and mentored throughout my newspaper career by a group of brilliant journalists and editors. It all started at the *Sunday Mercury* in Birmingham, where I began life as a trainee. My first news editor was Bernard Cole, who eventually went on to become the ITV *News at Ten* editor. Bernard, who sadly died too young, was as creative as he was inspirational. He imbued me with an unquenchable curiosity and taught me the investigative skills that have been so invaluable to me during my career. I have also learnt so much from other *Sunday Mercury* stalwarts, including Bob Haywood and Tony Larner, as well as Amardeep Bassey, Lucy Miles, Paul Malley and Martyn Leak.

I am hugely grateful to John Meehan, the former editor of the *Hull Daily Mail*, for giving me my first job in the lobby, and Martin Townsend, the former editor of the *Sunday Express*, who gave me my first job on Fleet Street. Martin was also instrumental in creating and backing the *Sunday Express*'s crusade on the contaminated blood scandal. I am equally indebted to Matt Gibson, who was my phenomenal news editor at the *Sunday Express*. He was a joy to work with and I still miss working with him every day.

Huge thanks also to former editor Martin Ivens and his deputy Sarah Baxter for giving me my break at *The Sunday Times*. I am enormously proud to have joined a paper with such an illustrious campaigning history. It was former *Sunday Times* journalists Margarette Driscoll and John Pavison who were among the first to raise the alarm and start leading the charge on behalf of the victims.

My thanks also go to Emma Tucker, the former editor of *The Sunday Times*, and her successor, Ben Taylor, for supporting me in writing this book and allowing me to use excerpts from the interviews I have conducted on the issue during my time at the

ACKNOWLEDGEMENTS

paper. I am also grateful to my *Sunday Times* friends and colleagues, including my legendary long-time partner-in-mischief Tim Shipman, and my deputy Harry Yorke, who held the fort while I took some weeks off to write the book. Thanks also to my news editors Lindsay McInstosh, Becky Barrow and Tim Rayment, and to the other great journalists I have also had the privilege of working alongside, including Gabriel Pogrund, Roya Nikkhah, Dipesh Gadher, Nick Hellen, Krissi Mursion and Katherine Forster. I have also been blessed with a group of hugely supportive friends, including Julia Breen, Helena King, Rachel Slowey, Jo Tanner, Kirsty Buchanan, Jacki Vause, Elaine Potter, Zoe Dobson and Cat Edney. To all my wonderful friends in politics, you know exactly who you are and I thank you for all your support over the years.

Thanks also to my parents, Sue and Chris, and step-father, Henry, and to my wonderful children, Luke, Sam and Grace, and step-children-to-be, Anna, Rachel and Maggie, for being so patient with me and not complaining too much when writing the book took me away from having fun with you.

Finally, the biggest thanks of all goes to my partner, Tom Harper, who fills every day with love, joy and happiness and allows me to live life in technicolour. This book would never have happened had he not given me the confidence and support to see it through, especially at moments when I did not think I would ever get to the end of the process. I am also hugely grateful to the team at Headline, including Holly Purdham, Emma Horton and Kirsty Howarth, who helped get this book over the line, and to Northbank's Diane Banks and Matt Cole for helping to transform an idea into reality.

Needless to say, however, any remaining errors are all mine.

Index

INDEX

INDEX

INDEX

INDEX

INDEX